Bonnet Strings

"This story includes all the elements of a good romance—attraction, danger, secrets, beautiful scenery, obstacles, culture clashes, and old-fashioned chivalry. You will cheer for Saloma and the sense of self God placed in her."
—*Shirley Hershey Showalter, author of* Blush

"Saloma Miller Furlong explores the complexities of duty and desire, defining the careful balance between familial responsibility and the pursuit of true love. You will rejoice with Saloma as she acquires independence from her previously cloistered lifestyle among the Amish and recall your own first glimpse of someone you knew would capture your heart—and therefore change your world forever. *Bonnet Strings* is a memoir not to be missed."
—*Jolina Petersheim, author of* The Outcast

"In this memoir of the *Bildungsroman* genre, Saloma Miller Furlong writes carefully and artfully of the inner pain and joy she experiences as she finds her way, both outside of her home community and inside it. In addition, her partner David's voice provides readers with a poignant lens with which to view Furlong's journey."
—*Vi Dutcher, professor of language and literature, Eastern Mennonite University*

"*Bonnet Strings* paints an intimate portrait of one woman's struggle to find an authentic path for herself among the Amish. Saloma Miller Furlong vividly portrays the warmth and love in her tight-knit community but also what it was like to try to live according to her community's strict rules. The reader cheers as Furlong overcomes obstacles to create a life true to herself and her faith."
—*Lucinda Martin, researcher at Research Centre Gotha, University of Erfurt, Germany*

Bonnet Strings

An Amish Woman's Ties to Two Worlds

A true story featured in the **PBS** *American Experience*
documentaries *The Amish* and *The Amish: Shunned*

Saloma Miller Furlong

with David Furlong

Herald Press

Harrisonburg, Virginia
Kitchener, Ontario

Library of Congress Cataloging-in-Publication Data
Furlong, Saloma Miller.
    Bonnet strings : an Amish woman's ties to two worlds / Saloma Miller Furlong, with
David Furlong.
        pages cm
    ISBN 978-0-8361-9858-4 (pbk. : alk. paper) 1. Furlong, Saloma Miller. 2. Amish
women—Biography. 3. Man-woman relationships. 4. Burlington (Vt.)—Biography. 5.
Furlong, Saloma Miller—Family. 6. Amish—Ohio—Geauga County—Social life and
customs. 7. Amish—Ohio—Geauga County—Biography. 8. Geauga County (Ohio)—
Biography. 9. Christian biography. I. Furlong, David. II. Title. III. Title: Amish
woman's ties to two worlds.
    F500.M45F868 2014
    289.7092--dc23
    [B]

                                        2013041020

For David
It is because of your understanding and quiet perseverance that our love not only survived but also thrived.

True love stories never have endings.
—Richard Bach

For Saloma
Your truth shines a light on the path to eternal love.

Contents

Foreword by Callie T. Wiser 9

Introduction 11

Part I

1 A Lifetime on Earth 22

2 I Lift Mine Eyes 31

3 Weighing Happiness 38

4 Liberating Linda 49

5 The Struggle Within 59

6 Gemini Twins 70

7 *Schmunzling* 80

8 Life in Open Throttle 89

9 Love Unspoken 99

10 The Loss of Linda 104

11 Wearing Amish 114

12 *The Cross of Hope: David Furlong* 123

Part II

13 Prodigal Daughter 130

14 A Leaf in the River 142

15 Just Friends in Ohio 150

16 Mixed Messages 161

17 My Name's Saloma! 173

18 Family Immersion 183

19 On the Other Side of the Desk 190

20 Trip to Vermont 200

21 The Silent Beauty of a Moonlit Night 213

22 *A Little Faith in Plain Country: David Furlong* 223

Part III

23 A Birthday Gift 230

24 Linda's Day in the Sun 238

25 A Rendezvous 247

26 Moonlight in Vermont 253

27 Trip to New England 263

28 A Yankee Wedding 268

29 By the Waterfalls 273

30 Mull of Kintyre 278

31 Fairy Stones 287

32 Sister Talk 293

33 Arm in Arm with the Future 301

34 Farewells 306

35 *White Knight: David Furlong* 317

Epilogue 319

Acknowledgments 327

Recipes 330

The Author 337

Foreword

I first met Saloma while researching a documentary about the Amish faith. I left her house many hours later, my cheeks tired from so much talking and laughing.

When she told me she was writing a memoir, I had a hard time imagining someone with such seemingly boundless energy for conversation actually sitting down alone in a quiet room, typing away.

But she, like all Amish people I've met, will do what she sets out to do. And she will do it well. In waiting more than thirty years after leaving the Amish to write this memoir, she has done herself and the reader a great service. She hasn't forgotten the feelings she had as she struggled with her decision to leave the church, but she has not used the memoir as a therapy session. The result is a story of empathy and depth that reveals the wrenching decision that Amish people who consider leaving their culture must make. It's not the "let's have some fun and taste the world" decision that people on the outside like to imagine. It's a decision about whether you need to leave behind everything you know in order to be your truest self.

Many of us who are not Amish are encouraged to find our own path, discover our destiny, and be who we want to be. We are not forced to choose between our family, community, and ourselves. Indeed, the hundreds of thousands of Amish who find identity, comfort, and hope within the Amish community don't have to make that choice either. Their choice to become members and live the Amish life doesn't feel like a wrenching renunciation of their true self, because their true self exists, happy and fulfilled, within the Amish community.

It is people like Saloma, who find themselves searching for some middle ground, who struggle. The Amish belief that you can't put your individual "worldly" desires ahead of the needs of the spiritual community is what has made them one of the most tightly knit communities in the United States. It also exacts a price from those who don't find their place in that community. The beauty of the Amish is that they believe the strength of their community depends on and is worth the price. The beauty of Saloma is that she has accepted that price and is determined to find her own way.

I should not have worried that my conversation-loving friend Saloma would feel lonely or disconnected banging away on a keyboard to tell her story. The reader is in a conversation with Saloma from page one. The conversation isn't one-sided, as some memoirs tend to be. It is a conversation that asks you to engage and that rewards you in return.

—*Callie T. Wiser, producer of PBS* American Experience *documentaries* The Amish *and* The Amish: Shunned

Introduction

If God had wanted me otherwise, He would have created me otherwise.
—Johann Wolfgang von Goethe

It was a mismatch from the start—being born with a nature that just did not fit into my Amish culture. For as long as I can remember, questions had bubbled up from within. I tried to emulate other girls who were quiet and submissive. I'd practice folding my arms in the demure way of Amish girls, looking down in front of me instead of looking directly at others and not talking. That never lasted more than five minutes before I'd forget and become myself again.

I was often labeled a chatterbox or a handful or, worse yet, *dick-keppich* (stubborn) and rebellious. It was a terrible feeling, knowing I didn't fit into the only community I knew. As I was growing up I learned—at least if I believed the preachers—that leaving the Amish was not an option. They claimed because we were born Amish, God wanted us to stay Amish, and if we didn't, then all hope of our salvation would be lost. I used to wonder, why would God give me this inquisitive nature if it's wrong to ask questions? If I asked this out loud, my mother would say I shouldn't be asking such questions or "it's just the way it is."

My first book, *Why I Left the Amish*, tells the story of my childhood and my teenage years. That story is framed by my first semester at Smith College, when I traveled back to my horse-and-buggy world for my father's funeral. It also tells the story of why

On picture day in second grade at my public school, my teacher said I could stay in the classroom because she knew that the Amish don't normally allow photographs to be taken of themselves. I popped out of my seat and said, "Oh, but my mother said I could be in the class picture!" So when it was my turn to have my individual photograph taken, I sat up on the high stool and smiled into the lights and the camera.

and how I left the first time and how I came to choose Burlington, Vermont, for my new home.

Bonnet Strings continues my story—a story of being torn between the Amish community where I was born and raised and the Vermont world where I experienced freedom when I was twenty years old. I reveled in my newfound freedom and established my life as "Linda," the name I took for myself. I made new friends, formed a social life, made plans to take college courses, and landed my dream job—a waitress at Pizza Hut!

I began dating a Yankee toymaker and street peddler, David Furlong.[1] Our romance was still young when the Amish came to Vermont from Ohio to bring me back into the fold. Thus began my nearly three-year struggle of deciding whether to submit my will and settle into Amish life, with its centuries-old traditions, or follow my desire for the independence that I had experienced during my four months in Vermont.

---

1. The Amish in Geauga County often use the term *Yankee* for the non-Amish. The late Stephen Scott, author of several books on the Amish, observed that no other Amish community uses this term. His hypothesis was that because people from New England settled that area, they were, quite literally, Yankees. Other Amish communities normally call them *English*.

Meanwhile, the Yankee toymaker did not give up his quest to continue our romance. I kept telling him, "I'm Amish, and you're not—this relationship is impossible." David, with his quiet perseverance, kept sending me cards, conveying that he had not given up hope that our love would survive. After two years of trying to make myself Amish and still feeling like a misfit in my community, I became keenly aware of David's outstretched hand that offered love and understanding. It seemed there was no contest.

And yet it was not as simple as that.

From the time Amish children can understand the concept, they know they are different from people "out in the world." The first things that identify them as different are the obvious ones, such as plain clothing, traditional dialect, and riding in horse-drawn buggies. Everything about their way of life and belief system shapes and reinforces this identity. With this "training," most people who are born and raised Amish are well suited for the life the community prescribes from the cradle to the grave. But occasionally there are people born into the culture who just do not belong there. I was one of those.

A psychologist once told me that most people who leave an insular culture usually need to find out who they are, or discover their "self," once they leave. He said, "You are different. I think you had a self *while* you were in the community."

I have contemplated this thought often. No wonder I had to leave.

When I was twenty-three years old, contemplating leaving again, with David waiting in the wings, I felt the weight of the deep and abiding traditions of my ancestors on my shoulders. This made the question of whether or not to leave a tough one. Eventually I took the hand that offered me love.

Bonnet Strings is a universal story of choosing between one's need for community and belonging and the desire for freedom to walk the path that is most authentic to who we are. This usually involves overcoming adversities and learning and growing through our struggles and the mistakes we make.

This book has three parts. The first part is about adjusting to my life in Burlington, Vermont. I met David two months after arriving there, which is about halfway through part 1. At the end of each part, David's voice comes into my story via a short chapter that he has written.

If I could have written *Bonnet Strings* without showing anyone in a negative light, I would have. Many of the people whose stories intersected with mine have matured and grown and have children of their own. Many events are central to my story, however, and would leave big holes if I were to skip them. So to protect people's privacy, I have changed some of the names and identities.

Throughout my book, I sometimes refer to the people in my community as "the Amish." It is only after I left the second time and began learning more about various Amish communities that I realized how much diversity there is among the Amish. And the diversity has increased since I left. Today there are more than 460 Amish settlements in the United States. There are as many ways to live an Amish life as there are church districts, with each bishop interpreting the *Ordnung* (set of rules) differently. But at the time, I definitely thought of the people in the community as "the Amish." To stay true to what I actually said in conversations, I have retained some of these phrases.

I have often been asked whether the abuse that I endured as a child and wrote about in my first memoir is prevalent. I always answer that I have no idea. Silence shrouds abuse among the Amish, just as it does in other cultures, and within an insular culture that shroud of silence is even thicker. One would have to be a fly on the wall in every home at all times to know the answer to this question. This is impossible, of course. And so it is also impossible for me (or anyone else) to know the prevalence of abuse in Amish homes and communities. I do know, however, that there are well-adjusted families in Amish communities, and so it goes without saying that I do not claim that my experiences are "the norm." I just have no idea how unique they are.

All four of my sisters left the community after I did, while my two brothers stayed. This is an unusually high number of children to leave the Amish, at least compared to the patterns in my home community. There are other families in which more than five people left, especially families with fifteen or more children. But I could find no other family in the directory of Amish in Geauga County in which all the women left and the men stayed.

Some people in my story have died since this story took place. Readers of *Why I Left the Amish* will remember my account of my father's funeral in 2004. My mother died a year later. My sister Lizzie lost her battle with cancer and died in 2009. We lost three family members over the course of five years. For the six of us still living, it seemed our parents' deaths were not nearly as difficult as Lizzie's. Neither of my brothers traveled to Lizzie's funeral. I tried communicating with them afterward with a letter, describing what it was like to be there when Lizzie died, the support of the church community she belonged to, and things I discovered in her paperwork that showed she was a lot more intelligent than we had ever given her credit for. I never heard from either Joe or Simon.

My first book came on the heels of Lizzie's death. Sarah and Susan stopped communicating with me after they read the book. Katherine, who lives in a group home in Kentucky, also stopped taking my calls when I tried to stay in communication with her.

In December 2012, Sarah and I began communicating again. When Sarah told me what upset her about the book, I realized that I could have been kinder to her and others in *Why I Left the Amish*. Sometimes sensitivity is not so much in what one tells as in how one tells it. Sarah and I have talked about how telling my story will reveal the parts in which she was instrumental in bringing me back into the fold. I have asked her what she would like for me to tell people about the ways in which she has changed, and why she would not do now what she did back then. She said the only way she can explain what she did is that she was still in the "Amish mindset."

Those who were born and raised Amish and those who were not often have two different understandings of what the "Amish mindset" is. Regardless of the diversity of Amish communities, certain things are universal in most, if not all, of them. Words are often inadequate to describe what this means, because being Amish is not just a religion or way of life. It is also a way of *thinking* and *being*.

Sarah said she had bought into the Amish way of thinking at that time when she believed the most important thing was to get me to come back to the community—even at the expense of any loyalty to me as her sister.

I understand what Sarah means. It was because of this mindset that I rejected David for more than two years. When you read *Bonnet Strings,* you will be taking the journey with me from my world of freedom in Vermont through two years and eight months back in my community as I tried to make myself Amish. If I've told the story well, you will know what it means to be torn between the two worlds. You will also gain more of an understanding of what Sarah and I mean by the "Amish mindset." If I make you feel this struggle, then I have done my job.

This Amish mindset is also what gives their communities cohesion. They are taught that what they do as individuals affects the whole community. This is something the mainstream culture could learn from. The Amish can also teach us that it takes a certain amount of self-denial or sacrifice to be part of a community. The cohesion in a given community is commensurate with the sacrifices we make to be a part of that community. Perhaps the reverse is also true: the strength of our personal freedom is commensurate with how much we have to sacrifice community to develop that freedom. And that is why the Amish have close-knit communities the rest of us often envy.

I recently witnessed firsthand the powerful draw that an Amish community has had on another young woman. She came to live with David and me after leaving one of the most conservative Amish groups, in which nearly everything is decided for the women. While living with us she established a business making baskets and baking, selling her wares out of our house. After six months of doing well in the outside world, however, she chose to return to her people. Even after enjoying a washer and dryer, dishwasher, and hot shower for six months, this young woman missed her community and family so much that she chose to return and no longer communicates with David and me. She had to sacrifice her personal freedom to be part of that community. Only time will tell which will be more compelling—her desire for personal freedom or her need for community. She is likely in that place of being torn between two worlds, perhaps denying herself even the recollection of what life "on the outside" is like.

Even though I do not regret my decision to leave the Amish, I understand why so many people in mainstream American culture are drawn to them. In this individualistic culture, people find themselves caught up in a rat race to own the latest fashions and technologies. Many people are taught that nothing is off limits—if they want something badly enough, they can acquire it or achieve it.

This is the opposite of what I was taught growing up. To be Amish we had to make sacrifices, including the temptation to "be of the world." We were told that you are either Amish or not—there simply is no in-between. For years after leaving, I fought against this belief. I kept telling myself I must have the best of both worlds. That is, I thought I could be "partly Amish": I could hold on to some of the Amish values yet still enjoy the freedoms I had gained and not have to put up with the restrictions of Amish life. But I now see that the Amish have a point—I cannot have it all. To have my personal freedom I had to sacrifice community and tradition. The values of the two cultures are so different that I had to choose between them.

Several years after I left the Amish the second time, I found the need to embark on a healing journey to deal with the complexities of the two worlds in which I'd lived. I felt there was a mutual betrayal. I had betrayed the vows I made when I was baptized into the community, but I also felt betrayed by the people in my community who had not been able to accommodate my personality. I was taught that God doesn't make mistakes. I reasoned that if that's true then I was meant to be an outgoing, feisty, and adventurous person with a voracious desire to ask fundamental questions. To try to mold myself into the Amish ways seemed like it was going against my own nature and God's purpose for my life.

While I was going through my most intensive therapy, I also grappled with my spiritual beliefs. I questioned everything I had been taught. I found many of the Amish beliefs punitive, especially the one about going to hell if I left the Amish. To reestablish my own beliefs, I had to ask fundamental questions: Who is God? What happens to our souls when we die? If there is such a thing as heaven for eternity, then wouldn't we be there now? Otherwise, how is it that we are living outside eternity while we live on this earth?

Gradually, as my search continued, I discovered that I had an innate belief that there is something greater than us. Our world and our universe just don't make sense without a source for everything. Eventually, I came around to believing in a loving and personal God who hears and answers our prayers.

I often feel in awe of God through nature, whether it's watching a male bluebird sidle up to his mate to feed her on one of the lower branches of the birch tree outside my window, watching an eagle soaring above the Connecticut River, or seeing the grandeur of the Swiss Alps or the Canadian Rockies.

Most Christians believe in Jesus Christ as their Savior. And this is where I come back to my Amish roots—at least to the less punitive beliefs. In my home community, we did believe Jesus came to earth and died on the cross so that we may have everlasting life. However, it is *Jesus on earth* or *Jesus as human* with whom the people in my community identified. They strove to follow Jesus' example and live their lives as he had lived his life on earth—even if it meant becoming martyrs for their beliefs. There was no separation between what they *believed* from the way they *lived*. Rather than going out and spreading the *gospel* of Christ, most Amish believe in living the *example* of Christ.

I espouse these beliefs. I also believe Jesus knew his purpose for having been born on this earth and that he lived his life in accord with that purpose. I believe God gave us the ability to know when we are living our purpose. As Thomas Merton wrote,

"The problem of sanctity and salvation is in fact the problem of finding out who I am and of discovering my true self."

Discovering my true self has included grafting my chosen faith onto that "old-time religion" of my childhood. Some aspects of who I am shall remain forever shaped by the culture of my childhood.

Part 1

1

A Lifetime on Earth

At the darkest moment comes the light.
—Joseph Campbell

In the darkest moment of my life, I was down to two choices. Both of them were a form of suicide—one mortal, the other spiritual.

I was twenty years old and living in constant fear of my father's next violent episode. It seemed there was no help for our family troubles. All the elders knew how to do was accept yet another one of his public confessions for "having gone too far."[2] I knew all too well the shame and indignation of sitting through one of those confessions in church. We would be required to "forgive and forget"—meaning we could never speak of it again. What made this experience all the more dreadful was when the bishop would say, "Well it's not entirely Sim's fault—if the wife and children weren't so rebellious, maybe Sim wouldn't have this problem." My father's name was Simon, and he was called "Sim" for short. It was clear the bishop did not know how unreasonable my father's behavior was.

After each of *Datt*'s confessions, the cycle of violence continued.

One day I discovered there was indeed help for our family, but I needed to reach into the outside world to get it: the county social

---

2. Donald Kraybill, author of numerous books on the Amish, describes this phenomenon well in a *New York Times* article: "Some Amish communities aren't fully aware that a psychological disorder may be underlying devious behavior. . . . They think that if the person confesses the sin, and we bring them back into the church, and we pray about it, everything is going to be O.K." Quoted in Malcolm Gay, "A Crisis in Amish Country," *New York Times*, September 3, 2010, http://nyti.ms/JDcH08.

workers. But I soon found out that, being twenty years old, I was not yet considered of age in the state of Ohio. The social workers could not intervene in an abusive home unless they had permission from someone in the family who was twenty-one or older, who could vouch for the abuse. Believing *Mem* was my best bet, I gave the social worker our address and then waited to find out if *Mem* would grant the permission.

Mem refused the help.

The social worker tried a second time.

At the time, I was cleaning houses for Yankee people six days a week. (The Amish in Geauga County often use the term *Yankee* for the non-Amish.)[3] The day the social worker called, all my hopes of living a normal, healthy life were dashed. I was cleaning the bedroom that used to belong to a daughter in the family who had died in a car accident months before, but I cleaned Pamela's room every two weeks as if she were still alive. When the social worker called to inform me that *Mem* had said no a second time, I hung up the phone and lay down on Pamela's bed. My soul cried out to God, why Pamela and not me?

I felt completely trapped. Now that *Mem* had closed the door to my only hope, I had to think about my other options. Lying on my back, with my wrist on my forehead, I thought that if I commit suicide, then I will surely go to hell—and right now. But if I leave the Amish, I'll go to hell too!

Then a daring thought surfaced: if I leave the Amish, then I'll at least have a lifetime on earth before I have to go to hell. And besides, what if the preachers are wrong?

Before I got up from Pamela's bed, I resolved one thing in my mind. I could no longer think about what was good for my family. I now had to think about what was good for me.

~ ❀ ~

---

3. As noted in the introduction, the late Stephen Scott, author of several books on the Amish, observed that no other Amish community uses this term. His hypothesis was that because people from New England settled that area, they were, quite literally, Yankees. Other Amish communities normally call them English.

My plans started forming in earnest one chilly Saturday night in October when I was sitting in the woods next to the cornfield, afraid to go in the house. That afternoon, *Datt* had been sawing logs in half so they would fit into the woodstove. It was one of the first times that fall when we needed the warmth from the stove for taking our baths. I was on my way to the mailbox when *Datt* looked up and said, "Lomie, take this wood in the house."

Before I could stop myself, I said, "No! I'm getting the mail."

Shock registered in *Datt*'s eyes. I knew I was in trouble now. His next reaction would be anger, and then his eyes would turn dark, like two shiny black coals, just before he would lash out at me. I ran out into the cornfield and then to the woods beyond. I hid there all afternoon, and now it was nighttime. I knew *Mem* would tell me it was my fault—we had to rally around *Datt* so as not to trigger his anger.

Mem had always played the martyr. She wanted us to feel sorry that she was in such a bad marriage. Once I pointed out to her

This barn sat on the small farm in Burton, Ohio, where I lived the first twenty years of my life.

that she was the only one who had a choice—after all, she had married him, but we children had absolutely no choice who our father was. I saw I had hurt her deeply and I felt guilty. Now I wondered if *Mem* brought some of her troubles on herself. She had turned down the helping hand of the social worker when it was offered to her—not once, but twice.

As I sat shivering on the stump in the woods on that October night, my anger helped to clarify my thoughts, and I found the resolve I needed to leave. I thought about who I would ask for help, how I would leave, where I would go, and how I would keep my secret long enough to make my escape. I decided I wanted to go to Vermont. I had never had a train ride, so maybe I could take a train to Vermont. I would ask Megan, one of the Yankee people I worked for, to assist my getaway. She was the one who had connected me with the social workers after I became upset and spilled my story following one of *Datt*'s violent episodes.

Long after dark, I tucked away my secret as I slipped inside to bathe and retire for the night.

At the first chance I could find to use a phone privately, I called Megan and asked if she would help me leave. She said she would, and we made plans to meet nine days later in her little town.

The next week, I said goodbye to life as I knew it: I went to my last church service; I cleaned each house for the last time; I had my last Amish date; and I lived the last day in my parents' house. Finally, the morning arrived when I would slip away to a whole new life in a whole new world.

I had gone to Middlefield the day before and withdrawn the contents of my savings account: just under four hundred dollars. It had taken me five years to save the money. My parents allowed me to keep five dollars a week of the money I earned. My employers also would give me extra money for my birthdays and at Christmas. Whenever I made a deposit in the bank, I would think in the back of my mind: It's there if I ever need it. Until now, I had never dared to think those words: if I ever leave the Amish.

That evening I packed the money into my little blue overnight suitcase, along with as many underclothes as I could, and a toothbrush, a hairbrush and comb, and several photos taken with a camera that my sisters and I shared in secret. Then I placed the suitcase in the back of the closet, hidden behind my long dresses, until it was time to leave.

On the morning of November 7, 1977, I waited in my room until my ride arrived to take me to work. *Mem* called out from the kitchen, "*Lomie, dei taxi is do.*" (Saloma, your ride is here.) I had hoped she'd be in the living room when she announced my ride, so I could slip out the door without her seeing me. But her voice came from the kitchen. I went down and came face to face with her. She looked pointedly at my suitcase and then at me.

"I'm babysitting tonight at the place where I'm working," I said.

"Well, you just don't let this happen too often!"

"I won't!" I said, as I went down the stairs and out the door.

As the driver drove past the kitchen windows, I saw *Mem* peering out the window, and I knew she knew something was up. My hand went up and I gave her a wave. Then I wondered if I would ever see her again.

～❀～

My plans came together at Megan's house. She asked me where I was going to go. I told her I'd like to go to Vermont. She asked me why I chose Vermont. I said I'd discovered Vermont in my seventh-grade geography book. Megan smiled, and she looked at me sideways. I quickly added that I'd been getting *Vermont Life* magazines for the last year. Hesitating, I said, "Do you think that's not a good idea?"

"No, I think it's fine. I'm just amazed that you picked it. If you're starting a whole new life, it may as well be someplace where you want to be."

"That's what I was thinking."

"Where will you stay?"

"Someone told me about YWCAs. I thought I might find one in Vermont."

"That's a wonderful idea. The best place to call is the chamber of commerce. And be sure to ask for a residential YWCA. Not all of them are."

After several phone calls, I found out the only residential Y in all of Vermont was in Burlington. I voiced my concern about living in a city, but Megan assured me Burlington was not a big city and that it probably had resources that the rest of the state might not. So I made reservations for a week at the Y in Burlington.

Next, I made a reservation for a train ticket out of Cleveland. The agent told me the best way to get to Burlington was to go to Port Kent, New York, and then take a ferry across Lake Champlain. I thought that was a good plan, so I reserved a ticket.

Megan took me to get a haircut, and I bought my first Yankee clothes that day. Later, when I stepped onto the night train from Cleveland, I felt half-naked without a covering on my head and with my knees showing.

◦~❀~◦

I arrived in Albany in the morning and then had to wait five hours for the next train bound for Port Kent, New York. That's when the adventure began. An astute conductor noticed my ticket and warned me that I was getting off at a stop in the middle of the woods where there were no hotels, no restaurants, and no phones.

I explained that I was taking the ferry across the lake to Burlington. He shook his head and said, "That ferry was discontinued twelve days ago."

It felt like someone had just dropped a stone into the bottom of my stomach. "How will I get to Burlington then?" I asked.

"If you want to get there by train, you'll have to go up to Montreal and then buy a ticket back down to Burlington. But there is a couple on the train who will be getting off in Port Kent. Let me see if they are going to Burlington." With that, he approached a couple in the back of the train and told them about my need for a ride. The woman shook her head and said, "No, no! Can't do that; she's a stranger!"

The conductor tried to tell her I was not someone to be afraid of, but she would have none of that. He came back to me and said, "Have your things ready and we'll just see."

When the train stopped, a woman approached the train, calling out, "Hi, Mom! Hi, Dad!" to the couple getting off.

The conductor leaned out the door of the train and called to her, "There is a young woman who needs a ride to Burlington. Will you give her one?"

"Sure, come along!" said the daughter, with a welcoming wave of her arm. The conductor nearly pushed me off the train as he handed me my suitcase and said, "Go! Go!" Then the doors closed, and the train moved on down the tracks.

I looked around me at the tall trees and the darkness. The conductor was not kidding; this was a stop in the middle of the woods. There was nothing left to do but to follow the family to the little white car that was parked not far away. The mother was saying to her daughter, "You can't do that—she's a stranger!"

"Oh, Mom! I'm a Vermonter!" the daughter said.

I thought, okay, so I at least I picked the right state.

I sat in the back seat with the daughter's eight-year-old son and the woman who thought "stranger" was the same as "evil." We drove through the hills and woods to the ferry farther south. When we were on the ferry, I thought it should be so romantic, coming to Vermont for the first time by way of Lake Champlain. The younger woman asked me what I was going to do in Vermont. I thought about making up a story, but I wasn't any good at that. So I told the truth. The mother said, "See! Now you've got a runaway in your car!"

When I stepped up onto the front porch of a stately brick house on Main Street that housed the YWCA, I knew my long journey from home was finally at an end and that I was entering a whole new world.

I rang the doorbell. The woman who came to the door introduced herself as Ana Mae. She led me to my bedroom behind the kitchen on the first floor. It was a tiny room with a faded gray carpet and a small closet. It was furnished with a dresser, a nightstand, and a single bed. The drab room felt like my own little domain, so it may as well have been a room in a mansion.

Ana Mae was talkative, saying the linens and towels were upstairs and that she'd be happy to show me around, and did I want to do that now or later?

I said I would like to do it later if that was okay. Until I saw the bed, I hadn't realized just how exhausted I was. With only one night's sleep in the last three, I felt overcome with fatigue. I closed the door, took off my shoes, lay down on the bed, and breathed a prayer of gratitude for my safe journey. Then I slid effortlessly under a soft blanket of sleep.

I awoke some time later to the sound of voices in the kitchen and the smell of toast. Someone was having a late-night snack. I realized I was famished. I turned on the light and combed my hair. Then I stepped into the kitchen, where two women were sitting at the counter, eating. We introduced ourselves. Maureen had long red hair and lively hazel eyes. Christine wore thick, heavy-looking glasses that kept sliding down her nose. She had long, stringy, dark hair.

This building in Burlington, Vermont, housed the YWCA where I first lived when I moved away from my Ohio Amish community.

Maureen offered me something to eat and I gratefully accepted. As we were sitting on stools at the counter, Maureen asked where I was from. As I told my story, more and more of the women residents joined the circle to listen in. Seeing the eagerness on these women's faces and hearing their questions spurred me on. Instead of seeing my life as unbearable and mundane—as I had when I was still living with my parents—I now saw it as unique.

After I told my story, Maureen gave me a mischievous grin. She said, "You are going to have so much fun!"

Ana Mae noticed I was tired, so she showed me to the upstairs bathroom with its claw-foot bathtub and to the closet where the linens and towels were kept.

As I slipped into the luxuriously deep bath, I knew I would not miss the baths of home. In cold weather, I would no longer have to pour heated water into the galvanized tub by the woodstove in the living room. In summer, I would no longer have to mix hot water from the stove with cold water in a garden sprinkling can and hang it from a nail on the ceiling in the basement for a "homemade shower." Now, as I sank into the warm water with only my head above it, the bliss of it all was like coming home to myself—a place where I had never been before.

2

I Lift Mine Eyes

My head is bursting with the joy of the unknown.
My heart is expanding a thousand fold.
—Rumi

The next morning, as I stepped out onto the front porch, I breathed in the crisp autumn air and looked out across Lake Champlain, sparkling under the November sun. It was framed by the Adirondacks on the opposite shore, and fluffy clouds hung in the blue sky above.

I realized no one in my family or Amish community knew where I was or that I had changed my name. I didn't think I could hide behind a name like Saloma, and I didn't want my family to find me, so I had decided to change my name to Malinda (Linda) Sue Miller. Everyone in my new world would know me as Linda.

I waited for the remorse and guilt feelings to set in. Instead, I breathed in the air of freedom. It was as if the lake represented my future—both exhilarating and terrifyingly open.

For months, I had admired this scene from a distance, through *Vermont Life* magazines. Now I was in Vermont for real—not there, back home in Ohio, afraid my father would come after me, but here—in Burlington. I had been living in constant fear of my father's next violent episode since there seemed to be no help for our family troubles.

Now, as I breathed in the crisp autumn air, I knew *Mem* was likely heartbroken that I'd left. She had probably been crying ever since getting the letter I sent before leaving Ohio that let her know

I was leaving home. Perhaps she had been lying awake through the night. I could just imagine her large frame moving slowly and sadly around the kitchen, from the counter to the oil stove and back again. Her fair, freckled skin was likely flushed from crying, her light blue eyes moist with tears. Causing *Mem* tears had always made me feel guilty. Instilling guilt was one of the tools she used to make me give in—to her, to Datt, to my brother Joe, to the church.

The brisk wind off the lake brought tears to my eyes as I thought: she even refused the offer for help from the social workers.

I could feel my chest expanding to make room for my heart, brimming with relief that I was no longer stuck in the world I'd left behind, and with joy for the new world I was experiencing as I looked out at Lake Champlain. I wiped my cheeks and turned to walk up the hill with a quick stride. At the top of the hill I stopped in my tracks. There stretched Mt. Mansfield across the horizon, with snow covering its top. White cotton clouds hovered above it in a light blue sky. The scene was enough to make me wish I were an artist like my sister Sarah. Yet I knew that even if I were the best artist in the world, I would not be able to capture that beauty on canvas. It would be but an imitation of the work of the Great Artist.

As I wrapped myself in the white sweater Megan had given me and stood in the wind, all I could do was cry into the November breezes. I kept thinking, why am I not laughing instead of crying? I hadn't comprehended that it would take time for me to adjust to being "in" one of the pictures from *Vermont Life*. I looked into the blue between clouds and pulled strength from its expanse. I thought of the psalm, "I lift mine eyes unto the hills, from whence cometh my help."[4] I had stepped into the world of the unknown. I imagined the clouds were angels, there to watch over me. Just as Megan had helped me plan and make my getaway, and just as the conductor and the Vermonter had saved me from being stranded

4. This verse comes from Psalm 121:1. I learned this and other verses from the King James Bible as I was growing up, although at that time I didn't realize that there are different translations of the Bible.

in the woods on the opposite shore of Lake Champlain, I hoped angels would continue to guide my way as they had on my journey out of the Amish.

I turned to walk down the hill to the Y, knowing there were things I needed to do. I had to find warm clothing for the winter coming on, and I needed to apply for a Social Security number. Ana Mae had offered to show me around the city. I had to prepare for my new life as Linda.

~⚜~

Several of the women residents at the Y were helpful in showing me around town. Ana Mae was older than most of the women at the Y. I judged she was in her early forties. She took me to the Social Security office, to a secondhand clothing shop, and to several food establishments to apply for jobs. She liked to talk about herself, but she also enjoyed being my escort as I found my way around town, which I thought of as "the city." She was with me the day I bought a long, black winter coat, which fit snugly at my waist with a flared skirt. It flattered my figure, and I tried not to notice when men stared. Ana Mae later told the women at the Y, "And they weren't staring at me. It wasn't me wearing the long, black coat."

During my first week at the Y, Maureen arranged with the director that I could receive free room and board in exchange for cleaning the common areas of the Y. I was used to cleaning the homes of many Yankee families per week, so this was easy for me. I soon found other cleaning jobs in Burlington. I knew this could sustain me for a while, but I wanted to move on to doing things I could only fantasize about before, such as working in an office or a restaurant.

Maureen took me to a place for drinks one night. In Vermont the legal drinking age was eighteen, while in Ohio it was twenty-one. But there had been plenty of beer at the Amish young people's gatherings. I hated beer, but sometimes I drank it anyway, just to be part of the crowd. Now Maureen introduced me to mixed drinks. I chose a piña colada. The waitress asked if I had a birth certificate to prove I was eighteen. Maureen laughed and said, "I can vouch for her—she's twenty." The waitress accepted that.

When she was gone, Maureen said, "Linda, you do look young, with your hair up like that." She had taught me several new hairdos by then. She loved to shampoo and blow-dry my hair. This time she had pulled my hair into a bun and pinned it at the top of my head. It felt so different from when my hair had been clamped against my head so my covering would fit over it. That stiff organdy *kopp,* which Amish women wear to symbolize their subservience to God and to the men of the community, was now a world away.

Christine wasn't immediately likeable, but she had an uncanny way of voicing my subconscious thoughts, which brought them to the surface. I sometimes welcomed this, and at other times I found it annoying. She also liked to eavesdrop. She seemed to have a barometer for private moments and was either right outside the door or finding her way into the middle of things that didn't concern her. But Christine also shared helpful information. When I mentioned that I would like to further my education, she told me about the program at the Church Street Center, where I could work in exchange for taking courses. Within a week, I went there to sign up.

When I arrived at the University of Vermont Church Street Center for Community Education, the woman at the desk turned around in her chair, shook my hand, and said, "Hi, I'm Barbara Lalancette. It's great to meet you." Her blue eyes sparkled. She explained they didn't have any work exchange at that time, but she invited me to have a seat and said, "Tell me about yourself."

I began telling my story. Barbara's eyes widened and she said, "I'll be darned! I used to live in Lancaster, Pennsylvania, around the Amish, and I even had a Mennonite boyfriend for a while."

As my story flowed out easily, Barbara shook her head and said, "Oh . . . my . . . God." I had never felt such a quick kinship as I did with Barbara. Before we knew it, we had been talking for more than an hour. She said it was time for her to go home, but added, "Linda, I am so glad you came! And if any work comes up,

I will be sure to call you. Here, if you could just write down your phone number, that would be great."

As I left, I was sorry the center didn't have any work for me and I wondered if I'd get to talk to Barbara again. Little did I know I had just met a lifetime friend.

Several days later, Barbara left a message for me to call her. She told me her mother-in-law wanted to invite me to Thanksgiving dinner at their house. At first I felt too overcome to respond. Finally I said, "Are you sure? I wouldn't want to intrude on the family."

"You aren't intruding at all. My mother-in-law said, 'Well, she must not have anyone to spend Thanksgiving with; why don't you invite her over?' Linda, we would love to include you." I let her know how touched I was by their kindness and accepted the invitation.

I wondered why I felt so unworthy of the kindness people were showing me. It was like seeing Lake Champlain and Mt. Mansfield for the first time: I couldn't take it all in at once. I wondered how in less than two weeks I could feel like I belonged in Vermont, and yet I never felt like I belonged in the community where I grew up. But I would only belong if I allowed myself to—accepting the kindness of strangers was humbling, but necessary.

∽❀∾

And so I spent my first Thanksgiving outside the Amish community. The Lalancettes welcomed me into their midst. Just as in my family, there were seven siblings, and I liked them all. The two pies I baked were a big hit. And my new best friend, Barbara, kept the discussion lively. The day went by quickly.

On the way back to the Y with Barbara and her husband, Rick, I thought about them all. What a tall and handsome family! Dennis was the tallest—someone said he was six feet five inches, and he was quite handsome, but he already had a girlfriend. Their cousin, Raymond, didn't, as far as I knew, but I thought he was quite a bit older than me. Still, if he asked me out, I decided that I would probably accept.

Back at the Y, however, I became restless. I tried not to think about missing anything about my old life among the Amish, which would have brought up a conflict I didn't know how to handle; yet, for the first time, the six hundred miles between my family and me felt like a long way.

Normally we got together on *Mem*'s side of the family for Thanksgiving. When all the cousins, uncles, and aunts came, there would be more than a hundred people. I wondered if the families had decided *not* to gather for Thanksgiving this time. This would be a typical Amish way for the relatives to show their sympathy for a daughter who had gone "out into the world." I tried not to think about that; otherwise I'd fall into the Amish guilt trap. I had often heard the preachers say it would be better to lose a child through death when she was still innocent than lose that child to "the world." They also claimed if you raise your children right, they wouldn't leave the Amish. This guilt trap made us children want to spare our parents the deepest of sorrows, and it made parents feel like failures if their sons or daughters did leave.

I wondered if *Mem* and *Datt* actually wished I had died when I was a small child, as I almost did when I was three years old. I had loved the feeling of holding a smooth marble in my mouth, even though *Mem* warned me not to. One winter night, as I sat on the top of the wood box, I had one in my mouth that slid into my throat and I couldn't breathe. *Mem* grabbed me, turned me upside down, held me by one ankle, and pounded me on my back three times. The marble popped out. The trauma was enough to cure my desire to feel the marble in my mouth ever again.

Was *Mem*'s sorrow greater now than if I had died when I was still innocent? She would have blamed herself then, and she was probably blaming herself now. I knew if I tried to imagine how much I had broken *Mem*'s heart, I would not be able to move forward with my new life. I would be drawn back into the fold and back into the family situation. All I had to do was imagine myself back in the house of my parents and I would feel the heavy blanket of dread again—being stuck with no one to help when things became unbearable. Maybe *Mem*'s heart was broken, but I had my own limits. On some level I knew my spirit would not survive if I went back to what I had escaped only weeks before.

I could not turn back now. Yet I was feeling homesick on my first holiday away from home.

I took out my diary and began writing.

I cannot help but think about the family today, especially Mem. I was determined I would not feel sorry for her again, but she has to be wondering if I have come to any harm. Maybe I should call Sarah at work and let her know I'm okay. I'm glad Megan insisted I write to Mem before I left, otherwise right now Mem would probably worry I'd been kidnapped or killed. At least the letter let her know I ran away, but she is probably thinking anything could have happened to me since then. I'll call Sarah tomorrow and let her know I'm okay.

I sat with my head in my hands and stared at the lamp on the dresser as I thought about how to let Sarah know I was okay without telling her where I was. I'd have to be very determined or else she would drag this information out of me. I decided to go down the hill the next day to the pay phone so the call could not be traced to the Y. The Amish might even involve the police because I was still underage in the state of Ohio. I'd rather be safe than sorry.

After putting away my journal and turning off the lights, I lay in bed and thought about starting a new job on Monday. Right now everything I did was unfamiliar. But, I told myself, it wouldn't always be like that. I had already made lots of friends in the three weeks I'd been in Vermont, and I felt I belonged there.

3

Weighing Happiness

No one saves us but ourselves. No one can and no one may.
We ourselves must walk the path.
—Buddha

A s I walked slowly down the hill on Main Street, I pulled my address book from my purse and looked at the phone number of Sarah's workplace. I dreaded the ordeal of calling, because I knew Sarah would ask where I was.

Sure enough, the first thing Sarah said when she answered the phone was, "Lomie, where *are* you?" It felt as though Sarah could suck me back into my old world just by invoking my Amish name.

"It's not important where I am. I just wanted to let you know I'm okay."

As if she hadn't understood, she said it with more emphasis, "*Lomie, wo* bischt *du*?"

"I am in a place where you won't find me. I will not tell you where I am, so do you want to waste my three minutes talking about that, or can I find out how things are going at home and tell you how I'm doing?"

"Fine! How are you doing?"

"I'm doing well. I'm living in a safe place with other women, and I've found work."

"So, if you want to know how things are going at home, I can tell you right now. If you had any idea how hard this is on *Mem*, you would come home."

"And make it hard on myself instead? Do you think she has thought about how hard our lives are?"

"I'm sure she has."

"Then why didn't she allow the social workers to help?"

"Oh, we told her you were the one who called the social workers, by the way."

"Thanks a lot; that makes me want to come back!"

"Just think about how guilty you would feel if something happened to *Mem*. And that is why I need to know where you are. What if there is an emergency?"

"I will check in with you every week," I said.

"Your three minutes are up," the operator cut in.

I heard Sarah ask, "Operator, where is this call coming from?"

At the same time the operator said, "Burlington, Vermont," I said, "Operator, would you please not tell her?" The operator sighed, as if she were *Mem*. Sarah said, "Where did you say this call is coming from?"

"I am being asked not to tell you," the operator said in a weary voice.

"But Operator, she ran away from home!" Sarah begged.

"I still cannot tell you," the operator said.

I waited for Sarah to hang up the phone before I hung up too. My breath was coming in gasps, and my hands were shaking. I shivered in the November air as I headed up the Main Street hill. I wished I hadn't told Sarah I would call her again. Now that I had promised her, they would certainly worry that something had happened to me if I didn't. But it was so risky. If the Amish found out where I was, they could come and take me back. I didn't want to lose my freedom to discover and become who I really was underneath the rules I had lived with for twenty years.

I wanted to meet someone I could love; I wanted to have a career other than cleaning houses; and I wanted to go to college, which would allow me to know what options were open to me. If I went back to the Amish community, I might never know what I was capable of. There I had few choices—either I would become a mother of many children or else an "old maid." If I became a mother, I would not have any way of deciding how many children I would have; most likely I'd have one per year. I wanted to be a mother, but I didn't want to become the little old woman who lived in a shoe. If I became an old maid, I'd have to eke out a living by cleaning houses or teaching in an Amish school. After five years, I was mighty tired of housecleaning. Teaching in an Amish school wouldn't be so bad if I could get training for it and if I could earn a living wage. Not getting paid enough often forced young Amish women teachers to live at home while they taught, and I knew I didn't want that.

I wished I had put up with the homesickness I'd been feeling the night before. Now I had opened the door to the Amish possibly finding out where I was. I knew I'd have at least another week without discovery.

❧ ✿ ☙

The second time I called Sarah, she was unrelenting. She pleaded into the phone, "Lomie, we *need* a way to get in touch with you in case of an *emergency*."

I assured her I would continue to call.

"But what if there is an emergency and you wouldn't know it for a week! Then what?" she demanded.

I didn't have a ready answer, and Sarah seized on my hesitation. She said she would keep my number and would only use it in case of an emergency, and she wouldn't give it to anyone else.

"But, Sarah, you know how Amish people go after those who leave. Remember the girl who had left the Punxy community and how they got together a vanload of people from the community and went and got her?"

"Yes, I remember, but I heard she was glad they did!"

"That does not mean I would be. Sarah, even you have thought about leaving. I would have thought you would be happy for me that I escaped our home life."

"Oh, but Lomie, if you only knew how hard this is on *Mem*!"

Sarah continued on about how *Mem* could have a breakdown, and then she launched into her emergency campaign again.

For an instant I imagined *Mem* lying in a coffin. People would all say she died of a broken heart. I wouldn't even be able to go to her funeral; I wouldn't be able to face all the condemning eyes following my every move. They would whisper in groups until I came near, and then they would quickly stop. And the worst part is they'd be right. It would all be my fault.

With a sinking heart, I gave Sarah my new name, my phone number, and my address. I could have kicked myself as soon as I hung up. But at least Sarah had promised she wouldn't give out my number.

That evening I was fixing a salad in the kitchen when Christine came in and said, "There's someone on the phone for you, Linda."

I sprinted up the stairs, wondering if Sarah had known something was about to happen—that she really was informing me of an emergency. I picked up the receiver and said, "Hello."

A breathy male voice, thick with reproof, came over the line, "Lomie! *Huscht du eniche idea was du am du bischt?*" (Lomie! Do you have any idea what you are doing?) I had heard that voice once before—the day Donny had called me at work to ask me if I would go steady with him.

"Who is this?" I asked. The heavy breathing was unmistakable, but I wanted him to tell me.

"Donny," he said.

"How did you get my phone number?" I asked.

"Sarah gave it to me." I had known she must have given it to him, but I wanted to hear him say that. I felt a flash of anger at Sarah for betraying my trust, and I said to Donny, "She told me she wouldn't give it away. Who else has it?"

"I don't know. But, Lomie, how can you run away from home like that? Do you have any idea what you did to me? And just think about what your parents must feel."

"My father doesn't feel anything for us except anger. Donny, you ought to understand why I did this. Do you remember the night we drove to your house after *Datt* threatened me? Have you forgotten that, or do you think *Datt* has suddenly changed?"

"Lomie, you have to learn to forgive."

"To forgive does not include allowing someone to abuse you. My decision to come back or not is tough enough; I don't need for you to pressure me."

"Lomie, why do you need to be so hard-hearted? Think about how I feel. I was so happy when you said you'd go steady with me. I thought you were too good for me."

I suddenly had an idea. I knew even if I was to go back to the Amish, I wouldn't want to be Donny's girlfriend. But I might be able to break up with him without destroying the small amount of confidence he did have. "Why would I be too good for you? If anything, you are too good for me. Your family is so happy, and your parents treat you well," I said.

"There are a lot of things you don't know about me. I never told you," Donny said, his breathing getting heavy again.

"Like what?" I asked. I really didn't want to know, but I said what he expected me to, as if he had put the words in my mouth.

"I want to tell you in person. I will tell you when you come back."

"Donny, I told you, I don't know if I am coming back. A lot depends on whether *Datt* gets help with his mental problems."

"Well, just keep in mind your promises to the church, that's all. And don't forget your *Mem*. How can you cause her so much heartache?"

"Donny, there came a time when I had to think of myself. And that's why I'm here and not there."

"Lomie how can you be so *dick-keppich* and hard-hearted?" I heard a click and then the dial tone. Being called *dick-keppich* (stubborn) was one of the worst insults I could get as an Amish person. It meant I just wanted to go my own way, when going the way of the church without question was the definition of a good person. This time it didn't hurt my feelings, but it didn't matter what I thought. Donny had hung up.

I stood at the top of the stairs with my arms crossed over my chest, trying to quiet the churning inside me. Donny was not the issue. I knew our phone conversation was the end of our relationship. It bothered me that the people in the community had my phone number and address. Before long the calls would come streaming in, and now that they knew where I was, they might even come and get me. I knew I could not stand up to them if they did.

Either I had to take my old life back and be Amish, or else I had to try, against all odds, to choose the life I wanted to live, completely separate from the life I'd known. I kept wanting to find a bridge between the two, but the Amish preachers always said either one is Amish or not—there is no middle road.

I walked through the hall and down the back steps to my room. Closing the door, I let the tears flow. Why, oh why did I let Sarah have my address? I could have given her my phone number without my address. Then at least they wouldn't know where I was. When I thought about Sarah's betrayal, I ground my teeth in anger. They can't make me go back—I just won't! With that, I dried my tears, washed my face, and went to finish my dinner.

<hr />

Sure enough, in the days that followed Donny's phone call, Joe, Sarah, Susan, our Amish neighbors the Gingeriches, Joe's sister-in-law Ada, and a host of others called. Letters arrived from my cousins in New York and Wisconsin, cousins and friends from my own community, and even some complete strangers. I realized someone must have announced my leaving in *The Budget*, a weekly Amish and Mennonite newspaper.

One evening, as I was cooking dinner for myself, the phone rang again.

"Linda, the phone is for you," Maureen said, as she came into the kitchen.

"Who is it?" I whispered as I looked at the receiver lying next to the phone on the shelf in the hallway. I knew it could be anyone from the Amish.

"Your mother," Maureen mouthed. I felt the blood draining from my face as she whispered, "Do you want me to tell her you aren't here?"

"No, I have to talk to her," I said. My chest felt hot and I heard my heart pounding in my ears as I reached for the phone. "Hello." I knew *Mem* could hear my fear.

"Hello, Lomie?" My knees felt too weak to hold me, but there was no chair in the hallway. I braced myself against the wall. I realized I had never heard my mother's voice on a telephone before. *"Mia hen an plan fa da Datt."* (We have a plan for *Datt*.) *Mem* knew what she was doing. By talking in Amish she was pulling me into her world from six hundred miles away.[5] "We have a plan for *Datt*, but we need for you to be here. We have a vanload of people who are ready to come up and get you."

I felt like I was going to choke for lack of air. I was sure *Mem* heard my sharp intake of breath before I said in a meek voice in her language, "But, why do you need me? Why don't you get help for *Datt*, and then I will come back?"

"The plan includes you. I can't explain it on the phone."

"Are you getting help from the social workers?"

"Like I said, I'll explain when I get there."

"Who all is coming?" I asked.

"Donny's parents, Bishop Dan Wengerd, Sarah, and Susan . . ." I wasn't listening to the rest of the names. I was thinking, why are Donny's parents coming? I haven't even met them. Now they were coming with *Mem* and a vanload of other Amish to claim me back into the community?

"*Mem*, I don't understand why I need to be there," I said again.

"We are hoping to be there by tomorrow night," *Mem* said as her voice took on a more determined authority, ignoring my question. I suddenly felt like I was ten years old instead of twenty. "I'll explain everything when we get there. We'll start at five o'clock in the morning." With her tone of voice, *Mem* may as well have been saying, "Lomie, you will do this because I said so!" I also heard her doubt, as if she knew she couldn't make me go back if I said I wouldn't. I knew she was relying on guilt. She would start crying if I told her I wouldn't go back. I would feel the same about hearing her cry from this far away as I would if I were standing next to her.

Mem wasn't taking any chances. "I have to go now," she said. "I will talk with you when we get there. If we don't make it by tomorrow night, I'll call you." I listened to the click as *Mem* hung up the phone.

---

5. The Amish speak a German dialect often known as Pennsylvania Dutch. We called this "talking in Amish."

As I hung up, I felt a hole in the pit of my stomach—panic. Why hadn't I told her she shouldn't come, because I wouldn't go back even if she did? I imagined her at our Yankee neighbors' house, where it was only by talking in Amish that she had privacy. For a minute I wished I had talked in English. *Mem* would have switched to English too. I wished I had forced her to expose to the neighbors what she had said.

The churning feeling was worse than it had been after Donny called. Anger, guilt, sadness, powerlessness, and determination all competed for the top position, but none of them won out. They kept roiling inside me.

I walked back into the kitchen, where my three friends looked at me with questioning eyes. They were quiet until Maureen burst out, "What language were you speaking?"

"Amish," I said. I suddenly felt as though I had turned all my feelings off, as a faucet at the kitchen sink turns off the flow of water. In place of the churning was a black void. I felt numb. "They are coming to take me back," I said in a flat voice.

Shock registered on all three of their faces. Maureen recovered first and asked, "Who? Your family?"

"My mom, my boyfriend's parents, the bishop, my sisters, and some others."

Maureen asked, "Linda, is that what you really want?"

"I don't have a choice."

"Why not?" Christine asked.

"Because I wouldn't be strong enough to stand up to my mother and all those people pressuring me to go back."

"So you could go somewhere and hide out," Maureen suggested.

"I couldn't do that to my mother."

"Why not?"

"Her life is tough enough," I said. "I've told you about my father."

"Your mother married him, though," Christine said in a matter-of-fact tone. She looked at me through her thick glasses. I knew she was right, but at that moment I didn't like her for telling the truth—that *Mem* had a choice and the rest of us didn't.

"I need to go pack," I said. I walked to the far end of the kitchen and into my bedroom, behind the back stairs. But I didn't pack. I sat on my bed and stared at the gray carpet at my feet. I wished I could shake this numbness, and then maybe I could think. I remembered this feeling from before. Like the day I found out the county social workers couldn't help my father because *Mem* wouldn't give them permission. That day, had I not felt so numb, maybe my anger would have been great enough to hurt someone, or burn a house down.

Now what would I be feeling if it wasn't for this numbness? Gray was the color at my feet and inside me. My thoughts were so clouded that it felt as though they were not my own.

⁓ ❀ ⁓

Mem called the following night. It was like my feelings returned as she said to me, "We are in New York State. We are staying here overnight, but we'll be there first thing in the morning."

"Okay," I said weakly. My knees felt as though they didn't want to support me.

Mem added, "The trip has gone well. We haven't gotten into any bad weather." She sounded excited, as though she was enjoying the trip. *Mem* didn't get to travel often; she had a scrapbook of pictures and accounts of a trip out West in 1950 when she was thirty years old and before she was married. But, of course, she would never admit to enjoying her trip to Vermont now.

"What time will you be here?" I asked.

"Probably around nine or ten," *Mem* said. "I have to go. My time on this pay phone is going to be up."

"Okay," I said.

After I had replaced the receiver, I stood there imagining my life as it had been, with the tension that lived in *Mem* and *Datt*'s house. At home, where I had not even one private space. Not a bedroom. Not a bathroom. Not a closet. Not a drawer. Not anything. And I had *Datt*'s judgmental eyes following me around— those eyes that could get wild when he was about to have one of his violent episodes.

I walked into the kitchen where Maureen was doing dishes at the kitchen sink. "I don't want to go back," I said.

"I can't believe you are doing this," Maureen said, and then a flood of words began, as if she couldn't stop them. "You are starting a whole new life here, and now you are going to throw that out the window! Think about all the good times we have had in just six weeks. You are just getting your feet on the ground, and now you are going to go back? To what? You were miserable there! I still say you could go somewhere else."

"Mom would be so upset. And it would make it hard for all the other residents who are here in the morning."

"We could tell everyone what is going to happen, and they can leave if they don't want to be here."

"That's an idea," I said. "But I need some time to think."

~⚘~

Back in my room the inner debate raged. Should I give in and go back to make *Mem*'s life easier? I wondered. Or stay with this new life? If it wasn't for *Mem*, the choice would be so easy. I've made new friends. I have a job I like . . .

Barbara will know what to do, I thought. I went to the phone in the hallway and dialed her number.

Barbara Lalancette became my mentor and friend in my life in Vermont.

Sure enough, Barbara helped me clarify my thoughts by asking the right questions.

She asked me what was prompting them to come. I explained what *Mem* had said—that they needed me to be there to get help for *Datt*.

"Do you think it's true?" Barbara asked.

"No, I think this is her way of getting me back."

"Do you want to go back?"

"No. But what I want to do and what I feel I have to do are two different things."

"What if you just tell them you don't want to go back?"

"I wouldn't be able to do that. I know if I stay here at the Y, they will convince me to go back."

I told her I was thinking of not being around when they came. "What would you do?" I finally asked Barbara. I wanted her to tell me not to go back. But she was too wise for that.

"I have no idea what I'd do. I can support you, but I can't make the decision for you. If you decide to leave the Y in the morning, you may use my house if you'd like. I'll leave my basement door unlocked and you can come through there."

"Thank you so much. You are such a good friend."

"You know it would be easy for me to tell you not to go back. We'll certainly miss you if you do."

"And I would miss you too. You and the rest of the Lalancettes made me feel at home on Thanksgiving. This has been the happiest six weeks of my life."

"I can see why this is a tough decision for you."

"I know. How do you weigh one person's happiness against another's?"

"I don't think there is an answer to that question. But, remember, kiddo, you are not responsible for your mother's life. The only person you're responsible for is yourself."

4

Liberating Linda

That's the way things come clear. All of a sudden.
And then you realize how obvious they've been all along.
—Madeleine L'Engle

As I soaked in the claw-foot bathtub, I wondered if this would
be my last "real" bath. Would I need to go back to using the
galvanized tub next to the woodstove in *Mem* and *Datt*'s living
room? I could live with that much more easily than I could stand
being monitored by everyone in the community or living in constant fear of being punished by *Datt*.

I remembered the time that I tried going out on a Saturday
night when I was eighteen and hadn't yet become a member of
the church. Other young people were allowed to go out on both
Saturday and Sunday nights, but whenever *Mem* or *Datt* had the
chance to be stricter than the rest of the community, they took
it. So after sneaking out on a Saturday night, I sheepishly came
back on Sunday afternoon and went directly to my room, knowing there was trouble in store for me.

My weekend had been a disaster. I had accepted a date with
someone I didn't know. He had driven me in his buggy to his
friend's house. There were three other couples there and we par-
tied for a while, drinking beer and hanging out in an upstairs bedroom. Then came the time when the couples paired up for the
actual date.

Not every Amish community practices bed courtship, but in
my home community they did. Even on a first date, the young

man and woman went to bed together. They were allowed to *schmunzle* (hug and kiss), but they were expected to stay chaste until marriage. I used to wish I could go out for dinner on dates so I could get to know someone before having intimacies with him, but this was simply not the way it was done.

Most of my bed dates had been disgusting. Some of the men had stinky feet. Others didn't know how to kiss without their teeth getting in the way, or they had roving hands. That night had been no exception. In fact, this guy's hands were more insistent than any of the others' had been. I kept pushing away his hands, but they kept coming back with more force. Finally I used the weapon I had found was effective: words. I said, *"Do net!"* (Don't!)

Sure enough, he turned his back and slept.

I awoke on Sunday morning with the young man gone from the bed. I got up and dressed. The other three women (whom I hardly knew) were cold with me, as though they knew what had happened and were on his side. I remember sitting on a buggy with one of the girls later that day and she kept handing me beers. I had not eaten for more than twenty-four hours, so they were making me tipsy very quickly. I remember drinking at least seven beers, and then I must have passed out. I also remember leaning on one of the women to get to the outhouse. She kept saying, *"Shteck dae finga in dae halz"* (Stick your finger in your throat), and said that if I could throw up, I would feel better.

When I was sober enough to face going home, I called one of the Yankee van drivers to pick me up. I didn't see my date again that day.

After arriving home and going straight to my room, I heard *Mem* lumbering up the stairs. I knew I still smelled of alcohol. Most Amish parents would look the other way as young people who had not yet joined the church drank, had cameras or radios on the sly, or did other things that weren't within the church *Ordnung* (set of rules). Then again, most young people were careful about hiding such things.

Parents were supposed to keep young people in line with the church teachings until they joined church and were baptized.

After baptism, young people were more accountable to the elders, and "sowing wild oats" was no longer acceptable. Young people also had to be baptized members of the church before they were allowed to marry. The final step into adulthood occurred when two people got married. Now the church had a full hold on their behavior. If someone got caught drinking alcohol, that person would have to make a public confession in church. Since I was not yet a member of the church, there really wasn't much *Mem* could do, yet I knew it wouldn't keep her from trying.

Mem nearly filled the doorway of my room, giving me no choice of whether she was going to come in—she just did. She said she was shocked to find out I had sneaked out the night before, and then she tried to extract a promise from me that I wouldn't do it again. I had already decided the whole ordeal hadn't been worth it—yet I didn't want to promise *Mem* I wouldn't ever do it again. After all, my date could just as easily have been a really nice guy. I wanted to leave my options open. So I used my usual defense, "But all the other young people get to go out on Saturday night!"

I was emotionally and physically exhausted, so when she insisted I needed to promise, I broke into tears. Then, out of nowhere, *Datt* came thundering into the room and pounced on me, slamming me with his hands and arms all over my head, my shoulders, my back, wherever the blows might land. I curled into a ball to protect my most vulnerable places. *Mem* managed to pull *Datt* away from me, and as she walked behind him down the stairs, she said, "That is the last time I will let *you* listen in."

I was as upset with *Mem* in that incident as I was with *Datt*. She couldn't always control *Datt*, but that didn't stop her from using him and the threat of his violence to try to control me.

Now, at the Y in Burlington, Vermont, my bathwater was cooling off. I really could not imagine going back to the oppression of living with *Mem* and *Datt*.

How can I forget *Mem* when everyone keeps reminding me of her hardships? I wondered. They were making me feel guilty for her mistake of marrying *Datt*. I remembered that summer day several years before, after *Mem* and *Datt* had one of their big arguments. *Mem* sat straddling a bench by the table in the dining end of the kitchen, snapping green beans for canning. Sitting in chairs at the table, we girls were also snapping beans. *Mem's* shoulders slumped over her work as she said in a rueful voice, "Oh . . . I hope you girls *never* have such a disappointment in your marriage as I've had." She moved her shoulders back and forth, as if she was trying to shake something from herself, and added, "Oh, I just *have* to be quiet."

"Why did you marry him?" I asked her.

Mem sighed and said, "I almost didn't."

"What happened?" I asked. *Mem* hesitated for so long that I thought she wasn't going to answer my question. Then she started slowly, as if she was reminding herself.

"I was living at my Aunt Em's at the time." *Mem* paused again and then continued in her hesitant voice, "I had been making suits for the Amish men, making braided rugs, and working at Spector's Dry Goods store in Middlefield. *Datt* and I were planning on getting married.

"One day I was sitting there, braiding rugs, when I started thinking about *Datt*. I knew he had problems. When I imagined living with him, I thought, wouldn't I just rather do what I'm doing now? So that Sunday night, I told him I didn't want to marry him. After that, I didn't hear from him for a few weeks. Then one day he drove in the lane. Aunt Em came to the bottom of the stairs and called up, 'Kettie, there's someone here to see you.'

"I stood at the top of the stairs and asked, 'What should I do?'

"Em said, 'Oh, I would let him in, he looks so forlorn.' So I did. *Datt* came up the stairs with his head hanging so low I wondered how he could walk. He said, 'Kettie, if I didn't know any better, I wouldn't be here right now.' I wasn't sure what he meant until he said, 'But I decided God didn't want me to be dead.' That's when I knew he meant taking his own life. I felt so sorry for him that I took him back," *Mem* concluded.

"Why didn't you tell your Aunt Em not to let him in, instead of letting her decide what to do?" I asked.

"Sometimes I wish I had," *Mem* sighed. "But it's not all bad. I did want to have children." Then she shook herself again. "Oh, I do have to be quiet," she said and got up to go to the outhouse.

I thought to myself as I sat there in the bathtub, I never would have married him! There is no way he would have tricked me into it. Then a thought hit me like a bolt of lightning. I sat upright and pulled the plug in the bathtub. I got out, dried off, and pulled on my nightgown. I went back to my room, opened my dresser drawer, and pulled out the letters I'd received from community members. I flipped through them until I came to the right one. I opened it and read it again. This time I was determined not to look away from its implications.

Donny had written that he could not sleep and that he felt he had to do something to make me come back. He assured me he was not running after me to go steady, but he wanted the satisfaction of knowing that I was Amish. Then came the part that was supposed to play on my sympathies: he had considered taking his gun off the wall and shooting himself, but he had decided God didn't want him dead.

I dropped the letter into my lap and stared at the wall. It was as if *Mem*'s decision to take *Datt* back had written the script for my life now. I had always thought of Donny as being my way out of my parents' home. But I had also sensed that Donny was unstable, and that if I were to marry him, my life would be like *Mem*'s.

As I read further, the resemblance between *Datt* and Donny sank in. Donny rambled on, describing how when he looked in the mirror he saw an eighty-year-old man instead of an eighteen-year-old boy; how he didn't want to date other girls until I came back and we'd had a chance to talk face to face; and how he had stopped taking his nerve pills because they made him feel sick. He acknowledged he should have told me about these problems, but that he hadn't been able to bring himself to do so.

I slowly folded Donny's letter. Would he also become violent, as *Datt* had? I knew one thing for sure. If I decided to go back to the Amish, I would break up with Donny, no matter what his reaction would be. I shuddered at the horrible realization that I could have felt trapped for a lifetime in a marriage I didn't want. I vowed I would never again say to *Mem* "I would not have married *Datt*," in that accusatory tone. I would have a better understanding of how that had happened.

I also heard Barbara's voice saying, "Just remember the only person you are responsible for is yourself."

Even if I don't have Donny for a boyfriend, I thought, I will still need to decide if I am going back tomorrow or not. It will be so hard to face Donny's parents, knowing I don't want to continue my relationship with him.

Getting up from the edge of the bed, I gathered the clothes I had taken out and placed them neatly back into my dresser drawers. I closed the empty suitcase and placed it in the closet. Unless I changed my mind in the morning, I would go to Barbara's house. I would feel bad for *Mem* and maybe I would be sorry, but it would be easier to take a train back to Ohio later than it would be to leave the community again if I went back and regretted it. I took my letters and stuck them in my purse. I would take them with me so *Mem* and the others wouldn't find them.

I switched off the light and got into bed. I looked at the patch of light on the ceiling, cast by the streetlamp in front of the Y. For most of the night, my thoughts tumbled in my mind until I dreamed I was back in *Mem* and *Datt's* house on a church Sunday morning. I couldn't find my white organdy cape and apron, and the church service was scheduled to start in ten minutes, but they were waiting to start until I arrived. When I finally found my cape and apron, my heart sank as I realized they didn't fit anymore, and now I had to go to church wearing everyday clothes. Otherwise, they wouldn't start the service. To go to church with anything but the usual clothes for that occasion was just not done. I imagined more than a hundred pairs of eyes on me as I walked in. I could see their horror at my improper attire. I had no idea what I would do. My panic was mounting when I awoke, breathing hard and crying out in Amish, "*Vass zill ich do?*" (What am I going to do?)

I awoke and I realized the dilemma I faced in real life was far worse than whether I was wearing the right clothes to attend a church service. I knew the decision I would have to make by morning would affect the course of my life. I had more compassion for *Mem* and the lifelong mistake she had made. But making a similar mistake was not going to help her, and it certainly wasn't going to do me any good either.

I began mentally drafting the letter for *Mem* that I would leave for her in the morning before catching the bus to Barbara's house.

❧

I awoke before sunrise and wrote *Mem* a note:

Dear Mem,

After you called last night I had a chance to think about the decision I have to make about whether to go back or not. I believe whatever help you are planning to get for Datt can be done without me. In fact, I will not come back to the community until he has gotten help. I'm sure the social worker who asked you for permission to help our family would still be willing to help, if you care to ask— her name is June Gotschling, in case you don't remember.

You and I both know that I wouldn't be able to stand up to all of you, and so I went someplace where you won't find me. I know this will be hard for you, but there came a time in our family situation when I had to start thinking of myself. I will not even consider coming back until Datt has gotten help and stops hitting us.

I should have told you not to come when you called the other night, but I didn't think you were taking no for an answer.

I am enclosing fifty dollars to help pay for your trip.

Sincerely,
Saloma

I wrote "To *Mem*" on the outside of the envelope and placed it on the windowsill next to the front door, in plain sight of someone entering.

Maureen came down the stairs as I was heading back to my room to get dressed. I told her about my plans and about the envelope. Her dimpled grin spread over her face as she said, "Linda, you are doing the right thing. Why don't you call my phone number in my room before you come back, to make sure they're gone?" I thanked her and grabbed my bag of embroidery. My stomach did nervous flops as I imagined how *Mem* would react to what I had written. But then I remembered how I felt when she told me I had to be there for *Datt* to get help. I wanted to add in my note to her, "I was there once trying to get the help for *Datt* that he needed, but you refused it." I decided I was already cruel enough without adding this. But I needed this anger to keep me moving forward, down the hill toward the bus stop, rather than caving in to the sympathy I felt for *Mem* and returning to the Y to wait for her and the vanload of people coming to take me back.

My mind began to play out the scenarios of what would happen if I did return to Ohio. I would have to dress, behave, and in every way *be* what the traditions prescribed for a young woman. These traditions had been set long before I was born. I would be banned from the church for two weeks, during which time I would not be allowed to eat with other members, which would make it difficult for me to partake in any community gatherings. At the end of two weeks, I would have to make a public confession on my knees for all the wrongs I had committed in my new life. As I walked up the steps at the front of the bus and dropped my quarters in the metal container by the driver, I kept asking myself: how can it be wrong, when it feels so right? I took a seat and looked at the Y as we went by. No sign of a van from Ohio yet—good. I could see my letter inside the window to the left of the front door.

I was restless at Barbara's house. I tried concentrating on my embroidery while their dog, Misty, lay next to my chair in their living room. At one point, when I could stand it no longer, I called

Maureen. She talked faster than ever as she said, "Don't come back yet. They're still here. You shouldn't have put the letter in the mail window—I had to chase the mailman down the street to get the letter back. But your mother has the letter, and I think they'll be leaving soon."

"Is Mom really upset?"

"We'll talk about that later. I need to go. They wanted me to tell them where you are, but I told them I don't know. Linda, I gotta go. I'll call you when they leave. What's your number there?"

Maureen called me around noon to tell me the Amish had left about fifteen minutes before. I decided to wait at least another hour, just in case they had left temporarily and would come back to the Y to catch me there.

At around two o'clock, I walked in the front door of the Y. Maureen bombarded me with her impressions of the men with their untrimmed beards and their pants with no zippers ("How *do* they go to the bathroom, anyway?" she asked with a grin); the women with their long dresses and their white hair coverings; how they talked in their own language; and how somber they were when they left.

"How did Mom react to me not being here?" I asked.

"Oh, she cried. She made *me* feel guilty, and I'm not even her daughter! I'm so glad you are still here. I could feel the oppression you were living with, and your dad wasn't even here," Maureen said. "Your mother was in your room when she started crying really hard. I guess she found your sheer stockings in your closet or something."

"Oh, yes, it's all about whether or not I'm wearing Amish cloth-ing, and this was probably a reminder to her that I'm wearing what I want . . ." My voice trailed off. If she didn't want to be hurt by the choice I was making, why was she snooping in my room? After all, this was my life—and the house I lived in. I remembered that whenever I had disagreed with *Mem*, she would say to me, "When *you* have a house of your own, you can do things *your* way. Until then, you do things *my* way." Well, now I am doing things my way, I thought.

As Christine entered the living room, she asked, "May I?"

"Sure, come in," I said. Christine added her impressions of what had happened, and before long there were five women in the group. I realized that in less than two months I had gained a new community. By refusing to be pulled into feeling sorry for *Mem*, I was liberating myself both from the constricted Amish way of life and from destructive family patterns. I was glad I hadn't given up my life as "Linda."

Little did I know how fragile my freedom was.

5

The Struggle Within

*If we had no winter, the spring would not be so pleasant: if
we did not sometimes taste of adversity, prosperity would
not be so welcome.*
—Anne Bradstreet

It was quiet for several days—no letters and no phone calls. I
already felt conflicted about the decision I had made and wondered if I should go back to the Amish. Then the letters started
to roll in—shaming me for causing my mother so much sorrow
and imploring me to repent and to come back to the church I
had promised to stay in for the rest of my life. One person even
wrote that she was concerned that I would lie in some fancy coffin
someday.

The worst letter came from my Aunt Katie, *Datt's* youngest
sister and caretaker for my grandmother. She didn't know how
to express her feelings, she wrote, but if I could only feel a small
fraction of their aching and grieved hearts, I would gladly return.
Like a fire and brimstone preacher, she told of people who had
visions on their deathbed. Someone saw a lake of fire with snakes,
worms, and people trying to crawl out. When they thought they
could reach the shore, more big waves came, and down they went
to the bottom again. Thousands of years would pass, and these
poor souls would be no nearer to escaping—eternity is forever
and ever. If we knew what hell was like, she wrote, we would be
more willing to follow Jesus rather than our own flesh.

Aunt Katie's rambling about eternal damnation reminded me
of those dark winter nights of my childhood, sitting on *Datt's*

lap as he looked at the pictures in a little black book that showed the devil with a pitchfork, ready to toss people into the fire. Aunt Katie then went on to make her admonishments more personal. She wrote that they had not told Grandmother that I had left, and they hoped not to have to tell her, lest it shorten her life. Here Grandmother was more than eighty years old, and Aunt Katie wanted to make me feel responsible if she died!

If I accepted the messages from the Amish, I would have to pay for my new life of freedom in the afterlife—there would be hell to pay—forever. And if I went back and accepted the Amish ways, there was at least a chance I could make it to heaven. I wondered if God really meant for us to lose the self to make it into his kingdom.

I sought help from the Scriptures by opening the Bible at random, but I found the conflicting messages there only confused me more. I found myself in tears more than once, often not even knowing what had triggered them. I confided in Barbara about the struggle I felt in my soul. She suggested I talk with a minister she knew and offered to make an appointment with him for me. I accepted.

~⁓ ❀ ⁓~

Reverend William Hollister's office was in the same building as the Church Street Center, where I first met Barbara. As I entered, he stood up, shook my hand, and asked me to have a seat. I sat down and folded my hands in my lap. I hardly knew where to begin.

"So should we start by you telling me why you're here?"

"I don't know how much Barbara has told you . . . ?"

"She only told me you were seeking counsel for a struggle you were having."

"Okay. Well, I will start from the beginning . . ." I poured out my conflict, starting with how and why I had left my Amish family and community and how the life I had chosen felt right until I considered the messages I was getting from the Amish. I was crying through most of the hour. I could tell he was overwhelmed by my emotions. He asked a few questions, which seemed irrelevant to me at the time: which version of the Bible the Amish use; how Amish ministers are appointed; and what the community believes about salvation. I understand now that he wanted to gauge how fundamentalist the Amish religion is, but at the time I just wanted practical answers.

After an hour, he indicated he had to go. He had not given me the answer I wanted—whether I would indeed go to hell if I didn't go back to the Amish, and ultimately whether or not I should go back. I sensed, even then, that he was too wise to give me the answer I so craved. He knew I was the only one who could make such a decision.

When I saw the Reverend Hollister drive off in a little white BMW, I thought it would be the last time I saw him. It wasn't. He would play an important part in my future.

～❀～

One evening in December, Maureen, a woman named Bernetta, and I were cooking our dinners when Maureen announced that a new woman was moving into the room behind the stairs, the one I had occupied when I first came. I had since moved to a bigger room upstairs. The new woman would arrive that evening.

We were still in the kitchen when we saw a pickup truck pull into the side parking lot. Soon a slight, young, dark-haired woman walked in. Her manner was tentative, as if she wasn't sure she had a right to be there. Right behind her was a young man carrying a pillow and a suitcase. Maureen introduced Janie to us, and the young man wearing a dark peacoat introduced himself as David. Maureen then showed them to the room behind the stairs. I felt almost as if someone was moving into my room. Janie and David brought in more of her belongings and David left as soon as he had moved Janie in.

Later that evening, Janie and I were having tea at the kitchen table when she asked me if my mother was still upset. Surprise must have registered on my face because she said, "I was here the day your mother came."

"You were?"

"Yes, I was talking to the director about a room. Your mother was very upset."

"Yes, I heard," I said.

Janie got a vacant look in her eyes as she stared off into a place behind my head. It reminded me of the look in my father's eyes when I was a small child and he'd talk to people only he could see while rocking in his rocking chair.

Then Janie started mumbling unrelated things: something about the Amish being close to God and how she needed to cleanse her body, which she was going to do with the right food and drink. I thought she was suffering from mental illness, and I wondered how we would be able to accommodate her in our shared space. I listened to Janie rant for a while and then excused myself and retired for the night.

❧

Barbara Lalancette's in-laws invited me to their house for Christmas Eve. Their house looked festive with the Christmas tree all decorated and lit. As a child, I had often admired our Yankee neighbors' Christmas tree from across the street and wished we were allowed to have one. Now I found myself sitting in a festive living room, drinking hot chocolate, and enjoying the company of Mr. and Mrs. Lalancette, their youngest daughter, whom they called "Little Linda" so the two of us wouldn't be confused with one another, and a nephew, Raymond.

Raymond invited me to go to the midnight mass, but I declined, saying I was still unsure of whether I would return to the Amish. If I went back to the Amish, I would then have to confess that I had gone to a different church. Raymond said he understood, but I sensed he felt rebuffed and he became quiet. Barbara's sister-in-law, Denise, arrived later that evening, and she and Raymond went to mass together. Mrs. Lalancette noticed I was getting tired, so she showed me to my room and I settled into bed.

Sleep did not come for a long time. I wondered what *Mem* was feeling. Would the family get together with the uncles, aunts, and cousins on Christmas, or was *Mem* feeling too ashamed? For the hundredth time, I felt guilty for causing *Mem* grief when her life had been filled with it already. How much was too much for her to bear? I tossed and turned. Finally, I asked God to send angels to guide my way. With the rhythm of the sound of my own heartbeat, I finally fell asleep in the early morning hours.

The sun was shining when I awoke. I showered, dressed, and went downstairs. Mrs. Lalancette paused in the preparations of her holiday meal and came up and put her arm around me. She said, "Our Christmas gift to you today is to pay for you to call your mother. I'm sure she would love to hear from you."

I wondered if Mrs. Lalancette had read my thoughts the night before. I was touched by her generous gift—not just the money, but the thought itself.

I called the Yankee neighbors across the lane from my family's house and asked them to go get *Mem* and said I would call back in ten minutes.

Mem answered the phone when I called the second time. She sounded surprised and a little sad. I tried to keep the conversation cheerful, even though that's not how I really felt.

"Are you getting together with your side of the family today?" I asked.

"No, we're just staying home." *Mem* said this with a sigh.

I waited, not knowing what to say. *Mem*'s sad voice continued, "Under the circumstances, I didn't feel like a big get-together."

"So are Joe and Emma and their family coming for dinner today?" I asked, trying to keep the conversation from going in the direction it had started.

"Yes."

"It'll be nice to see the grandchildren, won't it?"

"Yes, it will." *Mem* said. Then she became quiet. Finally she asked, "Where are you calling from?"

"The Lalancettes'."

"Who?"

"Remember the family I spent Thanksgiving with? They invited me for Christmas, too. I made three pies yesterday at my friend Barb's house. They have a dog, Misty. When I put the pies on the counter to cool, I asked Barbara if I should put them up higher, and she said I didn't need to worry; Misty wouldn't bother them. She apparently left for a while, and when she came back, Misty had eaten some of each."

"Oh my! What are you going to do about pies then?" *Mem* asked.

"Mrs. Lalancette said she has enough dessert and not to worry. She is paying for this phone call today. She thought you would want to hear from me on Christmas."

Mem remarked about how it was nice of them, and then she asked how big the family was, and I told her there were seven of them, ranging in age from twenty-nine to eleven and that one of the daughters, Denise, is the friend who I had been getting together with to quilt. I sensed that the happier I sounded, the sadder *Mem* would be. If I had sounded sad or wistful, she would have used it to urge me to come home. But I was starting to realize it might have been preferable to her subdued and sad mood coming right through the telephone wires.

I was relieved when *Mem* finally said that since someone else was paying for the call, perhaps we shouldn't stay on the phone too long. She asked me to thank Mrs. Lalancette for the call.

"Well, Merry Christmas," I said, trying to sound cheery.

"I don't think there is any chance of that," *Mem* said and then fell silent.

I didn't know what to say.

Mem said, "I should get back to my cooking."

"Okay, bye, *Mem*."

"Bye-bye."

I replaced the receiver on the hook and sat quietly at the top of the basement steps, where Mrs. Lalancette said I could go to have privacy. I stared at the basement wall. I had to collect myself and not allow *Mem*'s mood to spread. I wanted to be gracious to Mrs. Lalancette for the call, but I wondered if *Mem* and I might both have been happier if I hadn't called. I imagined *Mem* having crying spells throughout the day, which would get her sympathy from the rest of the family.

I reminded myself I had not left to make *Mem*'s life harder; I had left to make mine bearable. And part of that was making new friends. I decided I was going to enjoy the day. As I opened the basement door, I smiled and thanked Mrs. Lalancette for both my mother and me. I asked for an apron to wear and how I could help. She gave me potatoes to peel. Now that was something I could do.

⤞⚘⤝

The director at the Y told me there were two Amish families living in Shoreham, Vermont. I wished out loud that I'd have a way to get there to visit them. Maureen suggested she and her boyfriend, Gary, would drive me down if I would pay for their gas. I was more than happy to take Maureen up on her offer, since I was used to paying by the mile when I was Amish.

I dressed in my Amish gray dress, black stockings and boots, black coat, and a white scarf instead of a bonnet—I hadn't been wearing a bonnet when I left home. Maureen, Gary, and I headed south on Route 7 for Shoreham. It was a sunny afternoon, with the snow sparkling like tiny rainbow crystals. Maureen pointed out Vermont's two highest mountain peaks: Mt. Mansfield and Camel's Hump to the east. The Adirondacks framed the western horizon on the opposite shore of Lake Champlain. I was happy to get to see more Vermont scenery.

We stopped at a local store in Shoreham to find out where the Amish lived. The store owner hesitated to tell us until I explained that I grew up Amish and was visiting them. When we got back into the car, I had to ask myself the question: What exactly was I hoping to accomplish with this trip? Perhaps I was exploring the option of having it both ways: being Amish and living in Vermont.

The family I visited had eight young children. The mother of the children was friendlier than the father, who seemed to be aloof. Maureen, Gary, and I followed them to their barn. During the milking I asked if it would be possible for me to come and join their new community. She checked with her husband, and he said I would have to go back to my original community and "make things right" before they would consider it.

I spent the trip back to Burlington answering Maureen's questions about what we had discussed in the Amish dialect, but I was much more subdued than I had been on the way to Shoreham. Even though I felt some relief in knowing the Amish in Shoreham wouldn't allow me to join them, there was also a feeling of rejection in that.

When we got back to the Y, I walked down to McDonald's and bought two cheeseburgers, fries, a milkshake, and an apple pie. After eating all of it, I promptly went into the bathroom and threw it up.

~ ❀ ~

Besides my spiritual struggle, I also longed for male companionship. I had plenty of women friends: the women at the Y, Denise and Barbara Lalancette, and people I'd met at Zachary's Pizza, where I had gotten a job working in the kitchen.

After Christmas, I took a trip to Maine with Denise Lalancette and her cousin Raymond to see their Aunt Eve. Denise stayed to see her boyfriend, while Raymond and I drove to Freeport, Maine, to visit the L. L. Bean store. Then we ate at a seafood restaurant in Portsmouth, New Hampshire, and drove back through the White Mountains to Vermont. I liked Raymond, but he seemed uncomfortable around me unless we were with others.

After I had spent several weeks wishing for a date with him, Raymond finally asked me out to a movie. He was uncomfortable with the movie he chose: *Saturday Night Fever*. It seemed for him it was about the movie, but for me it was about the company. I liked being with him, even if the movie wasn't that good.

To encourage Raymond, I invited him to dinner at the Y. We ate in the formal dining room, and I chose the nicest plates from the Y kitchen. He appreciated the food I cooked, and we talked at the table afterward. After clearing the table, I suggested we move to the parlor, but he seemed to have a sudden urge to leave. I had no choice but to get him his coat and walk him to the side door. He stopped for a minute, and then he put his arm around my shoulders. Just when I was leaning in for a hug, he leaned down and kissed me lightly on the lips, and his arm lingered on mine for a moment. Then he was gone, leaving me standing there, wanting something but not quite knowing what. I wondered if I had expected too much.

Raymond called a few days later, asking me if I would like to go dancing at the Cobweb with him, Denise, and her boyfriend. I accepted.

The Cobweb was humming with activity. Denise's boyfriend taught me the basics of how to dance. I felt like a klutz, but he made it seem easy by naming the steps. Raymond was six feet four inches tall, to my five feet four inches, which made it awkward for us to dance together, so he and Denise danced together instead.

Some of the dances were square dances. I had always wanted to learn them, and with a caller for a guide, I soon learned the basic moves. I loved the whirling energy, and before I knew it, I had whirled the night away.

After climbing up into Raymond's truck, I shivered and blew on my hands, trying to get warm. As the truck warmed up and Raymond pulled onto Interstate 89, I told him how much fun I had and thanked him for taking me there. Then Raymond began telling me about a woman friend. They had liked one another as friends and had been corresponding for eight years. I sensed he was trying to imply that this is what he wanted from me—a friendship and nothing more. I became quiet, because I didn't know what to say: Are you saying you like me as a friend, and that's it? Is that why you didn't even give me a goodnight hug when I cooked a meal for you?

When Raymond pulled in at the Y, he parked his truck but left it running. He came around to my side of the truck, took my arm, and walked me to the door. He kissed me like he was getting that duty over with, and then he walked quickly back to his truck. I waved to him and went inside.

⚜

One night Maureen decided to teach me the fine art of getting dances and free drinks at a bar. We stood near the bar at The

Olde Board, looking aimlessly around as music blared from the speakers. Before long, a short man came and asked me if I would like to dance and offered me a drink. I didn't know how to say no, so I said yes to him and to the next two men who asked me the same question. We danced—or rather we faced one another and gyrated our bodies back and forth. One man kept bumping his clammy hands into mine.

I was not used to alcohol, so it didn't take me long to feel the effects of the three mixed drinks I had consumed. At some point it felt like my head was stuffed with cotton and I couldn't think straight. I don't know how I ended up sitting across the table from the man who had bought me my fourth drink. He was smoking a cigarette and leaning across the table toward me. Through the fog of my brain, I remember him saying, "You want to go to your place?"

I acted goofy on purpose. "Naw, I live with ten other women; can't do that."

"Do you want to go to my place, have a ball, and come back?"

"Naw, not tonight. I'm with my friend."

Later, in the car on the way home, Maureen told me, "Linda, that's the last time I'm taking you to a bar—you take all my dates."

"You can have any of those guys!" I drawled in my goofy state. I hiccupped.

The following morning as I slowly awoke from my drunken stupor, I realized I would have to temper my freedom with a little more discernment. When Maureen had told me I was going to have a lot of fun, I hadn't realized that her sense of "fun" wouldn't always be the same as mine. I thought about the man who had blatantly asked me for a one-night stand. I knew one thing for sure: I hadn't staved off the roving hands of the Amish men to give myself up to some stranger just because I was drunk. Going to The Olde Board with Maureen would not be something I would do again, I decided.

Turning men's heads was new to me. It seemed to me the Amish men had eyes for the popular girls only, and I was not one of them. Now I was constantly being confronted with unabashed stares. Once, while riding a bus from Burlington to Essex Junction, the bus driver kept looking back at me every time he stopped, and sometimes he even stole glances while he was driving. I couldn't wait to get off his bus. I knew that look; my older brother, Joe, could undress me with his eyes, and I hated it.

When I left the Amish, I was probably slimmer than I had been at any time in my life since my adolescence. Losing weight hadn't seemed to matter in the Amish community, because I was never going to be one of the popular girls. So it was flattering that men around Burlington found me attractive. But especially after my drunken encounter at the bar, I realized that any romantic relationship I got involved in would have to have more to it than physical attraction.

I was in this disquieting search for meaning in my spiritual life and open to a romantic relationship when I first got to know David.

~ 6 ~

Gemini Twins

Every moment and every event of every man's life on earth
plants something in his soul.
—Thomas Merton

I first met David when he moved Janie to the Y, but I didn't pay much attention to him because I thought he was Janie's boyfriend. He would visit her every few days, which reinforced this idea. Then one day when David came to see Janie, she was out. She had a tendency to wander away and then drift back to the Y, as if she wasn't really in her body.

Instead of leaving, David lingered. I had chickpeas cooking on the stove, so I walked into the kitchen to check on them. When Maureen introduced me to David, he shook my hand and then asked how Janie was doing. Maureen and I looked at one another, and then Maureen said something evasive. I decided it would be good for David to know that Janie was not easy to live with. I told him she wasn't eating properly, and that she had a way of showing up in a room, quietly, so we didn't know she was there, which was very startling.

"She's been like this ever since she broke up with her boyfriend, Richard," David said. I didn't know what to say to that, and apparently Maureen didn't either. After a pause, David added, "They experimented with drugs and she couldn't handle it."

For the first time it dawned on me that David may not be her boyfriend, but I wanted to know. "So she's not your girlfriend?"

"Not at all," David responded quickly. "I moved her here from her parents' house because she asked me to. I've been checking in on her because I know she's been unstable."

"What about Richard? Doesn't he have any obligations to her, since he's the one who messed her up?" I asked. I hadn't even had time to think about my question before the words tumbled out of my mouth. I had no idea at the time that I was responding in anger at how my older brother could do anything he wanted to us sisters and then not take responsibility for his actions, while *Mem* was always there to protect him.

David didn't seem to mind that I'd been so blunt, but Maureen suddenly decided she had to leave.

"Who knows?" David said. "She may have been unstable even before they were involved."

"Still, it seems to me Richard should have some obligation," I said.

"You've got to know Richard—he doesn't take responsibility for anyone. I just felt sorry for Janie, and didn't want her to feel stuck living at her parents' house."

I really wanted to retort, "So if you're not her boyfriend, why do you keep checking on her?" But out of politeness, I said, "It's nice of you to do that, then."

As I took the chickpeas off the stove and drained them in the kitchen sink, David asked me what I was doing, and I told him I was going to make a chickpea salad. He didn't seem to be going anywhere, so I offered him a seat. As I made the salad, he sat on one of the stools by the table and watched.

"Are you the Amish girl?" he asked.

"Yes, how did you know?"

"Janie told me she was here when some Amish people came to the Y."

"Yes, she told me she was here that day. I'd left the Y because I didn't want to return to the community."

"Why did you leave the Amish?" David asked, seeming genuinely interested.

"It will take a while to answer that, so would you like some chickpea salad while I tell you?" I asked.

"Sure," David said. Despite his calm and unassuming countenance, he could not conceal his pleasure that I'd offered to share my story and my food.

David seemed riveted as I told him my story. When I got to the part about my arrival at the Y, he regarded me carefully. "So, here you are."

"Yes, here I am."

David and I talked in the kitchen for hours. I learned that he was a toymaker and street peddler and that he and his brother had designed and made the display train I'd seen out in front of Magram's Department Store. I was impressed.

I told David more than I'd told anyone about my family. At the time, the only abuse I could give voice to was what I had endured at the hands of my father. Still hidden in my psyche was my brother Joe's brutality. I knew I didn't trust Joe, but I was not yet ready to remember the beatings, the psychological terror, and the sexual molestation that all had occurred before I had any defenses.

David asked about Amish traditions: What was it like to ride in a horse and buggy? What was it like to be baptized in the church? How were ministers ordained? Which technologies were allowed and which weren't? When I mentioned pictures I had of my siblings, he said, "I thought the Amish couldn't have their pictures taken."

"We had a camera on the sly." I went to my room and brought down the photos my siblings and I had taken secretly with our camera.

When David left, he shook my hand and said he had enjoyed the afternoon. I had too, and I told him so. That evening I wrote in my journal.

I had a long visit with David Furlong today. He is a toy maker and I found out he is the man who designed and made that train engine display down on Church Street. Wow, is he ever talented!

David had come to see Janie, but she wasn't here. I would have felt like I was entertaining someone else's boyfriend, except he claims Janie is not his girlfriend. But why would he move Janie in to the Y and keep coming back to "check on her" if he had no feelings for her? And what about her feelings for him? David seems like a nice young man, but I sure don't want to be someone's "other woman." Maybe it's another one of those "just friends" deals. I guess I don't understand Yankee men.

David was a toymaker and street peddler in Burlington, Vermont, when I first met him.

The next time I saw David was two mornings later, when he showed up at the side door. From halfway up the stairs, where I was sweeping, I called out for him to come in. As he stepped in, I wondered if he had come to see Janie or me. Then I chided myself for caring one way or another. After all, I had no claim on David just because we had talked for an afternoon.

"I came to take Janie to Fairfax to see Richard," David announced, as he closed the door behind him.

"I knew Janie was planning on going somewhere. She seems pretty happy about it," I said.

"Yeah, she asked if I would take her, and I said I'd be happy to." I looked at David to see if there was some deeper meaning in what he was saying. He looked like he was happy to get a break from her.

So was I.

"Taking a break from making toys today?" I asked.

"Yes, it's good to get out of the basement once in a while."

"It's a nice day for a drive into the country," I said. Just then Janie came around the corner with a duffle bag in her hands. She gave me a withering look, like she was telling me with her body language that she didn't like that I was talking with David, yet she seemed anxious to go see her former boyfriend. I sensed I was helping to weave a complicated web. Maybe I shouldn't have anything to do with David until their relationship was resolved.

Janie headed out the door and said, "David, are you coming?"

"Sure," he said. David looked up at me, still standing on the stairs, and said, "Bye, I'll talk to you later." I wondered when that would be.

The following evening when I was just sitting down for my break at Zachary's Pizza, David walked in. I invited him to sit with me. He started talking about Janie. "You know when we left for Fairfax yesterday morning? Just as I was going up the ramp onto the highway, she opened the door of the pickup! I got the feeling she was thinking of jumping!"

"What did you do?" I asked.

"I grabbed on to her and asked her what she was doing. She mumbled something about losing her knitting needle."

I listened quietly while I munched on my pizza. David reported that Janie decided to stay in Fairfax to be with Richard for a while and wondered aloud how long that would last.

I hoped a long time. It would be a relief for those of us at the Y to get a break from Janie's disturbed and disturbing behavior.

David seemed to notice I was quiet and said, "Anyway, enough about Janie."

I spoke before I thought. "You didn't come here to talk about Janie, did you?"

David seemed startled and hesitated a moment before he said, "No, I didn't." After another long pause, he smiled and said, "Do you like Chinese food?"

I suddenly realized David was about to ask me out. He was looking at me, waiting for an answer. I looked into his ocean-blue eyes. Out of nowhere, I felt sensations I had never felt before course through my body. I noticed the peacoat David was wearing, and how it accentuated his wide shoulders and slender body.

"I've never had Chinese food, but I sure would like to try it," I said.

David was looking at me intently. "There is a place near here called the Tiki Garden," he said. "Would you like to go there with me on Sunday?"

"Sure," I said.

David looked pleased, a smile playing around his full red lips. He pulled slightly at his sideburns and said, "Great."

"What time?" I asked. I forgot about the pizza I was eating as I watched David's face, looking for signs of what he might be feeling.

"Why don't I pick you up around eleven?"

"Okay. That sounds fine. I look forward to it."

We looked at one another for a long moment, until I realized where I was. "I have to get back to work," I said.

As David left, his slender legs taking long strides up the street, I knew this was the kind of date I had always dreamed of: going out for a meal at a restaurant and getting to know someone, rather than making out in "bed dates."

I decided David's relationship with Janie didn't matter. I was going to enjoy myself. After all, he wasn't asking me to marry him; he was only asking me for a date.

     ❀

Sunday morning dawned bright and cold. I dressed in my best clothing: a wraparound wool plaid skirt and a white turtleneck layered with a navy blue blouse. I ate an orange for breakfast and then waited for David to arrive. I felt nervous as I anticipated my first "real" date—the kind I used to fantasize about, though I never mentioned it to other Amish people. This was my chance.

I wondered if there were mores for dating someone Yankee. After our conversation in the kitchen, I imagined David would tell me if there were. I had shared more about myself with him in one conversation than I had with my Amish boyfriend, Donny, with whom I had been going steady for three months before I left the community. I admonished myself for making such a comparison; after all, this was only my first date with David. I didn't know him yet.

I hovered around the kitchen windows, putting away the dishes from the night before. I realized I was fidgeting. But right on time, David's yellow Datsun pickup came driving into the side parking lot. I watched him get out of the truck in his navy peacoat and dark pants. I greeted him with a smile, hoping my eagerness wasn't too evident.

On the way to the Tiki Garden, David asked, "How's your job going?"

"Oh, it's okay," I said. "My boss is really hard to get along with."

"That's too bad."

"I won't feel too bad about leaving when I start the waitress job at Pizza Hut. Oh, by the way, I got the job there and I start a week from tomorrow."

"Oh, that's great!"

"Yeah, I'm really excited about that."

"Are Amish girls allowed to waitress?"

"No. We basically have two choices—teaching school or cleaning houses."

"Whose houses did you clean?"

"Wealthy people who were not Amish. Most of my jobs were in Chesterland or Gates Mills, near Cleveland."

"I bet you'll be a good waitress."

"I used to watch waitresses at Belle's Restaurant in our little town of Burton, and I wished I could become one."

At the restaurant, an Asian woman greeted us and led us to our table. David said I should choose where I wanted to sit. I chose the seat that faced west so I could see Lake Champlain and the snow-capped Adirondacks on the other side.

David wasn't wearing his glasses, and I loved seeing his blue eyes. We looked at one another, and then David said, "We should probably order our food."

After looking at the menu, I said, "I've never eaten at a Chinese restaurant before, so I might need your help in deciding what to order."

David ordered a five-course meal for two with wonton soup, dumplings, two main dishes, dessert, and tea. Then he pulled in his chair and arranged his napkin next to his plate. "So, if you were back in your community, what would you be doing today?" he asked.

"It depends if it was our church Sunday or not."

"What do you mean by church Sunday?"

"The Amish only have church every other Sunday."

"Really. And what do they do on the alternate Sundays?"

"We called those our 'in-between-church Sundays.' We always treated Sundays as our Sabbath, which means we weren't allowed to work. We visited other people in the community whose church Sundays were the same as ours, we played board games with one another, and when we were children we went sledding in the winter."

"Were you allowed to do housework?"

"It depends. We were allowed to do the everyday things, like making meals and doing dishes, but we always cleaned the house and baked pies and bread on Saturdays to prepare for Sundays."

"Where did you go to church?"

"Oh, we didn't have a church building. We met in people's homes."

"In people's homes? How many people could you fit into a house?"

"I think there were twenty families in our church district. Some families were big, and others were younger couples just starting a family."

"How would you fit all those people into one house?"

"Basically at our house, we'd clean the house from top to bottom and move the furniture to make room for the church benches. Usually we set up the benches the night before. In the summer, some families would hold the services in the top of a barn or in a shop."

"That is so different than a Catholic mass with a priest conducting it from the sanctuary of the church."

When the waitress brought the wonton soup, I was glad for the interruption, because I didn't really want to think about what was happening at home. There were times when homesickness snuck out of the shadows and took me by surprise. I wondered if the closing hymn was being sung in our church district. I decided to change the subject.

"Do you have any brothers or sisters?" I asked.

"Yes, two brothers and two sisters."

"Where do you fit in?"

"I'm smack dab in the middle—I'm third, with an older sister and an older brother and I also have a younger brother and a younger sister."

"I'm third in line also, with an older brother and an older sister."

"Do you follow astrology?"

"I know I'm a Gemini, but I don't know much else."

"Oh, when's your birthday?" David said excitedly.

"June nineteenth."

David's blue eyes widened and a grin crept into his face. He rearranged his fork and spoon on his napkin and said, "You're not going to believe this."

"What?" I said, now curious.

"My birthday is the day before yours—on June eighteenth."

"Oh, really!"

"Does that make us the Gemini twins?" David asked, the grin having spread across his whole face. Little crinkles formed at the corners of his eyes.

"Oh, you're right!" I said laughing. "What year were you born in?"

"1954."

"So we are three years apart—I'm twenty."

David looked at me with those blue, blue eyes, and I could see that the attraction I felt for him was mutual. At that moment there was no other place I would rather have been than sitting at the Tiki Garden with David Furlong in South Burlington, Vermont, with the sun sparkling on Lake Champlain in the background.

7

Schmunzling

*A kiss is a lovely trick designed by nature to stop speech
when words become superfluous.*
—Ingrid Bergman

I had never felt such a lightness in my being as I did for several days after my first date with David. Going out on a date had been every bit as romantic as I had dreamed it would be, though David was very different from the kind of man I had envisioned I would be dating. I had always imagined that Mr. "Tall, Dark, and Handsome" would one day come along and sweep me off my feet with his charm and wit and that I would fall head over heels in love with him.

This was not at all what David was like. He was certainly handsome. But his was not the "sweep me off my feet" kind of charm. Rather, he had a calm demeanor that made me trust him implicitly. I could tell by the questions he asked that he was genuinely interested in me as a person and in the Amish lifestyle from which I had emerged. His approach to life in general was quiet, sensitive, and creative. It seemed to fit his personality to make wooden toys out of the basement of his parents' home rather than hold a mainstream job. I didn't know where our relationship was headed, but I looked forward to having another date with him when he returned from doing a craft show in Massachusetts.

❦

Denise Lalancette and I walked from the Y to the Gutterson Field House on the University of Vermont Campus to skate one

Sunday afternoon. The sidewalk had about six inches of slippery snow on it, and our feet kept sliding backward with every step we took. We talked about turning back, but then we trudged on. I had bought myself a new pair of white skates and was looking forward to skating on a rink, because in Ohio, I had only skated on ponds.

When we got to the rink, we donned our skates and joined the circle of skaters going in the same direction around the rink. As I slid around in the big circle, I thought about how skating was possibly the closest humans would come to flying. Then it all happened so fast, I didn't even have time to put my hands out. I caught the teeth of one of my skates on the ice, and down I went, face forward. As I picked myself up, blood was pouring out of a cut on my eyebrow. My glasses lay in two pieces on the ice. Denise and several others gathered around, and someone soon handed me a clean towel to blot the bleeding. People guided me into the back room, where Denise helped me out of my skates while I cried from the pain and indignation of having made such a public spectacle of myself. At some point I blurted, "What a bloody mess!"

Denise chuckled and said, "Well, at least you still have a sense of hummer!" Her use of the word *hummer* instead of *humor* made me laugh at the same time I was crying.

Someone gave me a ride to the emergency room, where a doctor stitched up the gash caused by the plastic frame of my glasses breaking and cutting my eyebrow. Then I got a ride back to the Y, where I took it easy for the rest of the evening.

I took my glasses to an optical shop on Church Street the next day to get them repaired. The person there said he needed to order them from Boston and thought it would take a few days. When I returned to the optical shop to pick up my glasses a few days later, I found out the snowstorm in Boston had delayed the delivery of the glasses. I was sorely disappointed, because the world was so blurry without them. I resorted to perching my glasses on my nose, with just the left half of the glasses in place over my ear. Finally, on Friday, I got a phone call, letting me know they had come in.

I must have written to *Mem* about my accident, because she asked if I didn't think I would get better care at home. I was learning that *Mem* and the other people in my community used everything they possibly could as leverage to convince me to come back. I thought about not writing back at all. I thought about throwing out their letters without reading them. But my curiosity was greater than my resolve to not let them get to me, so I read and kept the letters I received.

I took several days off from my new job at Pizza Hut. I hoped I wouldn't lose my job because of it. I found I liked meeting new

This photograph shows what I looked like during my time in Vermont after leaving the Amish.

people, which is what waitressing is all about. Counting the tips was another fun part; it was like getting a prize for the work I already liked doing.

On our second date, David and I ate at a restaurant in downtown Burlington. I had my coat on, ready to go when he arrived at the time he said he would. We decided to walk downtown, so we wouldn't have to find a place to park. It was a cold, snappy January night, with the stars shining brightly. We could see our breath, and the snow squeaked under our boots. I wondered if David would offer me an arm to lean on, but he didn't. We walked side by side and talked along the way.

As we were being seated at the restaurant, David looked at me intently and then said, "You've got a red nose."

I laughed and said, "So do you. Do you think we should offer Santa to be two of his reindeer?" David laughed heartily, his grin spreading across his whole face. I noticed he had a very wide mouth, framed by his red lips. I wondered what it would be like to kiss those lips.

We ordered our food. When the waitress left, David crossed his legs and bumped his knee into mine. The contact both surprised and excited me.

As we talked, he kept giving me an intent look from across the table, and then his knee or foot would touch me again. After the second time, I knew it was no accident, and I didn't want to move out of the way. Instead, I planted my knee in towards him.

At some point, David looked around, leaned toward me, and whispered, "See that woman over by the door?"

"Yes."

"She's both." David watched my face intently.

"What do you mean?"

"She's bisexual."

"Oh." I said, stumped. I had no idea what to say to this revelation. Hesitating, I asked, "How do you know?"

"She was the lover of a woman I knew from judo."

"What's judo?"

"Judo is a sport popular in Japan. I used to take classes at the University of Vermont."

"Oh, is it like karate?"

"Yes, it's sort of like that, but it has throws instead of kicks and chops. I used to travel to tournaments with my judo group."

"Okay, so, she was the lover of a woman in the group. How do we know she likes men, then?"

"She told me."

"She told *you*?"

"We were friends . . . just friends."

These Yankee men and "just friends," I thought. Why would a woman tell someone who is "just a friend" that she is bisexual? Unless she was trying to tell him something.

David noticed my silence. He asked, "Are there any gay people among the Amish?"

"Not that the Amish know about."

"What do you mean?"

"Well, I once saw something I could not explain any other way than two women were attracted to one another. When I mentioned this to my sisters, who were also there, they said I was full of beans. That is the Amish way—to refuse to acknowledge there is such a thing as women being attracted to women or men being attracted to men. When I mentioned this to my cousin, she thought about it for a moment, then she said bluntly, 'But . . . how can they?'"

David said, "Can what?" as his knee bumped into mine.

"Well, you know . . ."

"Ohhh, I get it. That's funny." David got an amused grin on this face. "I told my cousin they can at least *schmunzle*."

"What does that mean—*schmunzle*?"

"It means to hug and kiss."

"Okay. Now I know," David said, his grin getting still wider. He paused a moment and said, "Would you like another drink?"

After our second drink, I suggested we go back to the Y, where

we could get warmed up in the parlor. We walked briskly, antici-
pating the warmth of being inside. I told David how one night
there were people rushing by the Y on their way to the Memorial
Auditorium and finally Maureen had gone out and asked someone hurrying by where they were going. The person replied,
"Marcel Marceau!" and kept on going.

"Oh, yes, he is an internationally known mime," David said.

"What's a mime?"

"Someone who acts without words. It's rather hard to explain,
but he uses his body to convey emotions."

"Oh, that must be hard!"

"No, it isn't. You do it every day," he said, laughing.

"I do?"

"I'll tell you the next time you do it."

"Have you ever seen anyone famous?" I asked.

"I saw Arlo Guthrie in person at the Flynn Theater a couple
months ago and then I also saw Bob Dylan and Joan Baez at the
Shelburne Inn."

"Oh, I cannot stand Bob Dylan! But I like Bill Monroe, Charley
Pride, and Hank Williams Sr. Hank Williams had such a great
singing voice."

"How do you know?" he asked teasingly.

"The young people bring tapes of country singers to the singings and dances."

"They dance too?"

"They're supposed to sing hymns, but they end up in the barn
dancing to a kind of square dance."

"That's a surprise!"

As we walked past the parlor windows, I saw it was empty.
Good. I hoped the other women would give us some privacy. The
signals I had been getting all night from David told me he was
ready for some schmunzling. I knew I was.

I hung my coat over the newel post in the front hallway, and
David hung his coat over the top of mine. I invited him into the
parlor and told him to have a seat, pointing toward the sofa. After
closing all three doors in the parlor, I sat down next to him and

looked at him. His blue eyes sparkled and a grin spread across his face. He said, "Marcel Marceau."

"What?" I asked, puzzled.

"I told you I would remind you the next time you mimed."

"Oh," I said, laughing.

David moved closer and put his arm around me. Then he kissed me. His lips were soft and luscious.

~᠅~

For several days after our date, I could still taste David's kisses and feel his arms around me. I was still thinking about him at dusk when I stopped in at my favorite secondhand clothing store. I was looking through a rack of skirts when I saw someone cross-ing the street. He was walking with purpose and coming directly toward the door of Second Hand Rose. I startled when I realized it was David. I felt butterflies in my stomach, and my heart skipped a beat. For just a quick second, I wondered if he was following me. He looked at me as he came in the door. "Hi," he said.

"What brings you here?" I asked.

"I was next door visiting my friend Bill, and I saw you come in here, so I thought I would come and say hi."

"Where does Bill live?"

"See that brick building right across the street on the corner? He lives in the last apartment in that building."

Before I could say anything else, David said, "There is a popu-lar Italian restaurant next door named Boves. I was thinking of stopping there and getting something to eat. Would you like to join me?"

"Sure," I said. I made my purchases and then David and I headed next door.

After our meal, we decided to go to Nectar's for drinks and dancing. As we were walking along Saint Paul Street, I asked David where I could buy a tape player. He suggested Service Merchandise. I told him, "I'm thinking of buying a tape player, but if I go back to Ohio, then that would be wasting my money."

"You mean, to stay?" David asked, shocked. I explained that

if I did go back, it would be to stay. He asked me if there was any chance of that, and I felt the old murky uncertainty churn inside. I said I wasn't sure. The calm in my voice belied the turmoil I felt inside.

When we arrived at Nectar's, David asked me to dance. It was the first time we danced together. David had a funny grin on his face as he got up in front of me and danced. He looked amused and a little self-conscious all at the same time. I thought he looked like a blond Raggedy Andy doll with long, skinny arms. I wondered if I looked silly to him, too.

During the course of the evening, David had at least four drinks, and I was starting to feel a little tipsy after nursing my second. At some point, we decided it was time to go back to the Y. I invited David into the parlor and he readily accepted. He was even more ardent than the first time we had kissed in the parlor. And unlike the last time, when we took breaks and talked, this time he was kissing me nonstop. At some point, I pushed on his chest and declared that I was saving myself for marriage.

"Okay," David said as he sat up straight.

"Have you ever gone all the way with someone?" I asked bluntly. All of a sudden I wasn't sure I should have asked that question. Maybe he wouldn't want to tell me, and maybe I didn't really want to know.

"Yes, I've had a few girlfriends. But in each case they wanted to, or I wouldn't have."

David and I sat in silence for a moment. Then David started telling me about his former relationships. I was speechless. It seemed the drinks had loosened David's tongue. I just listened.

There was a moment of quiet before David asked, "What about you?"

"Several of my dates certainly acted like they wanted it, but I wasn't about to let that happen."

"What was the situation?"

"You are probably going to be shocked if I tell you. Most people outside the Amish are when they hear about our dating practice."

"Do you want to tell me?"

"The Amish in my community practice 'bed courtship.' A young man will drive the girl to her home and put up his horse in the barn, then come to her room and go to bed with her."

"Shocking!"

"Yes. They go to bed with their clothes on and they are not supposed to have sex. They are allowed to *schmunzle*, but not go all the way."

"So, is that all they do?"

"I don't know about other women. But I had my barriers."

"What happened if someone tried to do something you didn't want?"

"I fended off their roving hands. I found I could throw their hands off as many times as I wanted, but they would come right back. Then I discovered how to make them stop. It was eerie how it worked with every last one of them, like they were all made in the same mold."

"How?"

"Words. The minute I said 'Don't!' they would turn their backs and go to sleep. It was like magic."

He reached over and put his arm around me. "I can understand that you want to stay pure and I respect that."

As I looked into David's blue eyes, I felt drawn into them. We kissed. Knowing David could and would stop if I asked made me feel comfortable.

Before David left, I reminded him I would be cooking a meal for him on Friday night. "I wouldn't miss it for the world," he said with a cute smile as he pulled on his coat and reached to open the parlor door. I walked through the dining room with him to the side door, where he kissed me again. Then he opened up the door and a blast of frigid winter air, so cold it set my teeth on edge, came rushing into the dining room. I waved goodnight and ran up the stairs to bed.

8

Life in Open Throttle

We have to dare to be ourselves, however frightening or
strange that self may prove to be.
—May Sarton

During the weeks that David and I were dating, letters from Ohio kept arriving, putting constant pressure on me to return to my community and keep the promises I made when I was baptized. Each one seemed to have the same message as the one before—that I was causing *Mem* sorrow. The guilt threatened to set in. But I liked the life I was establishing, and I did not want to return to the Amish. I stuffed those guilt feelings out of reach so I could continue on with my life.

I was enjoying my waitress job at the Pizza Hut. After the initial weeks of training, I soon fell into a pattern. I happily replenished the salad bar, swept the floor, scrubbed the bathrooms, and did whatever else needed to be done. Some of the other servers avoided the more difficult tasks, but I was so grateful to have a job I liked that I was more than willing to take on anything I was asked to do.

At first, when David starting dropping by the Y without calling or planning in advance to see me, I didn't mind. But I soon found it annoying because I felt he was taking me for granted. I did not yet know David well enough to know it was his natural inclination to be spontaneous and it took a great deal of discipline for him to plan things in advance, as he had in planning our first dates. I only knew it was a lot less romantic for him to drop in and assume I wanted to see him than it was for him to call me up and give me a choice. Once he was standing at my door, I felt I didn't have as much of a choice. I knew I would most likely always say yes to going out with him, especially because Raymond Culligan hadn't even been in touch with me lately.

I talked to Maureen, who had become my confidante, about how I felt my relationship with David was "going too fast." Though I had a general idea of what I meant by that, I couldn't actually have articulated it. She agreed with me—that David was very intense with how often he came around, and she suggested that I ask him to call before he came. She added, "Besides, you might want to go out with Raymond sometimes."

"Exactly. Can you imagine if I had Raymond over for dinner one night and David showed up?"

Maureen got her mischievous grin on her face and said, "Oh, if your family could only see you now—going to the movies, going out drinking, going dancing, and now you've got two boyfriends on the hook."

"Not really—I'm not serious with either one of them," I said defensively.

"And why should you be? You're still young. You just left the Amish three months ago."

"I know. I sometimes have to think about that. In some ways it seems so long ago that I left, but in another way it seems like it happened last week."

"Do you think you'll ever go back?"

"I'm having too good a time to want to go back. But then when I get letters from the Amish, I feel really guilty."

"Why should you feel guilty? You aren't doing anything wrong—you're just making a life for yourself."

"Most of the time. Unless I go to the bars with you," I teased.

Maureen laughed. "Linda, you are just too Amish for your own good."

"That's what you say. My family says I'm not Amish enough for my own good."

I didn't have to wait very long to get a chance to talk to David about our relationship. The next time he showed up, we went out like we usually did and then ended up in the parlor afterward. I started out by asking David if he would please call before he showed up at the Y to see me.

David looked baffled. Then he said, "Well, I was in Burlington tonight already, so rather than go home and call, I thought I'd stop in and see if you wanted to go out."

"But this isn't the first time."

"No." David paused. "I can call first if you like."

"That brings up another thing. I feel like our relationship is going too fast. We haven't known one another very long. Under most circumstances, we might just be having our third date by now, but here we are seeing one another three or four times a week. I'm not ready for a serious relationship."

David was quiet. Then he asked tentatively, "Is this because you are seeing someone else?"

"I'm not seeing anyone else right now, but I might want that option. I cannot very well do that if you are coming around every night."

"Well, I don't come every night."

"But when you don't call first, I don't know when you are going to show up. So it takes away my ability to go out with anyone else, even with my girlfriends here at the Y."

"Okay. I get it. I'll call before I come." After a pause, David said, "Oh, and I meant to tell you, I'm going to be away next weekend at a craft show."

"Oh. Funny, Maureen invited me to go to her family's house in St. Johnsbury and to their camp in Peacham."

"Are you going?"

"Sure, why not? I'll get a chance to see more Vermont scenery."

❧ ✤ ❧

During the drive through Vermont with Maureen, it seemed as if winter struggled to keep its icy fingers on the pulse of the weather in Vermont. By mid- and late February, we sometimes were tapping trees to make maple syrup back in Ohio. I did not see any sugarhouses steaming in the frozen Vermont landscape.

First, we drove to St. Johnsbury to Maureen's family's home where we stayed overnight. The following day, Maureen, her mother, her five-year-old brother, Brian, and I drove to Peacham to visit their summer cottage. The snow was deep with a crust on the top. Little Brian, dressed in his snowsuit, crawled on his hands and knees while the rest of us sank through the crust with every step we took.

That afternoon, Maureen wanted me to go out snowmobiling on the dirt road outside the camp. She assured me it was safe because there was hardly any traffic on that road in the winter. Besides, we could stay on the side if a car did come along.

Out on the open road, Maureen taught me how to drive the snowmobile. As I started out slowly, she laughed at me and told me I drove like an old lady. So I squeezed the right handle of the snowmobile and gave it some gas. It was a cold but sunny afternoon. There was a long stretch of straight road ahead. We picked up speed, and I could barely hear Maureen yelling, "Linda, slow down!" The cold air stung my cheeks as we skimmed over the road. It felt like we were flying.

I hadn't felt so alive since I was a little girl, swinging high on the rope swing that hung from a tall branch of the oak tree next to the woodshed. Sometimes I would swing higher than the woodshed roof and I could hear the wind rushing past my ears. Just like now, when the air rushing past us was almost as loud as the engine of the snowmobile. The cold was exhilarating. Long before the bend in the road, I slowed down and stopped. Laughing, Maureen said, "Linda, that is the last time I'll let *you* drive!"

She positioned herself in the driver's spot; I grabbed her waist and held on. She turned the vehicle around and headed back to camp. On the way back, the wind was too strong for me to whoop and holler, though that's what I felt like doing.

On Sunday afternoon, when we got back to Burlington, Maureen invited me to go to a movie with her and a young woman, Patti, who had just arrived at the Y. I knew nothing about which movies to pick, so I left it to Maureen and Patti. Wrong decision.

We were not far into the 1978 horror movie *Coma* when I realized this was going to upset me. I did not want to see a whole warehouse full of bodies suspended from the ceiling in induced comas. I whispered to Maureen, "I don't think I want to watch this movie."

"It won't be too bad," she assured me.

It got worse. One woman became conscious, and a villain who was chasing her planned to kill her. I squirmed in my seat and said, "I don't think I want to see this."

"You can't walk out now," Maureen said as she put her hand on my thigh as if she were pinning me to my chair.

Perhaps I couldn't rip my eyes away from the horror on the screen, or perhaps I really didn't know what else to do, but I sat through the whole movie. By the time I left, I felt as though someone had raped my psyche—or else filleted it, and now the insides were showing. I was close to tears and kept saying, "Maureen, that was awful!"

"Linda, it's not real," Maureen said, giggling nervously.

"Yeah, well, that doesn't help. Someone had to think all that stuff up, and how sick is that. And I watched it—I can't believe it!" I was about to break into tears as we walked out into the lobby of the Flynn Theater.

That's when I saw David walking toward me. I was surprised and then a little annoyed that he hadn't called, as we had discussed. I hadn't even formulated the question yet, when David walked up to me and offered an explanation, "The craft show in Boston got canceled because of a snowstorm."

"Oh," I said. I saw David's eyes searching mine, and I knew my feelings showed; I also saw what seemed like hurt or distress in his eyes, but mine were so overwhelming I could not see beyond them.

"How was the movie?"

"Terrible!" I said.

Maureen and Patti had been talking to one another, and now Maureen said, "I didn't know she'd be so sensitive." She laughed nervously.

"Do you want to go somewhere and talk about it?" David offered me.

"Okay, let's go!" I said as I headed out the door. I didn't even look back. Maureen, Patti, and I had planned on going out for a drink after the movie, but I didn't feel like doing that anymore.

"Want to go to Hunt's?" David asked.

"Anywhere you want," I said. I'd been to Hunt's before, which was a bar and restaurant.

We walked in silence for a moment, and then I said, "That was awful! That was really awful! That was just awful!" With each proclamation, I became more adamant. I fought back tears. I really didn't want to be seen crying in public.

We found a table in the back of Hunt's, where I had my back turned to most people in the bar. There I started telling David about the awful images I had seen in the movie. He listened and then tried to console me the same way Maureen had: "Just remember, it's not real."

"That's what Maureen said, but then what does that say about the person who made all this up? It's downright evil!"

Some time later, I realized I would not be able to hold back my tears much longer. I asked David if he could take me back to the Y.

At the Y, we took off our boots and coats and headed to the parlor. Then I finally collapsed into tears. Without a word, David put his arms around me and held me. I told myself I shouldn't be such a crybaby, but the images from the movie were still flashing through my mind, and I couldn't help it. David's arms held me steady. He might not have understood why I was so upset, but at least he understood that I was upset. In that moment, it was enough.

It was as if everything the Amish preachers had warned about had come true—being enticed into the ways of the world, where

Satan would get his hold on us. And just by watching the evil on the screen, it seemed Satan had sneered at me, knowing he had sucked me into his lair. David's arms around me held me back from the abyss I felt I was about to fall into.

～❀～

It took days for the horror to fade. I struggled with the urge to go back to my community and give myself up to the rules of the church. I questioned my ability to deal with the outside world and the evils the Amish warned against.

On Friday morning, I saw David's pickup truck go down the Main Street hill. It was a cold, sunny day in late February. I hadn't seen him in several days, and I found myself missing him. I bundled up in layers and headed down the hill to Church Street. Just as I came around the corner, I saw David's display train set up near city hall. When I approached him, he had a wide, pleased grin on his face. "Hi, Linda," he said. "Imagine meeting you here."

David frequently peddled his wares on Church Street in Burlington.

"Yeah, how come you're down at this end of the street? Aren't you normally up at the top of Church Street?"

"Well, today there are a bunch of us peddlers out here to collect signatures for our petition. The store owners are trying to get us banned from the street, and we are fighting back by asking the voters whether they want us here or not. You want to sign our petition?"

"But I'm not a voter."

"That doesn't matter. It just shows support."

"Sure, why not?" I said, thinking, what if someone figures out my real name is Saloma, not Linda?

I took my glove off and tried to get my stiff, cold fingers to cooperate in signing "Linda." I felt like a fraud, just from the simple act of signing my name.

With his grin wide, David said, "We can't lose with your name on there." As he looked at me with those soft, liquid-blue eyes, I felt like I was going to lose myself in them. I held his gaze as I pulled on my glove.

Then David said, "I heard there is going to be a bluegrass band playing at the Ira Allen Chapel tomorrow night, and I was wondering if you'd like to go to it with me?"

"I would love to! What band is playing?"

"Well, let's see, I have the newspaper right here. It says J. D. Crowe and the New South."

"That sounds like fun! I've never been to a bluegrass concert before."

"Then this will be a first for both of us."

I felt like kissing David, right there on Church Street.

~ ❀ ~

Saturday night, as I got dressed to go to the Ira Allen Chapel, I chose my favorite wool plaid skirt, a white ribbed turtleneck, and a navy blue blouse to go over the turtleneck. I brushed out my hair and clasped it back, away from my face. As I surveyed myself in the mirror for just a moment, I realized I had never before seen myself as attractive. Perhaps David made me feel attractive because, in that moment, I realized if I saw someone else who looked like me, I would think she was good looking.

I looked at my dark hair and eyes, my clear complexion (what Maureen had dubbed "peaches and cream"), my bright red lips, and now my relatively slender body. I had struggled to lose weight for years and then tried crash diets, but none of them worked. Then I had started the nasty habit of purging if I felt like I'd eaten too much. It felt like I'd cheated to be thin. But I didn't want to think about that now.

When David arrived, I pulled on my coat and boots, and we headed out into the crisp wintery night. My teeth were chattering as I got into the pickup. "Boy, am I glad you have a heater in your truck!" I said.

"So am I!" David said, laughing. "But I don't know too many trucks that don't."

"I know buggies that don't, though."

"Oh man, on a night like tonight that would be cold! How did you stay warm?"

"That's just it: we didn't," I laughed. "But we'd at least try by wrapping blankets around ourselves and tucking them in around our laps. Some young men had storm fronts on their buggies, so at least the wind wouldn't be so bad."

"What are storm fronts?"

"They're like a windshield, but they're on hinges, so they can open or close."

"Still, I'm glad we aren't in a buggy tonight."

David found a place to park behind the Ira Allen Chapel on the University of Vermont campus. People were crowding in out of the cold along with us. We found a pew near the front but off to one side. I took my coat off and put it on my lap, then snuggled up next to David. To my surprise, he moved away, leaving space between us. I didn't think much of it, especially when the music started. And what great music it was—good old banjo-picking, fiddle-playing, foot-stomping bluegrass! My feet could not hold still. I looked at David, and he seemed pleased to see that I was enjoying myself. I couldn't tell if he was enjoying himself or not with the amused half-smile he had on his face.

That evening, I thought about a typical Saturday night at my parents' house. I realized if I was there now, I would be getting ready for church the next morning: taking a bath in the galvanized tub by the woodstove in the living room and ironing my white organdy cape and apron and my dress for church. I'd have to help my sisters empty the bathwater between baths, get *Datt*'s and Simon's suits brushed and hung up, and shine shoes. This would be after cleaning and baking all day.

Those wintery Saturday nights in my parents' home had a darkness all their own. And here I was, sitting in the light and airy Ira Allen Chapel, in Burlington, Vermont, with a handsome young man who seemed to care about me. I moved closer to David and snuggled under his arm. He was sitting at the end of the pew. He looked at me with a quizzical expression that seemed to ask, "What are you doing?" Then he gently but firmly pushed me away. Now it was my turn to look at him with a questioning expression. He had never turned away from any physical expression before. Then the next song started and I became mesmerized by the music again.

On the way back to the Y, I asked David why he had pushed me away. He apologized and said he was uncomfortable with showing affection in public.

"But all I wanted to do is sit next to you with your arm around me," I explained.

"I know it's my problem—it has to do with my Catholic upbringing."

I thought he would get over it, so I dropped the subject.

9

Love Unspoken

*The best and most beautiful things in this world cannot be
seen or even heard, but must be felt with the heart.*
—Helen Keller

D avid and I had never before seen one another three days in a
row, but it so happened that before we decided to go to the
bluegrass concert on Saturday night, I had invited him to come
and have brunch with me on Sunday morning at the Y.

Though that stretch of February days in Burlington seemed
to be the coldest February days I'd ever experienced, they were
also the sunniest. On this Sunday David arrived at ten o'clock as
planned. Most of the women at the Y were still sleeping, though
I could never be sure about Christine or another woman named
Edith. They could be lurking in the background, eavesdropping.
I decided I was going to be myself, whether they were listening
in or not.

When David took his coat off and hung it up, I put my arms
out for a hug and said, "You smell like the outdoors."

"Is that a good thing?" he asked as he gave me a tentative hug.
It seemed to me he was looking over my shoulder to see if anyone
else was around.

"Yes, I love that fresh-air smell."

"Oh good, and I love your breakfast smell."

"Okay, have a seat, and let's eat."

"Do you always talk in rhymes?"

"No, only for you," I laughed. "We used to say, 'If you say a
rhyme, you get to make a wish.'"

"So, are you going to make a wish?"

"I wish I could go driving in the Vermont countryside today."

"I'd love to take you for a ride. Where would you like to go?"

"I've always wanted to see the round church in Richmond. Is that far from here?"

"No, it's not far at all. I can take you there. But how do you know about the round church?"

"I saw it in *Vermont Life* magazine."

"You mean when you were still Amish?"

"Yes. I subscribed to the magazine. There were no rules to stop me, so I did it."

Over brunch, David and I chatted about Amish and Catholic church services. I learned that he could choose between going to church on Saturday night, Sunday morning, or Sunday night. He attended on Sunday nights to please his mother. Then I told the story of how my sisters and I once tried to skip church and how my father came back and walked behind us all the way to church, as if he were herding sheep. At first David laughed, but then we both became quiet. I got up and started clearing the table. "But let's talk about something else," I suggested.

On the drive out to Richmond, David said matter-of-factly, "See that house on the left, set back off the road? That's where I live."

"Really? Wow, that's a nice house!"

"You think so?"

"Yes!"

"I helped build it."

"You did?"

"Yes, back when I was still in high school. My family was living in Wappingers Falls, New York. I came up here with my dad and worked on it full time the summer I was sixteen."

I looked at David, wondering why he wasn't puffing up his chest with pride. I realized he would have been better suited for Amish life than I was. Seeing him in a different context from the YWCA parlor or the bars and restaurants of Burlington was somehow giving me a wider view of him.

Along Interstate 89 I oohed and aahed over the vistas of mountains and valleys. David looked pleased.

When David drove into Richmond, we did not see the church. He drove around the village several times, and we still could not find it. I assured him that just driving in the countryside was fun by itself. We headed east on Route 2, skirting around Mt. Mansfield and Camel's Hump, along the Winooski River. The dark, gray river changed with every bend. Defiant old maple trees with storm-broken tops lined the pastures, asleep under crusted snow. Silent barns and outbuildings seemed to cluster around white houses billowing white smoke from overworked chimneys. We topped a prominent point and saw Mt. Mansfield rise in all its winter glory, with a little village huddled in the valley below.

The raw winter beauty evoked longing in me. I knew I missed *Mem*, but I also knew my longing to see her was not enough to make me want to go back to my old life. Instead, I wished she could know the freedom I had, see the beauty of Vermont, and understand that the reasons I left did not include a desire to get away from her.

Though I could not convey all these feelings to David, I told him how I thought of my mother when I heard the song "Will the Circle Be Unbroken." He asked what the song was like, so I told him it was about someone's mother dying, and I sang the chorus, "Will the circle be unbroken / By and by, Lord, by and by / There's a better home awaiting / In the sky, Lord, in the sky."

"That's a pretty sad song."

"I know. But it sounds like I'm going to be the cause of my mother's death, at least if I go by the letters I keep getting."

"Really? Who's sending these letters?"

"Well, this past week, I got a letter from my Aunt Katie and a neighbor woman, Clara Yoder. It doesn't seem to matter who writes the letters, the message is usually the same—that I'm causing my mother sorrow. They don't know how she is going to endure it, and they make me feel like I am going to break the circle. My Aunt Katie wrote that she wants to ready herself for when she goes to her Maker and she hopes the same is true for the whole family. She underlined 'the whole family.' This, of course, is supposed to remind me that I will not 'be ready' if I don't come back and 'repent.'"

"Do the Amish believe you have to be Amish to make it to heaven?"

"Only if you were born Amish. Otherwise, you have as good a chance as anyone else."

"That's strange."

"Clara Yoder's letter had a different message. She told me how when she last saw my mother at church, someone asked her if she had heard from me, and Clara noticed her organdy cape was all wet with tears. Then, of course, I feel so awful to be the cause of my mother's sorrow. It makes me feel like I'm killing her."

"Could you go back and visit your mother but not stay?"

"Oh, no! The Amish would never let me leave again. The way it is now, at least I am far away from home, and I don't feel like they have power over me. If I went back, they would all surround me and convince me to stay."

There was silence between David and me for a moment. "Do they really have that kind of hold on you that you couldn't come and go on your own?"

"Oh, yes! Especially my mother—I feel so guilty. I wish I could build a log cabin in the woods in Vermont and have her come live with me, far away from the Amish."

David was silent.

⌘

Back at the Y, I invited David into the parlor. He had brought a little cedar chest of photos of his family members. When he showed me a photo of his mother, sitting in a wheelchair in a blue striped pantsuit with a birthday cake on her lap, David told how she had had multiple sclerosis since before she was married.

"Wow, and she had five children?" I asked.

"Yes, she did. She doesn't let anything stop her."

"I used to work for a woman with MS. She also had five children. She seemed to be the other way. She seemed to like to have other people do her work for her."

David was quiet for a moment. "I told my mother about you, and she'd like to meet you."

"Really?"

"Yes. Would you want to go and meet my family next Sunday?"

"Are you sure? Do you know it was just seven weeks ago today we had our first date?"

"It seems like we've known each other longer."

"Remember what I said about our relationship going too fast? Isn't meeting your family kind of serious?"

"It doesn't have to be."

I wasn't convinced. But I figured David knew the norms better than I did, so I said, "I guess I'm ready."

"It means a lot to me, you know."

David put aside the pictures and gathered me into his arms. I smelled his familiar smell of the linseed oil he used on his wooden toys. I wasn't sure how I felt about meeting his family, but I did know how I felt about David. I had come to trust him completely, especially after one of our nights in the parlor when I'd had too much to drink and had invited him up to my room. He had reminded me that I was saving myself for marriage, and he'd left so we wouldn't be tempted. Now I loved being inside the circle of his arms and hearing his heart beating in his chest.

It was dark by the time David left the Y. We had spent a whole day together, and I was not sick of his company. But he had to go to church, and I needed to write letters to my family.

10

The Loss of Linda

*If you follow someone else's way, you are not going
to realize your potential.*
—Joseph Campbell

On Friday night, I served a theater group at the Pizza Hut. We pulled tables together so they could all fit into one seating area. It was my first big group, and they seemed to appreciate my service. At the end, they apologized for giving me only a four-dollar tip. I told them that was just fine. I did not tell them it was the biggest tip I'd ever had.

After the group left, as I cleared the tables, I was startled to see David walking in. When I worked late, I usually took the late bus back to the Y. David had most likely gone to the Y and found out I was working.

I went up to him and said, "What are you doing here?"

"Edith told me that you were working late, so I thought I'd give you a ride home," he said.

"Oh. I don't get off work for another twenty minutes."

"That's okay, I'll wait." David sat at the booth where people usually sat when they were waiting for their orders.

While I was cleaning up, my boss told me someone wanted to talk to me. I went to the front counter, and two people from the group I had just served were standing there. They said, "We feel badly that we couldn't give you a bigger tip, so we would like to offer you these two tickets to our next play."

I must have expressed the surprise, delight, and appreciation I felt, because the two people seemed very pleased when they left.

I put the tickets in my purse and finished my work. I felt like I was walking on air, I was so happy. I was thinking about whether I should invite David to come with me to the play. Or should I ask Raymond? I hadn't seen him in a while, so maybe this would be a way to reconnect. But David knew I had the tickets, and it would be awkward not to ask him. He had, after all, come to take me back to the Y. But I didn't ask him to; he just did it, I thought.

In David's truck on the way back to the Y, he said, "That was very nice of that group. They must really like you."

"They were nice people, weren't they?"

"So are you going to go to the play?"

"I certainly hope to."

"Did they give you one or two tickets?"

"Two. I don't know yet who I want to ask to go with me."

"Oh." David looked hurt.

"You know that I've dated someone else in Vermont, don't you?"

"Is his name Raymond?"

"Yes, how did you know?"

"Edith told me. You remember the night you went to see that awful movie with Maureen and Patti?"

"Yes."

"Edith had told me that you were seeing a tall guy named Raymond."

"Oh, leave it to Edith! What business is that of hers?"

"So are you going to ask Raymond?"

"I don't know yet."

Back at the Y, I invited David in. He had gotten quiet since our discussion about the tickets. I sensed he was upset, but most people I knew would tell me when they were upset. David only came as far as the kitchen and then excused himself and left out the side door rather abruptly. I felt the emptiness inside me that came with conflict, and I reached for food. I started with graham crackers and milk.

I had just consumed the second cracker when the front doorbell rang. My first thought was that David must have left something behind. No, he wouldn't come to the front door, and he certainly wouldn't ring the doorbell. Then I thought, this is really late at night—should I even go to the door?

I was still chewing on my graham cracker when I looked down the hall. I thought I saw a light-green Amish dress through the window to the left of the door. Then I saw my brother Joe, like a dark shadow, through the window to the right of the door.

It felt like someone was playing darts, using my heart as the target. I was already in a forward motion, and the thought never occurred to me that I could turn tail and run. In fact, from the time I saw the dress, I felt like a marionette on strings. By the time my hand reached for the doorknob, my heart was racing. I felt trapped, like I had no choice in what I was doing.

I opened the door to my brother Joe and sister Sarah and invited them in. Sarah's face was as white as a sheet, like she was forgetting to breathe. It looked like she could faint. Joe, as always, was putting on a calm front. He looked around and said, "Wow, this is a big place."

"Well, come on in," I said as I motioned to the parlor. Joe sat down on the rocking chair, and Sarah sat down in slow motion, seeming frozen in panic as she had the day the neighbor's bull chased her and me across the yard. I had taken off running, until I realized she was not with me. I looked back and saw her running, as if in slow motion, with the bull right behind her. Fortunately, a neighbor intervened to save her. Now, in the parlor of the Y, I said, "Sarah, you look like you're about to faint."

"Well—you have to admit—this is rather unusual," she stammered, breathing hard.

I sat on the sofa and pulled my feet up underneath me. "So who else is in the van?" I asked.

Joe answered, "Dan and Nance Wengerd, Uncle Ervin and Sadie, and Une's Ada."[6]

---

6. In most Amish settlements, many people share the same first and last names. There was another Saloma Miller in my community, so to differentiate between us, our father's names were used before our own: I was called "Sim's Lomie" ("Simon's Saloma") and the other Saloma was "John's Lomie." The apostrophe is used for those who are not yet married. When someone gets married, she takes her husband's name before her own but the apostrophe is dropped, as if the husband's name becomes a prefix. So I would be called "David Lomie," and

My heart sank lower with every person he named. Dan Wengerd was the bishop of the church, Uncle Ervin was a minister in another district, and Ada was one of my closest friends in the community. Joe didn't even need to say more than Dan Wengerd for me to assess that I was not getting out of this one. He and the others in the van had a firm grip on the strings that controlled me, and he knew it. I could see it in his eyes.

"So when are we going back?" I asked, matter-of-factly.

"Oh, so you are coming back," Joe said, as if in great relief.

"Well, what did you think?" I retorted. "Do you really think I'm going to resist everyone in that van?"

"Well, we didn't know," Joe said. I was suddenly very aware of Joe's eyes undressing me. My Pizza Hut uniform didn't seem to cover me enough; I may as well have been naked.

"Let me go change," I said, as I ran up the stairs to my room, where I quickly changed into the light-gray Amish dress that I had worn when I left home four months before. I combed my hair and dutifully pulled it into a bun and covered it with my *kopp*. I decided I wanted Maureen to know what was happening. I knew she was in her room, because I'd seen her car parked outside. I knocked on her door and waited. No answer. I knocked again. No answer. I opened up her door and turned on her light and saw that she was fast asleep. What should I do? I wondered. I touched Maureen's shoulder and she startled awake. She opened her eyes. "Linda! You scared me!" she exclaimed. Then she looked at me again and said, "Oh, my God, what happened?"

"Shh!" I motioned. "Maureen, they came to get me."

"Who came to get you?"

I named them off. "Maureen, I'm not getting out of this one. I have to go back."

"Is that what you want to do?"

"It's not what I want to do, but I don't think I have a choice. Joe is capable of forcing me to get into the van, and I don't think the others would stop him."

Clara, a woman who befriended me as a child and who appears later in my story, was called "Olin Clara."

"Do you want to call the police?"

"I don't think so." I laughed nervously. "I don't know whose side they'd take. I'm still considered a minor in Ohio."

"Yeah, but you can't just go back."

"I have to get back downstairs. My brother and sister are waiting for me."

When I got to the living room, Joe looked at me and said, "*Oh na, sell iss so viel bessa!*" (Oh, now that is so much better!) I wanted to slap him, but instead I stammered something about the other outfit being what I had to wear to work and then I changed the subject.

"The one thing you may as well know is that I will not live at home again."

"You don't have to worry about that," Joe said in the buttery voice he used when he was trying to get someone to see his way of things. "Arrangements have already been made for you to stay at Urie Benders'."

I gulped. I would not have a choice.

Joe said it was time to talk to the others in the van and let them know what was happening. "Where is everyone staying tonight?" I asked.

"We're going to get a hotel."

"Sarah, do you and Ada want to stay here overnight?" Before the words were even out of my mouth, I wanted to bite my tongue. But it was too late. I had just locked the door to my own cage and thrown away the keys. Sarah and Ada were ensuring that I wouldn't slip away from them again.

Sarah went to the van, and she and Ada retrieved their suitcases. I showed them where the bathroom was, and then I showed them to the "guest room" with two single beds.

"Where are you going to sleep?" Sarah asked.

"In my room," I said. "Why? Are you afraid of the dark and need to be in the same room as your big sister?" I quipped.

"Well, you already slipped away from us once," Sarah said.

"So, if you want to make sure I don't do it again, you better not fall asleep. Oh, and maybe you should go to the bathroom with me, too, just to make sure."

"I can if you want me to," Sarah retorted.

"No, I don't want you to!"

Ada silently started removing pins from her dress to get into her nightdress.

I left them abruptly and went into the bathroom. I was shaking in fury. Everything I had worked toward in having a life of my own in Vermont was over. Slowly, I got ready for bed; then I lay down in my four-poster bed—most likely for the last time.

Once in bed, I could not calm down. I wanted to get up, get dressed, and run—to where I did not know, but away from the Amish and the trap that had been set for me. It felt like I was in one of my recurring dreams in which I was trying to go somewhere but something was preventing me from doing so.

I knew what I was up against.

Dan Wengerd. The bishop. The almighty bishop, who was now in his own bed in the hotel down the hill. He only had to say the word and any member of the church would have to obey. I recalled how only a year and half earlier, when I was "following the church" or taking instructions for baptism, he had asked me to make a promise he didn't seem to care whether I kept.

I didn't really want to "follow the church," but I was of the age that it was expected of me. And I knew if I didn't join church that summer, I would only make it harder on myself for the following summer because the pressure would only increase—unless I were to walk away from the Amish life altogether. I lacked the courage to leave and I lacked the conviction to join. So I took the middle road: I joined the church without conviction.

As I was taking instructions for baptism, the members of the church got a shot at correcting me, to make sure I was properly submitting to the Amish ways. *Datt* kept telling me I shouldn't be dancing at singings. I ignored him, knowing there wasn't much he could do about it, given he wasn't at the singings and because dancing was allowed before marriage.

Then one morning in the instruction class, the bishop started out by saying that "a brother" had come forward to say that one of us was still dancing and that this needed to stop. Dan shuffled his feet nervously and said, "So, ahhh . . . if that person will promise that she will stop, then we can continue on." With that he looked at me.

I looked up, stunned. "Me?" I asked. Before this, any promises I had made were made by all five of us who were joining church. Dan realized what I was asking. He said, "Well, ah . . . I guess everyone should make that promise, so . . . Noah, why don't you start?"

Dan got all five of the expected yeses, and then he moved on to the regular teaching session. I tried to swallow down my anger as I sat in front of the four elders and said nothing.

I gave up dancing as I had promised I would—until the day that one of the bishop's daughters was getting married. Out in the barn on that evening, the young people danced. Noah, who had promised along with me that his dancing days were over, was dancing along with everyone else. When I realized that Dan hadn't expected me to really give up dancing and that he had merely done that to satisfy my father, I joined in. It was through this experience that I lost all respect for Dan Wengerd, and yet he wielded so much power.

That night as I lay in bed, I recalled what it was like to be the scapegoat family in the community. Dan Wengerd and Uncle Ervin headed up two popular families in the community. From their high perch, they looked down on those of us who were at the bottom. And now they were here to gather me back into the fold.

Uncle Ervin commanded a great deal of respect in my mother's family and in every other facet of the community. He and Sadie had four sets of twins and fifteen children in all. They seemed to like the view that most people had of them: the model family. Ervin would strut when he walked in a way that made me think of a bantam rooster.

When *Mem* was young, she had a live-in job, working for Grace Bradley and her family. Grace and *Mem* developed a life-long friendship, even though Grace was not part of the Amish community. She would visit us when I was young. When I was a teenager, I used to help her clean house. One day she told me that my grandmother was a very stern woman. I immediately asked, "You mean my father's mother?"

"No, I am talking about your mother's mother," Grace said. "She once pulled your mother away from us to go and keep house for her brother Ervin when he returned from the Civilian Conservation Corps camp, where he'd been helping build the Hoover Dam as a conscientious objector during World War II."

"What Grandma did was a very Amish thing to do," I said.

"But your mother was of age. She should have been allowed to make that decision for herself."

Now as I lay in the four-poster bed at the Y, I wondered what that was like for my mother to go and keep house for Ervin. Did she take on that role willingly, or did she rebel against taking orders from him? For whatever reason, Ervin had become an authority figure in my mother's family, and then he had been ordained a minister, giving him even more power.

Sadie was a strong-willed woman. They maintained their model family status quite well, though they had also known sorrow. Elva, one of their oldest daughters, had contracted polio when she was little, which disfigured her. Then when she was a young woman, she was in a car-buggy accident, which left her fighting for her life for two weeks. She lost that fight at the age of twenty-two.

Now Ervin and Sadie were also sleeping in a hotel not far from the Y, waiting to take me back to my "rightful" place among the Amish.

And there was Ada, sleeping in the other room. She was Joe's wife's sister. When Joe was courting Emma, I would often spend Sunday afternoons with Ada and her other sister, Ella. We'd go to the singings together. Even though Ella and I were closer in age, Ada and I became closer friends. It was more pleasant to hang out with them on a Sunday afternoon than to spend Sunday afternoons at my parents' house. When Joe and Emma married, Ada and I drifted apart. Here in Vermont, I had gotten a few pedantic letters from her. She wrote that she could not imagine spending Christmas away from home. She also reported she had taken over one of my cleaning jobs and that when I left, one of the people I worked for nearly lost her mind. She said that this woman was shocked, but then who wasn't?

Ada had always assumed a certain authority over me. The Amish system of deferring to someone older (however slight) was automatic. If there was ever a question between what she wanted to do and what I wanted, it was expected that I defer to her, which I did. Now she was here at the Y to help ensure that I wouldn't slip away.

And Sarah, my sister. The good daughter. It would only seem reasonable that if *Mem* had five daughters, one of them should be the good daughter. Sarah was the middle child and the middle daughter. She had figured out how to please early on. I recalled how, when we were playing with our dolls as little children, I would catch *Mem* looking at Sarah with such love in her eyes. I would watch what Sarah did and copy her so that *Mem* would see me, too. In fact, I tried to be Sarah. That would only last for about five minutes before I'd switch back to being myself again.

Like the good daughter, Sarah was now staying here at the Y to make sure I returned home. Here to help Joe and the others.

And, of course, Joe was here—Joe who took pride in his ability to convince people to do what he wanted. He aimed to win. Every time. And with me he did. For when he couldn't convince me otherwise, he used physical violence. I could not run from him; he was faster. I could not hide from him; he was too perceptive. I could not fight him; he was too powerful. I could not outsmart him; he was too cagey. And I could not get help from *Mem*; she would let him do what he wanted. So if I crossed a line in my defiance of him and he came after me, I had to endure whatever pain he inflicted. Sometimes, after a thorough beating, when I was a crying heap on the ground and I would think it was finally over, he would give me a hard, brutal kick in my behind. The pain was excruciating. I could never figure out if he enjoyed inflicting pain or if he did it to maintain his dominance.

Joe knew, just by coming to the Y, that he would evoke fear in me. I had never won a fight against him before. If he decided it was necessary to grab me and physically put me in the van to take me back, the others would probably stand by and watch that happen. I realized any attempts at escaping this time could be disastrous. A thick gray blanket of dread weighed me down when I thought about leaving my freedom behind and returning to my old life. And yet I could not take a chance of losing my dignity altogether. I decided if I was going to have to go back anyway, I would at least go back with my dignity intact.

I thought of David. He had seemed upset when he left. I wished I had invited him to go to the theater with me. Now that chance was gone. And all those times when David and I had enjoyed one another's company—at the Tiki Garden, in the parlor, at the Ira Allen chapel, driving through the Vermont countryside, or anywhere else—were now at an end. Maybe someday I would find another romance, but somehow I knew I would never again find such an understanding friend as I had in David. He understood me in a way that no one else ever had. And now I would never have the chance to tell him so. The Amish had come to absorb me back into the fold, which was a world away from the one with David in it.

I felt the tears as they trickled down my cheeks and into my pillow. Four months ago, I had dared to leave the only life I knew for the promise of a better one. Now it was all slipping away. I felt keenly the loss of dreams, the loss of confidence, the loss of freedom—the loss of Linda.

11

Wearing Amish

Only in the agony of parting do we look into the depths of love.
—George Eliot

I awoke with a start from a dream I couldn't remember, yet it left me with a heavy, foreboding feeling. Then I remembered. Sarah and Ada were in the other room, sleeping at the Y to make sure I didn't leave. The leaden feeling followed me to the bathroom, where I ran water into the claw-foot bathtub. Unlike my first bath at the Y, when I filled up the tub and floated on the water, this time I bathed with less water. It was a utilitarian bath that fit my melancholy mood.

My mind was ahead of me, and I was thinking about the preparations I needed to make. I had to sort out my belongings. I would leave most of the food for the other women at the Y, but the dried food that I had bought at the co-op, especially the mint tea, I would take with me. My clothing I would give to my friends. But I would take my wool coats home with me; *Mem* could use those in a braided rug.

I dried off, wrapped myself in a towel, and slipped into my room. I saw the Amish dress I had laid over the chair before I went to bed and realized how the gray color fit my mood.

As I pulled on my dress and pinned myself into it, I felt myself become Amish again. Then I stuck myself as I pinned together the belt at my waist. How I hated wearing straight pins in my dress! The monotonous, gray feeling weighed down my limbs, and I felt as though I were slogging through mud. I pushed on, sorting my clothing and packing my underclothes and my two wool coats into my suitcases. I made my bed for the last time, and then I folded the rest of my clothes and left them on the bed. I would let the other women come and take what they wanted. They would have to throw out what they didn't want.

Down in the kitchen, I packed a bag of the food that I wanted to take with me. I set out breakfast for Sarah, Ada, and myself. They may as well eat with me, because the food we didn't eat would get left behind.

I looked at the clock. Seven o'clock—time to call Barbara. I just couldn't go back without saying goodbye to her. My hand shook as I dialed her number. Her husband, Rick, answered the phone. He sounded surprised. "Wow, Linda, you're calling early."

"I know," I said, as I struggled to keep from crying. "Is Barbara there?"

"Yes, she's right here." I heard him say to Barbara, "It's Linda."

Barbara's cheery voice said, "Hey, Linda! What's up?"

"I just wanted to let you know that I'm going back to Ohio today."

"What?! You're kidding me—why?"

"They came to get me."

"Who came to get you?"

"The bishop and his wife, my uncle and his wife, my brother, my sister, and a friend."

"Did you know they were coming?"

"No."

"Wow, they must really want you back, Linda." There was a pause for a moment. Then she asked, "But do you want to go back?"

"I don't think I'm getting out of this one. My sister and my friend stayed here overnight."

"You're kidding! Do you think they're making sure you don't leave again?"

"Yes."

"I'm on my way to work, so I have to go, but will you come by the Church Street Center so I can give you a goodbye hug?"

"Sure, what would be a good time?"

"How about around nine?"

"Sure. I'll see you then."

"Hang in there, kiddo!"

I hung up the phone and struggled to keep from crying. I would have to call David too. This could be tricky, especially if I didn't do it right. I didn't want the Amish to know anything about my relationship with David. That meant I could not do anything to show that I cared about him. And how could I be sure that he wouldn't show he cared? I decided I'd just have to take that chance.

I found his number in my address book. I hesitated. What if I got one of his parents? That would be really awkward, since I didn't know them. I didn't allow myself to think about the plans we had made for me to meet them the next day. I knew that was now impossible. I would wake up in my Amish world tomorrow morning. My arms and hands felt like cement as I dialed the number. I was suddenly very aware that Sarah and Ada would be listening from upstairs. I could not allow my voice to give away my feelings. My heartbeat pounded in my ears as I dialed the phone number. I hoped his parents wouldn't answer the phone.

A quiet voice answered, "Hello."

"Is this David?"

"Yes."

"It's Linda." All of a sudden I felt like a liar. I wasn't really Linda—not anymore.

"Hi, Linda. What a surprise."

"I'm going back to the Amish today," I said bluntly.

David hesitated, then said, "That's a shock. What made you decide that?"

"They came to get me."

"Who came to get you?"

After I named them, David asked, "Are you going to say good-bye to me?"

Now I felt like I had gotten into quicksand and I was slowly sinking. I tried to keep my voice from betraying my conflicting feelings. "I'm going to be saying goodbye to Barbara Lalancette at the Church Street Center at nine o'clock. You can come see me there if you'd like."

"I'll be there," David said.

David arrived at the Church Street Center soon after I got there with Sarah and Ada in tow. Like two shadows, they were following my every footstep. The others were at a dry goods store I'd told them about on lower Main Street, where they could buy dress material for incredible bargains.

David tried to give me meaningful looks, and then he motioned for me to follow him as he sauntered over behind a curtained-off area. He sat down and asked, "Is this what you really want?"

I already felt like a deer in the headlights, but before I could answer, Sarah and Ada came and stood next to me, Sarah on my right side and Ada on my left, with their arms folded across their chests. It seemed the turmoil I felt inside would wrench my heart in two: David and the nights in the parlor on one hand, and the

This building housed the Church Street Center at the time David and I said our goodbyes.

overwhelming presence of the Amish on the other. David gave me a look that seemed to beg me to give him some indication of my feelings. Sarah and Ada were also giving me looks, but of another kind. I felt as though I was caught between two worlds. I would have to keep my heart well guarded or else David would see what I felt inside: a tornado twisting and turning. I handed the two tickets to David that I'd gotten the night before from the theater group and said, "You may as well have these."

David took them hesitantly.

"I need to say goodbye to Barb," I said, and walked over to her desk.

My bonnet got in the way when I hugged Barbara goodbye. She toyed with my bonnet strings as she said, "Ah, Linda, I'll probably cry tonight, when I am all alone. I am going to miss you!" I had to go out the side door of the Church Street Center before I would burst into tears. I turned and waved to Barb. I got a glimpse of David, but I could not bear to see the look in his eyes. I turned and left.

I was heading to the bank with my two shadows just behind me when David called out to me. When I turned around, he came up to me and said, "I wanted you to have my address," and he handed me a folded-up paper. I could tell there was something folded inside, but I took it and tucked it into the pocket of my dress and said, "Thank you." I paused and then said, "By the way, my real name is Saloma."

"Saloma. That's a different name."

I turned to leave, without hugging him, without acknowledging all those nights in the parlor, without even admitting to myself that any of it happened.

"Will you shake my hand?" David asked my back.

"Sure," I said. I turned around and shook his hand. David tried to look me in the eye, but I would not return his gaze. "I will always remember you," David said. He was trying to break down the façade that he knew I was hiding behind. Perhaps I was wearing my Amish demeanor along with my Amish clothing. David could not reconcile the two Lindas or, more accurately, the Linda with the Saloma. In that moment, when David held on to my hand and told me he would always remember me, my façade nearly did collapse. I had to turn away and walk quickly toward the bank to keep that from happening. It never even dawned on me to wonder what Sarah and Ada thought about the interchange. I thought of them as my shadows, so it didn't really matter.

I withdrew all my money from the bank, and then we walked back up the hill to the Y. I wanted to say goodbye to my house-mates who had become my friends over the last four months. As I walked up the hill, one of my shadows fell behind. Sarah said, "Lomie, do you have to walk so fast?"

I hadn't realized before that I had taken on a whole different walk since I had left the community. My step was lighter, faster, and more confident. Sarah was asking me to change back to my old self. I waited for her and walked slowly up the hill toward the Y, wondering if it was for the last time.

I don't remember much about my goodbyes with the women at the Y except that I did try to tell Maureen I would miss her and all the fun we had. Spreading her fingers and gesturing with her hand in classic Maureen fashion, she said, "Linda, don't even start!" She looked like she was about to cry, and that was not something Maureen was comfortable doing.

"Okay, goodbye then," I said. I tried giving her a hug, but she went back inside and ran up the stairs to her room.

The Amish women had packed their dress material purchases into the back of the van, and we were all ready to go. I had to stop at the Pizza Hut to return my uniform and let them know I would no longer be coming back to work. Ada and Sarah followed me in. The manager looked at me twice before recognizing me in my bonnet. I explained that I had left an Amish community and that I was now returning. He kept looking at me, as if I were an impos-ter, though with Sarah on one side of me and Ada on the other, he could tell I wasn't making it up. After giving him my address where he should send my final paycheck, I made haste to leave as quickly as possible.

Back on the road, we headed down Route 7 to Vergennes to pick up Route 22A. I pretended to be happy, trying to strike up a conversation. I asked the women how they made out with the material, and they said they had bought several bolts of it. They oohed and aahed over how inexpensive it was, and they pointed to the back of the van, where bolts of fabric were piled up, along with the shawls and coats people had shed after the car had warmed up. When the mountain range became visible, I pointed out the two highest peaks in Vermont: Mt. Mansfield and Camel's Hump. Nobody in the van had much of a reaction, yet they looked in the direction in which I was pointing. I became quiet after that. I decided if they wanted to give me the message that this trip was serious business, and that they weren't here to have fun, then it would be better for me to be quiet. I retreated into my own thoughts.

I realized the four months I had lived away from the family and community had been both very long and very short—long because I had never before been away from the community, and short because so many exciting things had happened in that time. I tried not to think about what my life would be like back in the community.

Sometime after we had crossed over into New York State, Joe quietly told me that I should go up and sit in the seat between the driver and the bishop. I was to make any confessions I felt were necessary to be a member of the church. I realized I wouldn't even be granted the normal privacy when making these confessions, because the rest of the people in the van would be listening in. But then again, it wouldn't be private when the bishop announced in church what my wrongdoings had been.

I confessed to going to bars and getting drunk, wearing non-Amish clothes, and going to movies. I didn't mention dating. I decided that this should remain a private affair. And if they were going to allow me that privacy, they would have a chance at keeping me in the community. I hoped they would be wise enough to leave it alone. To my relief, Dan didn't bring it up. I also mentioned that I had some food stamps that I had received and I asked what I should do about those. He said, "Well, you can go ahead and use the ones you have; just don't get any more of them."

Bishop Dan explained that it was normal procedure for them to expel me from the church but that he thought I could be reinstated in three weeks. He said that Olin and Clara Yoder had offered that I could come and live with them for those three weeks. I wondered why I wouldn't be able to live with them for longer. As though Dan had read my thoughts, he mentioned that my sister Susan was living with them, and they thought having two of us living there permanently would be too much.

I took my seat again, and then I became really quiet. I lost myself in thoughts about what my life would be like now. I tried to push down the awful feelings of dread that all that freedom I had just begun to realize in Vermont was now at an end.

My thoughts were interrupted when Joe asked the driver if she would keep an eye out for someplace to eat lunch. Pretty soon she pulled into a restaurant, and we all piled in. The smell of old cigarettes and food, the look and feel of the place, and the people who were running the place all made me want to leave. I turned to the others and said in Amish, "We could probably find a better place than this." It was as if they were all deaf. I whispered to Sarah, "I'm going to find someplace else to get food," and then I headed out the door. I saw a grocery store not far away and headed there. Sarah came up behind me and said, "Maybe we should stay with the others."

"You can if you want, but I'm not," I said as I walked confidently toward the entrance of the Grand Union. Sarah followed without saying anything else. I wondered if she was given permission (or orders) to follow me.

I used my food stamps to buy apples, bananas, graham crackers and cream cheese, and milk. Sarah added the makings of sandwiches, and then we headed out to the van, where we ate. When the others came out, they asked where we went, and I said, "I wasn't going to get sick on that food, and it looked like I might have, had I eaten it."

The bishop's wife said in a reproving manner, "Well, sometimes one has to be satisfied with what there is." I took another bite of graham crackers with cream cheese and crunched, then swallowed down the reproach. I could tell that becoming submissive to the degree that was expected of me would not be easy. I wondered if it was going to be possible at all after my taste of freedom.

Several hours later, we took a break at a rest stop along Interstate 90. I chose a bathroom stall far away from the doorway. Sarah followed me to the adjacent stall. It was the one moment when I was out of view of everyone else. I took out the paper David had given me with his address on it. I unfolded it quietly so that Sarah wouldn't hear.

Sure enough, David had folded something into the paper. It was a little brown cross. I had never seen anything like it before, but from somewhere down deep, I felt the significance of the gift. I saw David's blue eyes clouded with sorrow as he'd handed me the gift. Here I was, halfway between my Vermont world and my Amish one, and I held in my hands the cross between my two worlds. I wanted to cry out my agony and have the whole world hear it.

As I sat there thinking of David, I heard my heart pounding in my ears. I wanted to scream out my rage against the injustice of how my Vermont world had been so suddenly and irrevocably wrenched away from me. I wanted to run and hide and make the Amish go back without me. I wanted to call the phone number on the paper David had given me and have him come get me. I wanted to do anything but come out of the bathroom stall where Sarah and Ada waited to escort me back into the van. And yet I knew that was what I had to do.

Slowly and quietly, I folded the cross into the paper and put it back into my pocket. I knew my freedom had come to an end.

12

The Cross of Hope

David Furlong

Gone—flitted away,
Taken the stars from the night and the sun
From the day!
Gone, and a cloud in my heart.
—Alfred Tennyson

I'll never forget the first time I noticed Linda. She struck me as a natural beauty with plump, rosy lips and a compelling smile. She had a milky white complexion and dark brown eyes that seemed to celebrate everything they saw. Her nose had a distinctive prominence that ended in a delicate pug that was so cute. Some unruly wisps of her dark brown hair fell around her ears, down the back of her neck, and against her smooth white cheeks. Her sensible hairstyle reminded me of the kind schoolteachers wore in the days of the one-room schoolhouse. She was shapely in all the right places and as sturdy as a country maiden. She radiated charm and I instantly fell under her spell.

Why didn't I notice her before? I wondered. Maybe she changed her hair.

I reached to shake her hand.

"My name is David. Nice to see you," I said.

"Yes, I remember you," she said with her calm, even voice. She shook my hand. I noticed her hand was the size of mine and she had a restrained, tentative grip.

I had gone to the Y to see Janie, who wasn't there that Saturday afternoon. Maureen had introduced me to Linda and then taken off. Linda and I were now alone in the kitchen. She took a pot of chickpeas off the stove and drained them in the sink in graceful, confident motions, moving about the kitchen in her bare feet. Her sturdy calves were barely exposed under a mid-length wool skirt. "Would you like some chickpea salad?" she offered.

"Sure, I'd love some." Linda moved about the kitchen, putting together the salad and adding the chickpeas and dressing. She served up a portion and handed it to me.

There was nothing coy about Linda. This had to be the Amish daughter; she acted like someone who knew her way around a kitchen, was direct, and had the solid body of a working girl. She was my kind of woman, and I knew it instantly. Any remaining interest in Janie dissolved in the clarity and simple charm of Linda.

Linda and I talked in the kitchen for hours. When I had arrived, the sun was as bright and as high as it gets in January. When I got into my Datsun pickup to leave, it was dark outside and I didn't care. I had just met someone extraordinary, and I sensed my life was about to change.

I was right. Taking Linda on a date to the Tiki Garden was only the beginning. I could see Linda's vulnerability—a kind of innocence in this new world she'd chosen. I wanted to get close to her, to protect her, to explore the new world with her. She had a remarkable sense of self, and she was refreshingly open, uncannily honest, and disarmingly naïve.

I remember well those romantic parlor dates with Linda. There is one night, perhaps even the last such night we had together, that is especially vivid in my memory. In a cozy embrace with Linda, I felt a presence in the room that had a spiritual quality. She had her head on my chest, and the room was lit by a single lamp on the end table next to the sofa. My senses were aware of something special around us—an aura of some kind—and my eyes searched the room for what that might be. I looked up at where the walls met the ceiling and the light seemed hazy there, like a photo that might have been taken through a layer of Vaseline. Was this an affirmation or my imagination? It seemed like angels surrounded Linda and me. Maybe they were acknowledging our attraction for one another as something holy.

Time seemed as frozen as Lake Champlain as I held her close to me. This was love, but I spoke not a word of it to her. I did not tell her how deeply she had touched me, and she said not a word of her feelings to me, as if we could not turn these deep emotions into words. So we held each other and felt what we could not say. This aura, real or imaginary, only intensified my feelings for Linda. On my way home, the stars were brighter than anytime I could remember, and I thanked God for the night.

Only a short week later, I was up early on Saturday, sitting in the living room of my parents' home, watching the sun come up over Camel's Hump. I had not gotten a good night's sleep. The night before, I had found out that Linda had been dating Raymond and was still interested in him. She had gone dancing with him and now might use her tickets to see a theater production with him. I wondered if she'd been intimate with him or if he was just a friend. I did not want to lose her.

The bright morning sun rose higher above the Green Mountains, warming the living room. I was thinking coffee would be perfect, so I set about making some. I had been planning to share my feelings with her last night, but things didn't go the way I'd planned. Tomorrow, after she meets my family, I thought, I'll share the lyrics to Elton John's "Harmony" tune and maybe we can talk about it. We talk about everything else. I just didn't want to come on too strong . . .

The phone rang, startling me out of my reflections. I wondered who was calling at seven o'clock on a Saturday morning. It was Linda, and I could tell by her lifeless voice that something was wrong. I thought she might have been hurt by my leaving so abruptly last night.

"Hi," I said. "You surprised me. Is everything alright?"

"I'm going back to the Amish today," she said in a voice so flat it did not sound like Linda at all.

The sun could have fallen from the sky and I would not have noticed. "Oh, what made you decide that?" I asked carefully.

"They came to get me."

"Who came to get you?"

That's when I learned that a contingent of her Amish community had arrived at the Y to take her back. I told myself that she wasn't running from me, that she was going back because she was afraid of them. She hadn't even known they were coming.

"Are you going to give me a chance to say goodbye?" I asked.

"I'm going to the Church Street Center to say goodbye to Barbara Lalancette at nine o'clock this morning; you can see me there if you want to."

"I'll be there."

As I hung up, I thought, if I *want* to! Is that all I mean to you, Linda? Of course I want to say goodbye if you're leaving for good! Now I heard my mother's wheelchair creaking down the hallway. She wheeled around the corner and into the kitchen. She must have seen that I was troubled. She asked, "Was that your girlfriend?"

"Yes, and she's going back to the Amish today."

"Oh no, that's too bad. I wanted to meet her!"

"The bishop and some others came to get her. I'm going to say goodbye to her this morning."

"I'll say a little prayer for you and her."

Her concern was enough to settle me a bit. I went into my room and sat at my desk and wrote down my address and phone number. I wondered what I could give Linda that she could remember me by. Then it came to me. I had bought a curious cross-shaped mineral called a "fairy stone" at an antique shop in Stowe weeks before. I'd been saving it for an unspecified purpose. What better symbol to give Linda than a cross?

As I approached the Y in my Datsun pickup, I could see Linda in her Amish clothes, walking toward Church Street with an escort on her right and one on her left. The stories she told me about the Amish suddenly became real. Now she was wearing Amish. Did that make her Amish? The woman on the phone: was she Linda, or was she some Amish person I didn't really know?

The solemn trio had arrived before me and I found Barbara talking with Linda. Barbara was toying with Linda's bonnet strings. She said, "Linda, I'm going to miss you. I'll probably cry when I'm alone tonight."

Linda gave me the slightest of acknowledgments with a half-smile and half-frown. She was pensive, quiet, and stern-looking in her full-length gray pleated dress with a short black waistcoat. Her black bonnet covered her hair and the side of her face. Her body was hidden in a veil of chastity. Even in my plight, I was aware of her startling beauty and the natural gracefulness the Amish clothing gave her. I sensed that she was torn in two, and yet there was nothing I could do to save her.

There was no light in Linda's eyes and no feeling in her voice. She seemed to be saying "Please let me go. This is my God-given destiny and I must submit to my people. I must go quickly before I completely break down." My heart went out to her, yet it was breaking at the thought of her spirit roped and bound by a force I could not change.

In the end, I made a choice not to push her, with the hope that somehow our affections would survive. Hoping that she would remember me, I handed her the piece of paper with my address on it. Concealed within it was the cross.

Part 2

13

Prodigal Daughter

[J]oy shall be in heaven over one sinner that
repenteth, more than over ninety and nine just
persons, which need no repentance.
—Luke 15:7

I awoke to the sound of a baby crying and a child playing. I had to remind myself that I was at my brother Joe's place. The group in the van had decided for me that it was too late to take me to Olin and Clara's house and that I was to stay at Joe and Emma's for the night. All the arrangements had been made for me. Sarah had so helpfully produced my pink nightdress, so I could be properly attired even while sleeping. Before going to bed, I had done stretches I had learned at an exercise salon in Burlington, where I still had two months left of my membership that I would not be able to use.

Sarah had looked up from the bed and said in her matter-of-fact yet critical tone, "What are you doing?"

"I'm exercising. I don't know about you, but I feel pretty cramped after that long drive."

"Where did you learn that?" she asked, as she peered over the top of the covers. I could tell she was trying to be critical. I knew her style—put me off guard with her criticism but at the same time get me to divulge the information she wanted. Usually that made me angry. This time I said with confidence, "At Elaine Powers."

"Elaine Powers, what's that?"

"Does it matter? I can't go there anymore now, can I?"

"I was just asking."

"And I was just saying."

"Lomie, you don't have to blame me for anything. If you had come back on your own, we wouldn't have had to go and get you."

"You wouldn't have had to come and get me, even if I didn't come back."

"So you are going to blame me. Is it really worth going to hell after you die for the fun you'd have living a Yankee life while you're on earth?"

"How do you know that I'd go to hell?"

"You know that's what we've been taught."

"And how do we know that what we were taught is right?"

"Oh, Lomie, nobody can reason with you! You are just too *dick-keppich*!" With that, Sarah rolled over on her side and was quiet. I finished my exercises and then got in on my side of the bed.

Now it was morning and I was still lying in bed, while Sarah was out helping Joe with the chores.

I thought about all the other things I had started in Vermont that had to be aborted. I had worked in exchange for courses at the Church Street Center; now I could not take those courses. There was my job at Pizza Hut. And there were the theater tickets for the play I couldn't go to.

And hardest of all was the relationship with David. I sensed he was devastated when I left. I could not look at him at the Church Street Center, because I knew I would betray my feelings if I did. Though we had never verbalized our feelings for one another, I knew he cared deeply for me, judging by how often he wanted to see me and that he wanted me to meet his family. Now I would not have a chance to share these feelings with him. I felt ashamed that I hadn't asked him to go to the play with me. He was, after all, the one who came to the Pizza Hut to give me a ride. I had probably sown doubt in David's mind about any feelings I had for him. And what was worse, I would now have to deny any feelings I did have.

Four months earlier, when I left the Amish community, I made a sudden change from my familiar Amish life to the unknown outside world. But the transformation from being Amish to becoming myself as Linda had occurred naturally, because it was my choice. Although I had thought transitioning from the world of the unknown back to familiar surroundings would be easier than going the other way had been, I now realized that going the way of freedom comes more naturally than working against it. I wondered, is it better to have known freedom and lost it than to never have known it at all? I decided on the spot that the answer for me was a definite yes. No matter what happened, no one could ever take away those four months of freedom I had experienced.

I knew the Amish thing to do would be to get up and help with whatever needed doing. My limbs felt lethargic, and I didn't want to get up. I was glad it was an "in-between-church Sunday," but Emma could probably use help with making breakfast.

I got up and pinned myself into my Amish dress, combed out my hair, and pulled it up and clasped it to my head, the very same way I'd promised the hairdresser in Chesterland just months before that I would never do again. Then I covered my hair with my *kopp* to show my subservience to God and to men.

~ ❀ ~

My whole family got together at *Mem* and *Datt's* house on my first day back in the community. When I saw *Mem*, I put my arms out and gave her a big hug. Showing affection with hugs or kissing was just not done in my community, but now that I had been hugging people for the last four months, it was natural for me. *Mem* and I had never hugged before. She squeezed me back, and when I looked into her blue eyes, they were wet with tears. I could tell that she liked the hug—almost as if she had been hungering for it all her life.

On my first day back, I was treated like the prodigal daughter. *Mem* had butchered chickens the day before. We feasted on fried chicken, mashed potatoes and gravy, fried carrots, homemade corn relish, fresh homemade bread, and pumpkin and apple pies for dessert. I knew my formal penance would come later, after the

following Sunday when I'd be placed in the *Bann*.[7] I wasn't looking forward to making a public confession, but that would not be
as hard as learning to obey the rules of the church after living free
of them in Vermont.

After spending most of the first day at *Mem* and *Datt*'s, I packed
my clothes and went to Olin and Clara Yoder's house, where I
had always felt welcome. Olin Clara was the one person who
had taken me under her wing when I was trying to find myself
at eleven years old. She had asked *Mem* if I could come and work
for her on Saturdays. I knew, even back then, that Clara didn't
need the help. She was trying to make my life easier, and she was
showing me what "normal" Amish life was like. Perhaps she had
seen a kindred spirit in me, even though she was old enough to
be my grandmother.

"*Salomie, cumm on rei*" (Saloma, come right on in), Olin Clara
said when I arrived. "Susan, will you show her which room she'll
be in?" My sister Susan, now seventeen years old, had also moved
in with Olin and Clara. I tried not to feel envy, since I had fanta-
sized about living with them before leaving home. I didn't think
it would be possible, given that young people were just not given
the chance to live in other people's homes unless they were "of
age." This was twenty-one in my family, though in some other
families it was twenty. Later I found out that Susan had been given
this opportunity after I left because people were afraid she would
also leave if she wasn't given dispensation from living in our parents' house.

Susan helped me carry my bags upstairs, where I hung up my
dresses and put away my underclothing. She asked me if I wanted
to go to the singing, and I said no. I knew I had to have time to
sort myself out before attending the young people's gatherings.

Before Susan went out that evening, Olin and Clara asked us
to sing with them. It was clear Susan's heart was not in it. When
we were upstairs afterwards, she told me that the singing was all
for show and that Clara was just concerned about her reputation.

---

7. Pronounced *bahn*. I was being placed in a temporary *Bann*, which means I
was being shunned during that time.

"How do you know that?" I asked.

Susan explained that one afternoon when she had had young people over, they had put beer on the upstairs windowsill to cool off. Someone driving by had noticed the beer and mentioned it to Olin and Clara. Clara had admonished Susan, saying that it "doesn't look good."

When Susan and I both lived at home we had often banded together and rebelled against our parents. But now I found myself seeing Clara's point of view. I was quiet for a moment and then said, "I don't know about you, but I am very thankful that they are letting me live here. If that means that I don't cool beer off in the front window of their house, then that's fine with me. I don't have to live in fear of *Datt*'s outbursts, and I have a roof over my head."

"You just don't get it, do you?" Susan said, as she got up to leave the room.

"No, I suppose I don't," I said.

The next morning Susan boldly told me she had dated Donny. I didn't think Susan was even attracted to Donny, so why would she have dated him? And why would he ask her for a date? When I was in Burlington, I thought several times about how I did not understand Yankee men. Now I realized the Amish man I had been going steady with was no easier to understand. I was surprised how neutral I felt about Susan dating Donny.

Despite our very different priorities and points of view, Susan and I were both bulimic, and I felt guilty for that. We were eating Olin and Clara out of house and home. Susan was very slim at the time, and yet she didn't see herself that way. I was also the slimmest of any time in my adult life, but I didn't want to gain weight. My eating disorder matched my need to stuff all those feelings I didn't know what to do with.

On Saturday night, a week after I returned from Vermont, I was bathing in Clara's bathroom when I caught a glimpse of myself in the mirror. Was it my imagination, or was that a bump on my chest? I turned this way, then that, looking at one side, then the other. There was something protruding from just above my left breast. I pushed on it, and it felt hard, like a rib. I pushed on the other side, and it was clearly missing the protrusion. I finished drying myself off and put on my nightgown; sure enough, I could see the bump right through the nightgown.

I needed to know if this was all my imagination. I was too embarrassed to ask Clara. And Susan was gone. I went to bed and worried, convinced that whatever was wrong with my chest was going to cause me to die young. I was only twenty years old. If I died, would I go to heaven? Would my coming back to the community increase my chances of that?

By the time I went up to my room and blew out the oil lamp, I was sure that something was very wrong with me. Was it breast cancer? What else could it be? I shed a few tears, feeling sorry for myself. Then I curled into a fetal position and fell asleep.

Hours later, I became dimly aware of noise outside my door, but I willed myself deeper into sleep. Then I startled awake when I realized Susan was asking me if I would allow a date into my bed. She asked if it was "okay for Enos Kurtz."

"What?" I asked incredulously.

Susan repeated her question.

"No," I said, and turned my back. I was really angry that she had woken me up. Now the memory of the problem I had discovered while bathing came back to me, and I didn't want to deal with it.

Susan left my room. A little while later, she knocked on my door again, came into my room and said, "You *have* to take him— he came with my date and me, 'cause I told him . . ."

"No, I *don't* have to take him," I said.

"Lomie, what am I going to do?"

"I don't know—that is *your* problem. You got yourself into this fix, and you can get yourself out of it. Now leave my room and don't come back." I turned my back and willed myself back into a deep sleep.

The next day was the church Sunday when they would be placing me in a temporary *Bann* for two weeks. I was expected to stay home. While the others were at the service, I roamed about the house alone, crying and feeling scared.

When Olin and Clara returned from the church service, I asked them if they would need to shun me, which would have meant I could not eat with them.

"No, it's all worked out," Clara said. "We feel because you have come back and are 'making things right' that it's different than if you had stayed away."

I felt unworthy. I must have looked sad and teary-eyed, and they probably thought it was contrition. I wished I had someone I could talk with who could help me sort out all those complicated feelings.

***

The Thursday after I was put from the church, my cousin Junior married my friend Ida. I would have been invited to be "table-waiter" at their wedding, but since I was under the *Bann*, Sarah became table-waiter in my place. That Thursday was one of the loneliest of all my Amish days. I was in the community but not part of it, which made me feel like an outsider.

The next day, I walked home to visit *Mem*. I gave her the two wool coats I'd been wearing in Vermont. My plan was to tear the coats into strips for her to braid the wool into a rug. I was about to start cutting up the black coat when *Mem* said, "Why don't you put it on?"

"What?" I asked. I thought I had misunderstood her. It was as if she had just asked me to strip off my clothes.

"I don't think that's a good idea," I said.

"Go ahead—no one else has to know. I just want to see what it looks like."

Reluctantly, I pulled the coat over my Amish dress. Wasn't *Mem* the one who had cried over my sheer stockings when she saw them in Vermont? Wasn't putting on a "Yankee" coat one of the things I wasn't allowed to do any longer? Wasn't I going to be making a public confession for having worn Yankee clothing? Why does *Mem* want to see me in this coat?

Mem looked me up and down in a way that made me think she liked the coat. It was almost as if she longed to have worn such a thing herself. "Well, I'm glad you aren't wearing that anymore," she said abruptly.

In that moment, I realized that *Mem* was of two minds. She wanted me to be Amish, yet she herself longed for nice things not allowed by the church *Ordnung*. She espoused the Amish ways most of the time, yet she sometimes rebelled against them. She didn't like being submissive to *Datt*, yet she tried whipping me into submission many times when I was growing up—even to the point of sending Joe or *Datt* after me to make me give in.

I took off the coat, and we began tearing it into strips. I knew *Mem* would eventually braid them into a woolen rug for a Yankee person and wondered what she would be thinking. Would she remember that she asked me to put the coat on? Would it occur to her what a double message that was to me?

~❀~

After two weeks of being out of the church, the day came when I needed to make my public confession and be reinstated. I dressed in my baptismal clothing: my black dress and white cape and apron. Then I walked up Hale Road and Burton Windsor Road to the Shrock home where the church service was being held. I felt many pairs of eyes on me as people gathered for the service. I folded my arms over my chest in the usual humble-young-Amish-woman pose. The women shook hands with one another, which was customary, and visited before filing in to the service. I walked in behind Sara Mae Gingerich, who was one day older than me. Behind me came her sister, Liz. The men all sat in the living room, while the women sat in the kitchen.

One of the singers announced a number in the songbook and everyone turned to that page. Then one of the men began "fore-singing," leading the German chant. The other men joined in, and then the women's higher voices joined in from the kitchen.

My heart skipped a beat when the bishop, two ministers, and the deacon filed upstairs for the elders' meeting. I knew that I was expected to follow them. I waited long enough to hear the men's feet hit the landing above the stairs, and then I slowly climbed the stairs and found the room they were sitting in. I sat down on the bench facing them, as I had when I took instructions for baptism. Back then there had been five of us young people. This time I was all alone.

The bishop started by quoting Scripture in German and then reflected on it. Then each of the other men took turns explaining Scripture with much emphasis on the shepherd that leaves the flock to go find one lost sheep. John Detweiler said he couldn't help but believe that the angels in heaven were rejoicing today.

This photograph shows me dressed mostly in my Amish church clothes, although I would have been wearing a black *kopp* for church instead of a white one.

I wanted to believe that, but I wondered if that was really so. Then the bishop had me repeat after him German words that professed that I still wanted to make my public confession. I focused on the things that I *was* actually sorry for: going to bars, getting drunk, and watching movies that I felt were evil. For good measure, I also confessed to having worn Yankee clothing. I knew that I was really supposed to feel sorry for leaving the Amish. But I thought that being truly sorry for some of it was more honest than pretending I felt sorry for all of it.

Bishop Dan then said I could return to the service downstairs. Even though the people were still singing, I felt the community watching as I took my seat.

The singing stopped soon after the elders came back. Then Joe Byler got up and preached the first sermon. When he was done, he said it was now time to kneel, and everyone turned around and knelt by their backless bench for several minutes of silence. Then we all rose and stood while the deacon read Scripture. This was the time when many of the young people would leave for a break. Today I thought it was a good idea to stay standing in the service, even though I usually looked forward to this break in the middle of the three-hour service.

When the deacon finished reading the Scripture, everyone sat back down and John Detweiler rose for the second sermon. He focused on renewing our faith in the church, and he repeated the idea that the angels in heaven are most likely rejoicing this day. Then he told the story of the prodigal son and quoted in German the Bible verse that says God is more joyful about one sinner repenting than he is about ninety-nine people who are believers. I asked myself: does God see me as a sinner who is asking for repentance? Is it right for me to be here when my heart is still in Vermont? I knew I *should* feel happy and be ready to ask for repentance as everyone was expecting, but I had so many doubts.

My mind soon wandered to Vermont, even though I tried to keep it in the church service. What was David doing? What would I be doing if I were still in Vermont at that moment? I steered my thoughts back to what the preacher was saying. Finally, about an hour after his sermon began, he led us into another prayer as everyone knelt by the benches. He read from the German prayer book, and then we all took our seats. We heard benedictions from Bishop Dan and Deacon John. Then came the moment I'd been dreading. Bishop Dan asked that members stay seated. That's when all the children and young people who were not yet members of the church left. I followed. The first part of my confession would happen with me gone—the bishop would lay out the reasons for my confession. I stayed in the washhouse, where the wringer washer was, so that I could easily be summoned.

I waited for what seemed like a long time. Then the deacon came to the door and motioned for me to come back into the house. I walked up to the bishop in the living room, and he indicated that I should kneel before him. I did.

I knew I should be feeling more humble than I ever had before, but as I kneeled on that living room floor, I felt like I was doing so with dignity. I had never experienced grace and humility together, and I would have thought of them as opposites. Now I wondered if the people around me could see and feel the grace, dignity, and humility I felt as I knelt before them. Just for a short moment I wondered what it would be like if David could see into my world, but I quickly dismissed that thought because I knew this could never be.

I repeated after the bishop the German words that were supposed to redeem me. In the act of kneeling in humility, I did feel redeemed. I imagined a circle of angels looking down on me and smiling. It felt like I was looking at myself from a distance, kneeling on the hardwood floor of the Shrocks' living room while at the same time I was looking down at myself, wearing a white starched and ironed cape and apron over my black dress. The white was like the lightness of the heavenly, winged angels that hovered just above me, while my black dress kept me earthbound. Heaven and earth came together as I knelt before everyone in the church.

Bishop Dan brought my thoughts back to earth when he asked that a "sister" come forward. There was a moment of hesitation. Then one of the older women came forward and offered me a hand. I stood up, and we exchanged the holy kiss. Bishop Dan announced that I was once again a "sister in the church" and asked me to take my seat. He then announced where the next church service would take place and dismissed the congregation.

I knew what had just happened would never be spoken of again. It was the Amish way to "forgive and forget" after someone had made a confession. I normally had to discuss my experiences to fully process them, especially something so out of the ordinary. In this case, I would not have that chance.

Maybe that was just as well. Words were inadequate to describe the experience. I had expected that I would feel emptied out, as I had when I was baptized, but instead I felt a spiritual lightness in my being. I had never experienced anything like it, and I wondered if I ever would again.

~ 14 ~

A Leaf in the River

*If you don't know where you are going, you'll
end up some place else.*
—Yogi Berra

During my transition back into my Amish community, I resigned myself to the Amish belief that God preordains everything that ever happens to anyone on earth. I wanted to believe that I still had a choice in determining my future, yet I had lost all confidence that it might be so. I was like a leaf that had fallen into a river. I was being carried along with the current, with no way of determining which way to go or where I might land.

Twenty-two days after my return to the Amish community and one day after I made my confession in church, I moved to the Benders'. I don't recall anything about my move. I would have been moving my clothing from Olin and Clara's house and then collecting everything else from *Mem* and *Datt*'s house. My belongings were meager at that time: woven rugs; bedding, which included a state flower quilt that *Mem* and I had made together; a sewing basket; stationary, report cards and other memorabilia from my school days; letters I'd saved; my "pretties" that decorated my room, including several candy and fruit dishes that people had given me over the years and a "pin dish" that held straight pins on the dresser; and of course my *Vermont Life* magazines.

I don't remember any interactions with my family members as I moved, nor do I remember what emotions I was having. Did *Mem* cry? Or was she cheerful as she helped me gather my things?

Was *Datt* there? What mood was he in? I can only speculate why my memory of this time is so full of gaps. It seems that, whenever I had conflicting emotions at that time in my life, I would somehow flick a switch, like a safety valve, and turn off all feeling. These incidents remain the holes in my memory.

What I do remember is setting up my room. When I was done, it had a light, open, airy feel to it, quite unlike the rest of the Benders' house. The windows in my bedroom were unusual because they were low, from the floor up to about my waist, because of the sloping ceiling. There were Amish curtains covering the windows for privacy. I arranged my clothes in the closet and the dresser and bureau in the room. I ironed my embroidered dresser scarves and arranged my pretties on top of the dresser and bureau and on my nightstand. There was no need for my oil lamp, since the Benders were using electricity in the house. They were living on a farm that was owned by a Yankee farmer, so they were allowed to have amenities that *Mem* called "handies," which other Amish people didn't have: a telephone, electric stove, refrigerator, freezer, milkers, a cooling system for the milk, and tractors on the farm.

I made my bed with my quilt, and the handwoven rugs coordinated well with the turquoise quilt. When I was done, I surveyed my room. It looked immaculate, and I kept it that way. It was the only order to my life during my stay at the Benders'.

My arrangement with the Benders was that I would help Liz with the housework in exchange for my room and board. Urie and Liz had only two children, so it didn't seem like it would be hard. They also had a hired hand to help with the milking and other work on the farm. So there were usually six of us at the supper table.

I had taken a job in Burton, only a few miles from the Benders. I took care of a woman who had multiple sclerosis and needed a personal care assistant. In addition to taking care of her, I ended up doing laundry and housework every day of the week. Then when I returned to the Benders, I would find a sink full of dishes and floors that needed sweeping. I found myself the housemaid to two families. In both cases, I had signed up for something I hadn't intended to.

I must have shared my feelings about my living situation with Barbara Lalancette, because she responded with sound advice in a letter to me:

> *Sounds like an interesting living situation you've got there. Be careful not to overcompensate by working too hard or you'll become bitter.*

I'm sure I was feeling that it was impossible to work too hard; after all, Urie and Liz were sparing me from living in my parents' home. I kept telling myself that I had a lot more freedom at the Benders'. And so I continued to do exactly what Barbara warned me against.

❧ ✿ ☙

Before I moved to the Benders', I had made an appointment with a doctor in Burton about the bump on my chest. While I was at his office, I thought I would also find out why I was not getting my period. It had been a year and three months since my last one. The doctor sat behind his desk and asked me questions. Finally he came around to the one that made me blush. He apologized that he had to ask me, but he said it was required of him as my doctor: "Did you ever have sexual intercourse with anyone?"

"No," I said. I remember wanting desperately for him to stop asking me questions. I also wanted the floor to open up and swallow me. I felt such guilt and shame—guilt because I felt I was not telling the truth, given what had happened when I was eleven and Joe was fourteen, and shame at having to reveal anything to this stranger sitting across the desk from me.

Then I was led to the examination room and told to take off all my clothing, put on a gown, and prepare for an examination. I had never heard of such a thing. When the doctor came back into the room, a nurse came with him. She patted my shoulder and said that she was there for moral support.

I needed it. No one had ever told me what it was like to have an examination. The position I had to assume was horrifying, and had the nurse not been there, I would have wondered what the doctor was up to. I was wondering what this had to do with not getting a period. But I succumbed to the authority of the doctor the same way I succumbed to the authority of the Amish men all my life. Thankfully, I survived it.

When the doctor finally examined my chest, he said that he thought the bump was a fused rib and that I had been born that way. I wondered why I had never noticed it before. Then I realized that I had never stood in front of a mirror after bathing, as I had when I was at Olin and Clara's. The doctor sent me to the hospital to have an X-ray taken of my chest, just to be sure. He also sent me home with hormone pills, and within a few days I got my period.

The X-ray results showed that it was indeed fused ribs. I had mixed feelings. Part of me was expecting to have a physical ailment. At least that way I could have pointed to a reason for the psychological pain that I was feeling.

Then I did develop a physical ailment. At first the symptoms were like those from the flu, but then I began feeling lethargic and I didn't feel like getting out of bed in the morning. I finally decided to go to the doctor I had seen before. He diagnosed me with mononucleosis and said I would need lots of bed rest.

I soon became really tired of being in bed, especially after I began feeling better. I wondered if I really did have mono, given I had recovered so quickly. Perhaps I had a mild case of it, I told myself. I didn't want to think about the other possibility—that I was making myself sick with my disordered eating.

❦

Whenever I received a letter from Vermont, I would take it to my room, sit on the edge of my bed, and savor the feeling of being transported back there, at least in thought. I was sitting in this spot when I opened my first letter from Maureen.

3/28/78

Dear Linda, (Saloma, I mean—I keep forgetting)

I can't believe I'm sitting here writing you—in Ohio no less! Vermont misses you. I must admit I miss talking to you. We did have some good talks!

Maureen couldn't remember my name was Saloma because I had truly *become* Linda, and that is who Maureen knew—outgoing, fun-loving, energetic, feisty Linda. She didn't know Saloma—the Amish me. Now I had to forsake all those qualities I had developed as Linda. I had to hide my intelligence under my *kopp*, lest I show *hochmut,* or pride. I had to quell my desire for freedom. I had to restrain my natural curiosity. Above all, I had to submit to the rules and ways of the church.

Maureen knew just how to intensify my longing for my life in Vermont when she wrote that Vermont (and, specifically, she) missed me. I felt a tug in that direction.

Maureen then addressed the surprise element of my Amish escort back to the community:

Do you think you would of gone home if they wouldn't of come for you? I couldn't help but dislike Ada or your sister for just coming without giving you any notice. I think that was rather dirty! You should of had time to say bye to people you wanted to, and give a little notice at your job. Oh well, that's over and done with now. Are you happy at home? Can you look at both lifestyles now, and make a decision of which you were happier in?

Maureen was right—I was blindsided. They knew that showing up without letting me know they were coming was their only chance of getting me back. I tasted the bitterness of regret when I thought about all I'd left behind in Vermont.

Maureen's question—which life was I happier in?—bothered me. I only wished that I could answer her question with the same clarity with which she had asked it. If I looked at it purely from my own point of view, then the answer was clear: I was certainly happier in my Vermont world. My freedom was about me as an individual. But Amish people carried a sense of duty or obligation for the community as a whole that other people didn't understand. To be born and raised and then baptized into the community was a covenant not to be taken lightly. Being back in my Amish world was about community and something greater than myself, and it didn't have to do with my personal happiness. And yet I found that no matter how hard I tried, I just could not fit into the community in the way that was expected of me. I often wished I could hold on to that moment of grace I had encountered when I made my public confession, but that seemed like a distant dream.

Maureen's letter continued:

Yes, David has been over quite a few times. Linda, he really cared for you and I feel you should at least write him a letter. At least let him know what you've been doing. I'm sure he'd be really happy to hear from you. I don't think you realized how much he cared for you. I think he at least deserves a letter. He's really lonely without you!

I wondered if it was true that David cared so much about me. It seemed odd that he had never told me, considering we talked about many other intimate matters. Thinking about the feelings I had when I was with David and imagining that he felt them too, I knew he must have been devastated when I left. I would sometimes take out the little brown cross he gave me and feel it between my fingers while remembering specific moments we shared together. I recalled our first date at the Tiki Garden, the first night we'd kissed and talked about miming, the night at the bluegrass festival, and the ride out into the country on that Sunday afternoon when we were looking for the round church of Richmond. Now all I had to remember David by was the little cross. And he had nothing of mine. Maureen had a point. I should write to him.

It may seem that Maureen was contradicting herself by telling me how much David cared about me and then writing what followed:

Raymond called for you the day after you left. I told him you had gone back to Ohio. He couldn't believe it! So apparently, he didn't know you had left. So I wonder why he was calling! He told me to tell you he said "hi" when I write you. I'm surprised his family hadn't told him. Just your luck, he was probably calling you to go out on a date or something.

In the context of our talks, however, this was not a contradiction. We both felt that men could ask anyone they wanted, while women had to choose from those who asked. Maureen

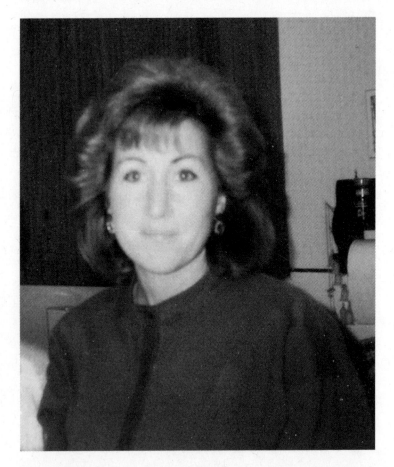

Maureen stayed in touch with me after I returned to my Ohio Amish community.

had supported me dating David and Raymond at the same time so that I would have a choice. I knew that I wouldn't be able to sustain both relationships long term. It was already becoming a problem, considering my interchange with David just before the vanload of Amish showed up at the Y.

Maureen went on to write about how she wished I could see Vermont in the summer, because it's even nicer than the winter. Pizza Hut was advertising in the paper for help—most likely for my job. She had been thinking about the money I spent at Elaine Powers; it was too bad I couldn't get my money back. It must have been awkward for me to see my old boyfriend, and how weird that he'd gone out with my sister! She was back with her boyfriend, Gary—she can just hear me now—she supposed she was pretty stupid. She signed off saying I should take care of myself and write to her soon.

After reading Maureen's letter, I found myself staring off into the middle distance, deep in thought. On the one hand, I had my family and community and now some independence from my parents. To have that, however, I had had to forsake the freedom of making my own choices and my love of Vermont. I remembered the feeling of zipping along on that dirt road in Peacham, holding on to Maureen on the back of the snowmobile. How I longed to see the vistas of the mountains and valleys that had come to symbolize freedom to me. Instead, here I was, living in a sodden, drab existence, where it seemed like spring herself could not show her face.

Just when the longing for my life in Vermont was becoming so intense that I was ready to cry, Liz called up the stairs and said supper was ready. I checked myself in the mirror, wiped away the beginnings of my tears, flicked the switch to turn off my feelings, and went downstairs for supper.

~15~

Just Friends in Ohio

Be not angry that you cannot make others as you
wish them to be, since you cannot make yourself as you
wish to be.
—Thomas à Kempis, *Imitation of Christ*

My first letter to David has been lost, but his response to it has survived. There is no date on his letter, but his address is written in capital letters at the top of the page.

Dear Linda,

Sorry I haven't written sooner but I was waiting to hear from you before making contact. I wanted to find out from you just how things are going back in Ohio. I'm sure your mother means a lot to you and for her sake it's good you're with her.

Your sister Sarah seems like a pleasant girl. She looks like my sister Claire.

Do you remember that theater group you served at the Pizza Hut your last night? I talked to three of the members and they missed you at that Friday night performance. They told me that after the show they looked for their waitress in the audience, but could not find her. You impressed them.

I saw a little Bluegrass on ETV the other night. Doc Watson and his son, Merle, played some tunes. They sang one of your favorites, "Will the Circle Be Unbroken."

Anyway, write soon. I miss you. David

That single page of David's handwriting did not convey the intimacies that we had shared with one another. But I knew that was just as well. It was impossible for David and me to have a romantic relationship—I was Amish and he was not.

After I received David's letter, he and I talked on the phone several times and arranged for him to come and visit me. I kept telling him that we could only be friends, which caused him to change the subject every time. I knew he didn't understand that our romantic relationship could not continue. I decided it would be important to convey that to him when he visited.

David and I made plans for him to come to my workplace at the end of the day. We'd go to dinner at his sister Bernadette's house in Cleveland that evening.

On the appointed day, David arrived right on time. I invited him in to the house where I worked, but we did not even shake hands. I didn't want to show my feelings in front of anyone, especially because I was unsure of them myself. It was a strange feeling to see David in *my* world.

When David and I got to his truck, we decided to visit my sister Susan at work. On the way over, he asked how I was doing and I said that the rainy and wet weather we'd been having for weeks was getting to me. I said, "Sometimes I wonder if the sun will ever shine again." Even as I said it, I realized I was talking about more than the weather. I hardly knew how to relate to David, alone in his truck. I had already decided I was going to treat him as a friend only, which meant I couldn't show him the real Saloma. Perhaps I didn't even know who the real Saloma was.

We found Susan washing walls in the home she was cleaning for a Yankee family. She was friendly and invited us to sit and have something to drink, but I could tell she was preoccupied, so we didn't stay long. On the way back to the Benders', we saw the bishop in Burton Station, driving his buggy through the flats. I hoped he hadn't noticed David and me together. Judging by what happened in the coming weeks, however, he probably did see us.

I decided I wanted David to see where *Mem* and *Datt* lived, down at the end of the road. My plan was to turn around at the end of the driveway and leave. My heart was pounding in my chest as we neared the house. Lo and behold, there was *Datt*, chopping wood next to the driveway. I panicked, and then remembered a back road that was muddy in the spring that went east toward a golf course. "Go down this road!" I said to David, pointing toward it. He did, rather quickly, but I got the sense that *Datt* saw us. He had stopped chopping wood and was staring at us.

When we got back to the Benders', David and I sat in the kitchen, talking. I was aware that Liz could be listening in. I suggested to David that he go upstairs with me to see my bedroom. He tentatively followed me upstairs. When we stepped into my room, his eyes darted this way and that, conveying how uncomfortable he was. I was trying to keep my voice the same as usual, telling him about the quilt *Mem* and I had made and how it felt really good to have a room of my own. David shifted his weight from one foot to the other. Then the hired man, whose room was down the hallway from mine, walked by. He'd gone to his room at a very inopportune time. Even though I didn't plan on doing anything other than show David the room where I was staying, I would have preferred doing it without a spy around.

I motioned to David and we went back downstairs. I offered him lemonade, and then we sat at the kitchen table and talked some more. David's shoulders relaxed, and he seemed more comfortable talking than I did. I knew that Liz was somewhere in another room. When she was listening in, it seemed like she was everywhere and nowhere at the same time.

Sometime during our conversation, I must have told David (and myself) how we could only be friends, which brought up the issue of our relationship. He said he had noticed that I sometimes gave mixed messages. "How so?" I asked.

"Like this," David said as he made a beckoning gesture with his right hand, as if he were saying "come hither." He put up his other hand in a "stop right there" gesture, like a police officer stopping traffic.

I sat there, stunned. David knew me better than I knew myself. His gesture summed up the conflict I felt within. The reason he didn't believe me when I said we could only be friends was because I had not yet come to terms with that myself. Going from our romantic Vermont relationship to our Ohio relationship of "just friends" felt as unnatural as not being allowed to tell anyone Amish about my experiences in Vermont.

David told me that he had brought photos with him that I'd given to Maureen when I left the Y. One of them was of me standing with my hand on the back of a rocking chair in the parlor of the Y. I was wearing my favorite plaid skirt and blue tights with a white turtleneck and blue shirt. As I looked at them in his hands, I had the sudden impulse to destroy evidence of that other me—Linda—who David knew in Vermont and was now trying to evoke.

"Let me see them," I said, pretending that I simply wanted a closer look.

"Why? What are you going to do with them?" David asked. He was laughing nervously, as he pretended he was going to keep them from me. I lunged for them, and he relinquished them.

I headed straight down the stairs to the furnace. I opened up the furnace door, and in they went. When the green flame started curling the edges of the photos, I had a moment of stinging regret. I wanted to pluck them from the fire. But it was too late. Those images were lost to me forever, and I knew it. I felt, even in that moment, that I would someday regret it intensely. I felt as if I had swallowed a peach pit, which now sat in the bottom of my stomach.

When I came back to the kitchen, David asked, "What did you do with them?"

"I burned them!" I said, as if I were confident in what I had just done.

"Why did you do that?"

I could not answer him. Maybe it was because I detected that David was trying to get me to feel regret for the life I'd left behind in Vermont. Meanwhile, I was trying desperately to prove to myself and everyone in the community that I was committed to the Amish way of life. Maybe it was an act of self-preservation.

The face of my Vermont self looking back at me would have intensified the conflict between my two selves beyond my ability to handle it. Either way, those photos were gone forever.

That evening, as David and I headed toward Cleveland to visit his sister, I described some of the challenges I'd faced since my return to Ohio, including my physical ailments, all without telling him about my eating disorder. When I told him about my fused rib, he couldn't imagine what it was like, so I said, "You can feel it." I took his hand and guided it to my chest, just below my collarbone. He looked surprised when I did it, and I suddenly wondered if he thought I was signaling to him to "come hither." I really just wanted him to know what it was, I told myself.

The sun was setting as we neared Cleveland. I remarked how beautiful and red it was. David said offhandedly that it was pollutants in the air that made it that way.

"You're kidding!" I said.

"No, I'm not."

"I've never heard that before," I protested. "I thought God made the sunsets the way they are!" I felt physically ill with the thought that people could sully something as natural as the sunset. I wanted so much for David to be wrong.

When we arrived at Bernadette's house, I forgot about our conversation as David introduced me to her and her husband, Don. Dinner was cordial, but I felt out of place in my Amish garb, and I was much quieter than my normal self. After dinner, Bernadette got into telling family stories. She had a lusty laugh for a woman of her small stature. Don seemed disengaged from the conversation.

David drove me back to the Benders', and I invited him in. We sat in their living room and talked for a while. Even though the house was quiet and it seemed like everyone was sleeping, I knew that Liz was nosy and could be eavesdropping, which put a strain on the conversation.

When David was ready to leave to go back to his sister's house for the night, I stepped outside with him, and we looked up at the stars. He said he really enjoyed visiting and hoped it wouldn't be long before we would see one another again.

It felt like someone had started turning a paddle wheel inside me. David had conveyed his feelings so naturally by simply stating his desire to see me. If he was thinking of coming back to visit, did that mean he was my boyfriend? Did I want him to be my boyfriend? Would that mean he would join my world, or I would go back to his world? Where did I want to be?

My uncertainty about the future and what I wanted it to be, along with all the "shoulds" of my Amish life, were enough to make all my feelings roil inside me. It was so uncomfortable that I didn't want David to be there anymore, conveying his feelings to me.

David's voice brought me to the present—standing there outside the Benders' house, under the stars, after having spent an evening with him "as a friend."

David was asking, "May I kiss you goodbye?"

"No," I said.

"May I give you a hug?"

"No."

"Then will you shake my hand?"

"Sure," I said and put out my hand.

David took my hand in his. Perhaps all those feelings we used to express on the sofa at the Y were channeled through our hands. That handshake under the stars was the most loving, most tender handshake I'd ever gotten from anyone. It held a longing and a desire that I couldn't even name.

Later I wouldn't be able to remember David's parting words—only the feeling in my right hand when I was lying in bed, staring into the starlight through the low windows of the bedroom where I slept. I was glad I was alone and in the dark with the feelings I didn't want anyone else to know about. I knew if I was going to stay Amish, I could not have any doubts about that choice. The people in my community would soon detect any feelings of ambivalence. If people suspected that I was unsure, they would watch every move I made. I had to show them I could be trusted before they would trust me.

Except I wasn't sure I trusted myself. All those feelings I had for David that I had wanted to tuck into a tidy package labeled "just friends" insisted on spilling out and messing things up. My right hand still felt warm with the love that David had wrapped around it. I brought it up to my face in a soft caress, the way he often had when we were together. Then, slowly, the tears came.

～ ❁ ～

When I awoke early to go out and wash the milkers in the barn, it felt like David's visit had happened in the distant past, not just the night before. This time I turned the shut-off valve to my feelings slowly and deliberately. I reminded myself that I had the freedom to choose not to live in *Mem* and *Datt's* house. The situation had changed at the Benders', so that I no longer was responsible for the housework. Instead I just had to get up early and wash the milkers. I was beginning to think about changing my work situation, too. And besides all these choices, I was allowed to have David visit me. That had to count for something. Little did I know that this was about to change.

For a few days I didn't notice anything different. Then I noticed that Liz was no longer making it a secret that she was listening in when I made phone calls to my Vermont friends. And there was a subtle shift in attitude—as if Urie and Liz were resenting something that they weren't communicating to me. I didn't really want to know if something was wrong, so I didn't ask. Yet the doubt clouded my certainty about the choice I'd made. At times I thought back to the night that David had visited me and wished, once we were truly alone, that I would have asked him to take me back to Vermont. I asked myself why I hadn't come clean and admitted, even to myself, that the life I had started in Vermont was preferable to living my Amish life. Why was I so committed to living the life that just didn't seem to fit me?

I knew I didn't have the courage it would take to leave again. I had no money—not even the four hundred dollars that I had saved up before I had left the first time. I also did not want to become dependent on David while establishing myself in Vermont all over again. I would have been committing myself to that relationship when I still wasn't sure about it.

Because I was not willing to think about the implications of losing my living situation, I continued on as if I hadn't noticed anything different with Urie and Liz. If they kicked me out, I would really wish I had asked David to take me back to Vermont. I had no way of knowing then how much I would be affected by what others thought in just a few short weeks.

The letters I received from my Vermont friends were the highlight of my life. This correspondence was a welcome reprieve from the conditional approval I was getting in my community, where most people treated me warily, as if they were waiting for me to betray my mixed feelings about being there. I was especially happy to hear from Barbara. I received a letter from her soon after David's visit:

Dear Saloma,

Thank you for another newsy letter. It sounds like you are as busy as ever. David stopped at the Center yesterday and said that he went to visit you. What a shock! He said that he went to see his family (relatives).

The fact that Barbara found David's visit surprising made me realize that I may have been the only person who thought it was natural for David to drive from Vermont to Ohio to see me. This caused me to examine my motives. Could it be that I wanted to stay in contact with him because I knew he could be my avenue out of the Amish should I decide to leave again? I could not push David away any more than I could hold him close.

Barbara went on to write about work and her plans to attend school full time in the fall. I was struck with how committed she was to her schooling. From deep within my being came a longing for a chance at that kind of learning experience. I wanted to search for answers to the fundamental questions that kept boiling up from within, no matter how hard I tried to squelch them. Even when I was a little girl, I had questions. I would sometimes lie in a field and look up at the clouds and wonder if there was anything beyond the sky. I had dreamed of traveling to places where there were mountains, lakes, and oceans. After getting a taste of traveling to new places, here I was again, confined to this little bit of northern Ohio, in a community where intellectual learning wasn't valued or even allowed. And Barbara had the freedom to go to school as long as she wanted to.

I folded Barbara's letter and lay back on my bed, staring at the ceiling. I wondered why the walls of my room suddenly felt so confining. I told myself anything was better than living in *Mem* and *Datt*'s house. Yet, each time I received a letter from Vermont, I felt like a butterfly confined by a jar, its wings beating against the sides without a sound.

⚜

Only days after David's visit, I got my first letter from Raymond. He started out writing about his job, the winter weather, and skiing conditions. Then he came around to writing about our relationship. He said he was sorry he hadn't been able to say goodbye to me and that he was certainly surprised. He said that, to be honest, he had enjoyed those meals I had cooked. He explained why he hadn't asked me out that much; the age difference bothered him. He wrote that he was glad I had enjoyed the trip to Maine and New Hampshire.

I sat on the corner of my bed and pondered. In one way I was relieved to know the age difference was the reason for the distance I'd often felt from Raymond. In another way, I was disappointed. There wasn't any way for me to make myself older, so that meant a relationship with Raymond would have been out of the question even if I'd stayed in Vermont. I was glad he was honest with me, but it made me wonder if the distance in space and culture had made it safe for him to be honest about his feelings.

I wrote a letter in response to Raymond's:

Raymond, I am so glad you were honest with me. I'm glad you enjoyed those meals. I'm sure you didn't enjoy them more than

I enjoyed the places you took me, like the Cobweb and of course the trips. I was sometimes conscious of the age difference too, but I never gave it a second thought. I still have memories, cause I sure enjoyed your company very much.

I wrote about a few other things, and then signed off, "Yours truly, Linda." I wonder whether I did this consciously or unconsciously. Did I become Linda when I wrote these letters to my Vermont friends?

❧ ✿ ❧

David's first letter after our visit felt like I was having a conversation with him. Even though he was the master of understatement, his feelings were evident.

5/11/78

Dear Linda,

I was very happy to see you and be able to talk to you. The evening at my sister's was the most fun I've had in a long time. Thank you for a good time. I did intend to write sooner but for some reason could not finish a letter.

I got an opportunity to speak to Barbara Lalancette. I met her the day you left but I didn't say much to her at the time. Everything you said about her is absolutely true. She is exceptionally nice. Her eyes are full of life and her friendliness is genuine.

I have been reading everything I can find about the Amish. Much of what I've read verifies what you've told me. I would like to know more and would like to go to a Sunday service.

I still miss you but I'm looking forward to seeing you in the future. The fact is I just like being with you. You are a special person to me and always fun to be with. It's nice to know someone so pleasant and attractive as you.

David

As I sat in my letter-reading place, on the edge of the bed in my room, I thought about the contents of David's letter and remembered in detail the times he and I had gone out together and the intimacy we had shared in the parlor of the Y. It seemed to me that he had come very close to saying he loved me in his last paragraph, but I was glad he had refrained. I knew I would have had to reject him altogether if he had. And he was complicating things further by his interest in Amish life. Would I even want him to be Amish? It would make it possible for us to be together, I thought. But do I want to be with him and be Amish too?

Deeply embedded in my subconscious mind was the association I'd made between David and the freedom I'd experienced in Vermont. For David to join my Amish world would bring my two worlds together. But what if I eventually decided that I wanted to leave again? What then?

I felt like a fly caught in a spider's web. The more I struggled against the web, the more I found myself entangled. I folded David's letter and put it in a drawer. The letter may as well have been labeled "Can't handle this."

Mixed Messages

Trouble is easier to get into than out of.
—Amish Proverb

Only days after I received David's letter, I had to move out of the Benders' house. I was in the process of writing a letter to him when "the talk" took place. My letter, dated May 15, 1978, recounts what happened:

> Quite a bit has happened since I came home from work. Liz had a talk all ready for me. She told me I have to find another place to stay. I was so shocked! Although like I told you yesterday things aren't like they used to be. They just don't like it that I eat separately from them and everything. So I told her I realize this arrangement was a mistake. Maybe I shouldn't have, but I same as asked for another chance. I'm not ready to make another move at all. I know where I could go. My brother offered me I could stay at their place. I might yet, but it would save a lot of complications if I could stay here. Down there you just have so many neighbors, you don't have very much privacy. At this point I don't know what I want. I have so many decisions to make all at once, it seems.
>
> During our talk Liz said some things I'm glad I know. There are some rumors going around. Somebody asked her if it's true that I have a boyfriend and he came and is trying to get me to go back to Vermont. (It was during your visit.) I don't know what she said. Then also somebody said something about all the mail I get

from Vermont. Whoever said it thought I should forget about the time I was gone. I told her, I'm sorry, I don't see it that way. I feel that I made a lot of nice friends and I want to keep in touch with them, and that it's nobody else's concern. She said people are concerned if I have too much contact with everybody in Vermont I might get a longing to leave again. So I said that there is only one way I would ever do that and that's if I had no other place to live other than with my parents. We finally talked out our differences and she said she wanted to talk to Urie about it. So she went to the barn and said something to him about it. Now after dinner and the children are in bed we're going to sit down and discuss it. So far Urie hasn't ever discussed anything with me. There was always Liz in between. I thought if all three of us come to an understanding, maybe things would work out.

I did go to my parents' house yesterday. Everybody was there, even Joes and the babies. So I think it was a happy Mother's Day for Mom. Susan had made a cake and decorated it. We had all kinds of eats. I always do come away from there with a heavy heart for Mom, though.

I wasn't really surprised when you wrote you want to attend an Amish church service. Actually last Sunday in church I had to think of you, when a visiting bishop said in his sermon that if people are interested in our faith and ask us about it, we have no right to give them an answer that would mean as much as "it's none of your business." I couldn't help but let my thoughts go further. I even imagined you becoming an Amish member of the church. That would be really nice. But, still I don't know if I'd want you to. I still get the feeling you would do it because you have an interest in me. If that's it, forget it, David. Even when I picture you an Amish person, I still see you as a friend only. It's kinda too bad, in a way, that I can't return the feelings I know you have for me. But that's just the way it is, and I can't help how I feel. I'm being quite honest with you, so that you know ahead of time there is no way there can ever be more than a friendship between us. Actually it's quite tempting to try to make it work, *'cause like any young person, I long to have companionship. But, that would put me in the same place I was in with my other boyfriend. I don't need that.*

Gotta go. Urie's ready to talk. Be back.

This is now Tuesday afternoon, at work. I was too crushed last night to finish this. I couldn't believe all Urie said. It started out how I figured it would, but ended quite differently. I got the feeling he would give me another chance if it wasn't for something I didn't know about. Someone came to him and said he should go to the church [to make a public confession] because of that visit you paid me. Urie said as far as he could see it was only a friendly visit. The other person said if it happens too often he should do something about it. I have the feeling he just wants to wash his hands of the whole thing. Then he also said things about Mom that really hurt me. He thinks Mom talks too much to us about Dad. I told him she wouldn't be human if she didn't have to unload her burden to someone. He said that she should do it to her brothers or sisters or elders of the church. I told him they don't understand 'cause they haven't gone through it.

Last night I felt I lost my independence and my freedom to make my own choices. I was never so hurt. I cried so hard as soon as I got to my room. I felt like the world came down around me. This morning as I was waking up I remembered all about it and felt the hurt all over again.

I gave my brother's address again before signing off with "Keep in touch. A friend, Linda."

Fitting into my Amish life, while still putting up a fierce battle to preserve my core self, was not easy. It was evident that my quest to fit into the community was in conflict with my desire to be free in the "come hither" and "stop right there" gestures that David had so aptly conveyed to me. I was stressing the "just friends" in words, but the content of the letter was pouring out my heart and soul in a very intimate way. And signing off as "Linda"? I was still preserving the persona I'd developed in Vermont.

And that is how I landed at my brother Joe's house. He and Emma lived on her parents' farm. Sarah was living there in exchange for helping Joe with the milking every morning and every night.

It didn't take me long after my move to start thinking the Amish way. I tried burying the memories of my Vermont life, and I no longer thought of myself as Linda. I did all this because I wanted to convince myself, as well as Joe—who I thought would convince others—that I was making myself Amish. After all, if I was going to survive in Joe's house, I had to stay on his good side—and that meant seeing things his way.

For me to be on Joe's good side meant someone had to be on the wrong side. Often this was Emma. If they disagreed about anything, he would win the argument—every time. One day I witnessed one of his put-down sessions in which he didn't just belittle her but attacked her ancestors, one generation at a time. It was really hard to keep quiet as he spewed his venom, but I also knew the consequences if I came to Emma's defense. Nonetheless, I waited until I had a chance to talk to Joe alone. I broached the subject by asking him if he didn't think he'd been too hard on Emma that morning. He said, "Yes. . . . but when I get started, I just can't stop."

"Doesn't that mean it's your problem more than hers?"

"Yes, I know." Joe bent over and busied himself at his task of cleaning a bearing of some kind in his milkhouse. Then he straightened up and turned to me and said, "You know, I'm doing you a favor allowing you to stay here, and what goes on between Emma and me isn't really any of your business. Just stay out of it."

"I just think Emma deserves more respect," I said, as I walked back in the direction of the house.

It seemed to me that Joe was just a bit kinder to Emma after that—at least when I was around. I didn't dare believe I had influenced his behavior.

I often helped Emma make breakfast while Sarah helped with the milking. After work each day, I helped with whatever needed to be done.

Emma's parents and sisters lived in the big house, also on the farm. One day, Emma's sister Ada and I were folding diapers for Emma out by the clothesline. We were talking about a cleaning job I had before I left for Vermont. Ada had taken over the job and she was now thinking of quitting. I suggested that maybe I could work for that family again.

As Ada busied herself making very precise folds in a diaper, she asked, "Well, do you want to know the truth?"

"Sure," I said.

"She doesn't want you."

"Why is that?"

"She said that she doesn't trust you. She's afraid you might leave again."

I wasn't ready for the blow that Ada had dealt me. She had helped bring me back to the Amish, and now this. I was crushed. I excused myself and went to my room to feel my pain in private.

Eventually I did with these feelings what I did with all my uncomfortable feelings. I tried, in the form of food, to stuff them but they wouldn't stay down. I eventually went to the outhouse that was set up over a little creek and rejected it. I watched as the vomit curled and flowed out from under the outhouse into a whisper of the brook. The flowing water helped to keep the secret of my feelings—and my eating disorder.

~⚜~

Several times on Sunday evenings, my brother Joe drove Emma's sisters and me in his surrey to the singings. We were usually a jolly bunch heading up the hill toward Huntsburg or up Clay Street toward the young folks' gathering. One evening, I found myself alone in the buggy with Joe on the way to a singing. It was a summer evening, with cool breezes as the buggy wheels crunched along on the gravel road. The conversation started out with Joe warning me about men's intentions, and then he started asking me if anyone had ever "gotten anywhere" with me. I told him I didn't want to talk about it.

But Joe did. Before I knew it, he was telling me inappropriate things about a young couple. I told Joe I didn't want to hear about that. He ignored me and said something even more inappropriate.

"Joe, I don't want to talk about this stuff."

"Well, what do you want to talk about?"

"Nothing."

"Oh, so that's how you thank me for taking you to the singing—you give me the silent treatment."

"Don't then. Let me off and I'll walk to the singing."

"Whoa!" Joe said, and I climbed off the buggy and started walking.

❧

My family wasn't sentimental about birthdays. So on the day I turned twenty-one, when Joe asked me to go to the back pasture and bring the cows home for milking, I did it without suspecting anything. As I was walking up toward the barn, I saw neighbors gathering and then realized they were having a party for me. My family came and so did several people from Uncle Ervin's family, as well as Emma's family and my friend Betty and her sister Ruth. Betty was just a few days older than I, so this was a joint birthday party. I wasn't shy by nature, but I didn't know how to act, knowing this was all part of their efforts to make me feel welcome in the neighborhood and the community. I felt unworthy.

I was glad that, during most of the party, people seemed to simply be using Betty's and my birthdays as an excuse to have a get-together. Then the gifts came out. There were little gifts of stationary, new stockings, towels, and sewing items. Susan had wrapped a small present in a creative way. When I unwrapped it, I found an Ohio blue-tips matchbox. I wasn't too sure I trusted it, so I cautiously opened it up, just a little. Catching a glimpse of long spider legs, I tossed the matchbox across the room. Had I seen the whole big plastic spider all at once, I would not have been able to control my reaction. But there was no screaming or hysterics, which is perhaps what Susan expected to evoke, given my spider phobia. I ground my teeth in anger at the thought of losing control in front of all those people on my twenty-first birthday.

It may be that Susan saw the spider gift as a harmless prank. She might even have accused me of having no sense of humor when I didn't laugh. But I also knew that this was her chance to get me back.

Our rivalry was a long-standing one that started when we were still very young. I always claimed that the two of us were too much alike to get along, but she hated hearing that. From what I could tell, she wanted to be as different from me as possible. Susan had many reasons not to like me. I was three years older, which made me three years more powerful. And the small amount of power girls in my community had was fought over more fiercely than the power that the men had at the top of the hierarchy.

I abused the power of age over Susan more than once as we were growing up. I tattled when she held her dress up to make it shorter and then walked past the basement windows to "mirror" herself. I tattled when she was supposed to be working but was petting the little barn kittens instead. If she became upset, her eyebrows would turn straight up and then I would tease her and call her a name that a Yankee man gave her. And I sometimes slapped her if I was upset with her—at least until she got old enough to fight back. After that, we had many physical fights.

In my family, we operated with the notion that the way to gain self-confidence was to break down others' confidence. It didn't seem to dawn on any of us that this just resulted in nobody feeling good about themselves. Giving me a plastic spider for my birthday was likely Susan's way to get back at me for all the times I had lorded my power over her.

~ ❀ ~

Marty was a popular "date" in the community. He and Susan had several dates. One night he danced with me at a singing. And then he dated Sarah. The two of them invited me to go to his house with them one Sunday afternoon. I visited with his sisters for a while, and then Sarah, Marty, and I went to one of the upstairs bedrooms to talk. Tagging along with my younger sister on her date made me feel old and lonely. At some point, I was lying down on a bed in the room and closed my eyes. As I was lying there, I found myself in a place between awake and dreaming, between imagination and reality. I allowed myself to go back to the place that felt more like years than only months ago when David and I had first entered the parlor at the Y with the intention of sharing our first kiss. I could just taste the sweetness of it, so soft and

This photograph of me in my Amish clothes shows me standing in front of my mother's flower garden.

gentle, yet so passionate. I could feel the first hug from David, like our arms were made for entangling and embracing one another. In my imagination, I transported myself to the parlor at the Y. I wanted to close the doors so David and I could be alone in that place where time stood still.

Sometime later, Sarah woke me up because it was time to go to the singing. She claimed I had talked in my sleep and said something about closing a door. I knew it would have been more than one door I was closing—because there were three in the parlor I'd been revisiting in my dream.

Marty seemed to be dating the spectrum of Sim's girls. After several weeks of dating Sarah, he asked me for a date. I knew this could not be serious, since he was five years younger than me. But no one else was asking me for a date, so I figured, why not? I knew he would never pick me for his girlfriend, so I thought I would find out what it was like to have a date with a popular guy. I found out what it was like—steamy. How was it that a sixteen-year-old could be so experienced?

When Marty asked me for a second date, I accepted. We went to his friend's house on Saturday afternoon, and then we went to a young people's gathering that evening with Sarah and her date. As is customary when men drive young women to the youth gatherings, Marty put his horse in a neighbor's barn, and we walked to the gathering from there. Normally, the young women would walk on ahead, because the two young people wouldn't want to be seen walking together. But Marty asked me to wait for him, and then we walked together. We talked a little bit on the way, but mostly we walked in silence. For just a quick second, my mind skipped years into the future, and I felt like I was walking alongside a husband of many years. I came back to reality by reminding myself of the impossibility of such a thing—Marty was just a kid. And he liked all young women—including my sisters.

Nonetheless, when Marty drove me back to Joe's house that night, I was looking forward to it. The *schmunzling* was even more passionate than it had been the first time.

Just before dawn, Marty was becoming more insistent and wanted to go further than I did. In the back of my mind a little voice cried out, "Don't—it's a trap!" I knew all too well the consequences of giving in to temptation. It must have been my intuition that got me to react as I did. I said, "I have an idea."

"What?" he asked.

I didn't say anything. Instead, I went to the window that opened to the porch roof and slid it open. I took two woven rugs and laid them out on the roof, then two pillows. I climbed out and whispered, "Come on! We can watch the sun come up!"

Marty looked baffled, but he followed me out onto the roof. I instinctively knew that I was safe out there with the sun coming up. And I was right. It was my best defense against the temptations of bed courtship.

I don't remember whether it was my choice or Marty's, but after two or three dates we stopped seeing one another. Perhaps our age and maturity difference was too great for either of us. I continued to go to the singings, often with Joe's sisters-in-law, but I was no longer asked for dates. I don't remember who told me this, but apparently word got around: "She left once, she could leave again."

It didn't occur to me to just say, "You're right about that," and leave.

~❀~

A few days after I turned twenty-one, Urie Byler came to visit me. He was the superintendent of all the Amish schools in the area. He had been the teacher at Meadow Glow School the first year it opened and the upper-grade teacher when I was in the third grade.

Urie had come to Joe's house to invite me to supper at his place the following Wednesday night. He said that someone would pick me up. I accepted the invitation.

That Wednesday night the board members of Meadow Glow School and the head teacher, Erma, gathered at Urie Byler's house for supper to ask me to teach the lower grades in the same school I had attended after it was built when I was in the third grade.

Even though I had enjoyed the public school more than I had the Amish school, I was happy going to school anywhere, and I wished I could still be a student. Being a teacher would at least put me back in a learning environment.

I felt inadequate for the job, especially when I found out that there would be twelve first-graders coming in. The normal way for the grades to be divided between two teachers was for the lower-grade teacher to teach first through fourth and the upper-grade teacher to teach fifth through eighth grades. This particular situation, however, would have meant that the lower-grade teacher would have thirty-eight students while Erma, the experienced teacher, would have twenty-three. Urie Byler advocated for us to break up the classes differently. Perhaps Erma could teach first, sixth, seventh, and eighth. I suggested I teach the upper grades, but Erma didn't want that—the upper-grade teacher was always the head teacher.

I asked how I would get to the school each day, and someone said that the Troyers had a house they were willing to rent to me and that I should talk with them.

After I accepted the job as teacher, I got a letter from Urie Byler:

I remember when you were in my school at Meadow Glow about 1965. If I remember right, you were sort of my little pet, at least some of the pupils thought so. Since then my mind has been with you a lot, and certainly wish you the best. I'm sure you deserve it, and if at times you don't feel so well, remember there is always a silver lining to every dark cloud, and that God has a purpose in everything. All he expects is faith and patience. . . . You'll never know how happy Mom and I were to see you back, and then that eve when you were here and your board came to hire you as a teacher. That eve this big old so-and-so actually bawled a little to think of the great change in your life, and that you are joining our teacher's group. Prayers always are answered if we give them enough time. When I was in the hospital this last time—well, my thoughts were with you, and this made my pains lighter and easier to take, and especially our young folks. We need more like Saloma.

Getting this kind of encouragement from someone I looked up to is what made me believe that I was doing the right thing by teaching school and accepting my Amish life. Someone believed in me, and I now had a respectable role to play in the community.

I knew if I did what was expected of me, by fall I could be a schoolteacher and live in a little house of my own.

~ 17 ~

My Name's Saloma!

Is it really so difficult to tell a good action from a bad one?
I think one usually knows right away or a moment
afterward, in a horrid flash of regret.
—Mary McCarthy

By the time I received David's response to the letter in which I had described the situation with the Benders, I was already turning away from him and the memories we had made together. Even though I had no privacy in Joe's house, I kept the letter.

Dear Linda,

You surprised me with your letter. I thought I'd never get one from you. I do understand that you are working much of the time and your free time is very valuable to you.

I'm sorry to hear you've had some difficult times. It sounds like some of it is a result of my visit. If that is true I am sorry only to you. My visit was strictly friendly and I had no intention of talking you into coming back to Vermont. You and I know that but unfortunately some people are suspicious. I would not be afraid to tell them to mind their own business, but I do realize they think it's for your own good.

Linda do you think someone wanted you to end up at Joe's? After all Joe can keep an eye on you and there is no telephone to contact those Vermonters. I kinda think that move was planned. I could be wrong but you would know.

I'm beginning to see how important your freedom is to you. You must not lose it. Your independence is too much a part of you. (Maybe more than you realize.) It sounds like you could use a little encouragement in maintaining your identity as one who is capable of making your own decisions. I think you will surely die emotionally if you lose the independence you have to make decisions. You have a strong head (strong will), Linda, I could see that from the start. I like that quality about you. I mean you're very determined once you've set your goals. There is much I could say about this but I would rather talk to you in person.

To be Amish is not easy. That I can see. I do think that way of life is closer to God than the world I live in. It seems to be not only a religion but also a way of life. It may be right for me but I don't know. I can now truthfully say that I would do it for myself and definitely not to get close to you. I'm taking my lifestyle more and more seriously as I see how blindly most of society lives. I do believe in God and I believe He will direct me to my rightful place. I sense something in me. It's like a hunger for truth but I don't know where to find it. Something we can talk about later also.

Now Linda I like you as a friend and wish you would stop going through all that "friends only" stuff every time we communicate. Do you really think it's necessary to keep saying, "we can never be more than friends," it sounds so melodramatic. I have no intentions of becoming one of your ill-fated boyfriends. Anyway you can get any Amish boy you want, if you put your mind to it. In my opinion you are just as attractive as your sisters Sarah and Susan if not more so!

I wish I were with you when things looked bad for you. You must know by now that this friend does care about you even though you're six hundred miles away.

David

In the letter, David also offered to come and bring me back to Vermont for a visit. I had been planning a visit with my friends, but now things had changed. I knew one thing for sure: there was not going to be a trip to Vermont, and most especially not with David. I told myself I didn't care what he did. He could join the Amish if he wanted to, but it wouldn't really affect our relationship. If I was going to step into my role as teacher, then continuing my relationship with David was out of the question.

I didn't respond to David's letter. Because I no longer had access to a phone, that meant no more communication—or at least I thought so. So when I read the letter David wrote to me dated July 6, I was annoyed with his persistence.

Dear Linda,

This is the first chance I have had to write since I sent you that card for your birthday. Now that you are twenty-one, has anything changed for you?

I almost made it to Cleveland about two weeks ago but my show schedule prevented that. Are you still at your brother's? I would like to visit in July and maybe take Maureen with me. If I do come I would like to meet your mother and father. I would also like to meet Joe if he could stand it. Write and let me know what you think. It would probably be around July 14 or so. I have one more show this weekend in Massachusetts and then I'm free for a while. I think the Amish would feel less suspicious of me if I can get to know more of them. My interest in the Amish way of life persists, and I have been considering the possibilities for some time on a serious level. This is part of the reason I want to visit. My business is a major consideration to a change of lifestyles. I would want to continue it even if I lived the Amish way. Anyway this is not the time to get into this question.

Tuesday, the Fourth of July, was great! I only wish you were here to enjoy it with me. After weeks of work I took the day off and went to a bluegrass festival. But not just any festival: a festival that featured your favorite: Bill Monroe. It was fantastic. The people called him Uncle Bill. I got a chance to talk with him after his first set of songs. He was very pleasant and easy to talk to. I told him about you and he signed a little paper for you. I would like to give you that paper he signed. Linda, the day was enjoyable and the music superb, but it was not complete without you. I must tell you about Bill Monroe and my little talk with him. I liked him and I must thank you for introducing me to bluegrass.

I want to hear from you, so please write me soon. Write to me before I show up at your front door. I do wish you were here for that fine show. Some other time maybe.

David

I lost no time in reacting to David's letter. My Vermont world was now encroaching on my Amish one. First, I'd been thrown out of the Benders' home and ended up at Joe's house, which was marginally better than living at *Mem* and *Datt's* house. Now I had a chance at playing a respectable role in the community, and I did not want to mess that up. I wrote a letter to David, trying to cut him off at the pass.

David,

A few lines in a hurry before I go to work. I see where I'll have to take time to write to you, whether I want to or not.

First of all, I cannot with a clear conscience push you off about becoming Amish (or in other words getting to know their ways more). BUT, not in Geauga County! I know the perfect place for you and that is Mio, Michigan. I know most of the people there and I am convinced that they would be much more willing to take in an outsider than people around here. The person I would advise you to see is Melvin Gingerich. He lives in Mio. His address is . . . They would welcome you much more than these people here, if you are sincere, and believe me, they can tell!

Next, I have some explaining to do. I should not have let you come visit me. I can see my mistake now. I didn't realize at the time that I was leading you on. In my eyes I wasn't doing that, but in yours I was. I'm sorry.

You asked me what I think about you coming and meeting my parents and my brother. The answer is no, no, no, NO! Don't you dare! What would be your gain? Not me! Cause David even if I wasn't Amish, or you were, I don't want you! Can't you see that? I've been trying not to hurt you, by pushing you off, but you just wouldn't take no for an answer. So this last letter did it, I'll have to come right out and tell you. So if you really want to become Amish, and you are not doing it to be close to me, prove it by taking my advice about Mio, Michigan and stay away from me. And don't make this letter an excuse to come see me.

By the way there is probably some questions you have like the time you asked me whether I think we would still be together if I hadn't come home. I didn't really say. What I would have liked to say is the only reason we would be together would be because I wouldn't have the nerve to tell you off, and I couldn't have gotten rid of you. The more somebody clings to me, the more he turns me off! So any other questions you would have would probably be the same, I didn't have the nerve. So just forget it, O.K.?

Good-bye,
Saloma Miller

This was the first letter to David in which I signed off as Saloma. This shift was obviously an abrupt one, as was my shift in attitude toward him. I hoped the letter would end our relationship.

Three days after I sent the letter to David, Sarah and I decided to go with our neighbors, Betty and Ruth, to the Akron Reservoir for a Saturday afternoon canoe ride. Sarah and I rented a canoe, and Betty and Ruth rented another. We set off across the water, two canoes carrying four Amish girls, paddling through the lily pads and watching the birds in the trees along the shore. Sarah was a bird expert and knew the names and calls of them all. We stayed alongside the other canoe and meandered across the reservoir.

Around noon, we decided to paddle to the little store on the opposite shore to get some snacks. I remember buying way too many things: bags of chips, donuts, milk, and a few other items.

My eating problems had worsened after I moved to Joe's house. I rarely ate anything without gorging myself. Then I would go to the outhouse over the running brook and throw it all up, watching the evidence of my disordered eating flowing away with the water.

But I don't know how I knew I was going to binge that afternoon. Canoeing with my sister and friends could have been fun, but as Sarah and I paddled along, I ate everything I bought and then felt the familiar urge to rid my body of everything I'd just eaten. I told Sarah to steer over to the shore into a wooded area. I got out of the canoe and walked into the woods. Finding a place that would be private and out of hearing distance of Sarah and our friends, I dug a hole with my foot and purged. I could hear Sarah talking with Betty and Ruth.

I was just finishing covering over the spot with leaves when I heard a man's voice. Then I heard Sarah saying, "Are you David from Vermont?"

I heard David say, "Yes."

I was so shocked I couldn't move. My two worlds had collided. My Amish one excluded David, and I had let him know that. I thought, why is he here? Doesn't he understand? Then it's time to make him understand! I set my jaw and headed for the canoe.

One glance at David in a little rowboat only intensified my anger. He was wearing a maroon-checkered shirt, open in the front, so that his dark chest hair was visible. Even when we were together in the parlor, I had never seen his chest. I had caressed it, but he'd always had it covered. But I didn't want to think about that now.

When David saw me, he said, "Hi, Linda. How are you?"

As I stepped into the canoe, I demanded, "Didn't you get my letter?"

"No, I didn't. What was in the letter?"

"Well, since you didn't wait for it to get there, I'll have to tell you face to face!"

With that, I started flinging my anger at David in the form of insults. I told him he couldn't take no for an answer; that I was

Amish and he was not; that I didn't want to be his girlfriend; that he had his nerve showing up without an invitation; and now he should just go away and leave me alone.

Sarah talked to me in Amish, giving me more fodder. David didn't seem fazed by my fury, which made me even angrier. "Okay," he said. "I will go if that is what you want. But before I do, I'd like to give you something." He pulled his rowboat up next to our canoe and handed me a piece of paper. On it was Bill Monroe's signature, autographed to me—Saloma. Not Linda, but Saloma.

I read the note, and then I dropped it into the reservoir as I looked David straight in the eye. I wanted for him to know how desperately I needed for him to leave me. The conflict he had caused by showing up was too acute. I felt it all throughout my body, and my mind was desperate in its will to survive. For months I had been trying to reconcile my Amish world with the Vermont world. The pressure from the people in the community to forsake the Vermont world was constant and unrelenting. And now David's insistence on having a relationship with me was just as persistent. I had not yet figured out what I wanted myself.

Here I was, torn between the two worlds. It felt like an army of ants was scurrying around inside my mind, arranging my thoughts and feelings to alleviate the agony.

David's liquid-blue eyes that had conveyed his feelings for me in the parlor of the Y were clouded with hurt. He said, "Okay, if you really want me to leave, I will." He quietly turned his rowboat in the direction of the boathouse. "Bye, Linda," he said softly.

"My name's Saloma!" I snapped.

"Bye, Saloma," David said, kindly, and then slowly rowed away. His arms made arcs in the air with the oars of the boat. I could feel the burden of sorrow that was weighing him down as I watched that checkered shirt retreating. With each push of his oars, he pushed himself off into the distance. My agony was intense when David was there, but it was only a small sample of the overwhelming regret that washed over me like the water from the reservoir. I had the sinking feeling that I would never see him again. Oh, no! What have I done? I thought. What *have* I done?

Sarah said something in Amish about him finally getting the message.

"What business is it of yours anyway?" I retorted.

"Lomie, I thought I was helping you," Sarah said. She seemed surprised that I was lashing out at her.

I realized how often Sarah had led me away from my heart's desires. She had convinced me to go steady with Donny. She had gotten me to reveal my whereabouts when I was in Vermont. She had given out my phone number and address even though she had promised me she wouldn't. She had stayed by my side to ensure that I would not escape from the vanload of Amish. Now she had fueled the venom I used to make David leave—possibly for good.

My body reacted before my mind. I stood up in the canoe and started rocking it back and forth with my legs. Sarah clung tightly to the sides of the canoe and said, *"Lomie, huck ana!"* (Lomie, sit down!) I didn't sit down. I rocked the canoe some more. I turned around and looked at Sarah as she desperately clung to the sides of the canoe. Her face was red in her panic, and she said, *"Lomie! Ich wess nett fovass es da David dich vill enichha!!!"* (Lomie! I don't know why David wants you anyhow!!!)

Neither Sarah nor I could swim. The reservoir was deep. David was gone. These were my thoughts as I tempted fate with my dangerous rocking of the canoe. It was as if I was observing someone I didn't really know who was rocking the canoe.

Then it hit me. If I wanted to tempt fate by standing in a canoe in the middle of a deep reservoir without a life jacket, I had no right to take Sarah with me. No matter what she had done, she did not deserve to die for it. On some level, I must have been aware that Sarah was just trying to do the "right" (Amish) thing in all these instances, just as I was trying to make myself Amish again when I burned the photos David brought from Vermont and when I so brutally rejected him only minutes earlier.

Of course Sarah would be confused by my actions. I was confusing myself. When I came back to my senses, I sat back down in the canoe and behaved myself. I took up the paddle, and Sarah and I paddled slowly across the reservoir. By now, David was only a speck in the distance.

~୬ 🕸 ୧~

When Sarah and I got back to Joe's house, Joe played it cool. He waited for me to talk with him about what had happened. As if I was allowing him to put the words in my mouth, I asked him if he wanted to go for a walk, which he said yes to—coolly—as if he were doing me a favor.

As we sat on the banks of the little creek in the back pasture with Joe's fishing rod dangling in the water, he smoked his pipe. At the time, he hadn't yet rebelled against the rule in church that disallowed cigarettes for married men, though pipe smoking was allowed.

Why did I ask Joe to go for a walk? Why did I seek confirmation from him, of all people? Perhaps I thought Joe's perception of my "conviction" would make a difference in the rest of the community. I was trying so hard to prove to myself and to the community that I was really Amish and that I could fit into that lifestyle.

Joe showed his most sympathetic self in the dilemma that David had caused by showing up. He described how David had come to the porch and asked for me. Mostly Joe puffed on his pipe and listened as I told him how I had told David off. I don't remember him saying much, except at some point he said, "You know what I wondered?"

"What?"

"I wondered if he's even all there."

I hesitated. Joe was looking at me, gauging my reaction to what he'd just said. I knew he wanted me to agree with him. In the past, he often got me to verbally agree with him and then later I would wonder why I had done so, for I surely didn't agree. This time he had misgauged.

"David is actually quite smart. He couldn't run his own business if he was retarded," I said.

"Like I said, I just had to wonder. But you would know better than me." With that, Joe dropped the subject.

I was keeping a diary at the time of David's visit. It was a *Vermont Life* datebook that he had given me as a gift when he came to visit me at the Benders'. It had enough room for only a few sentences each day. On July 15, 1978, I wrote: "Sarah, Dan's Betty, Ruth, and I went to the Akron Dam today. David Furlong came to see me. I told him off!" I noted that I'd spent $5.50 that day. From the entry the following day, it seems as though my Amish life didn't skip a beat: "I went to church at Al's Lester's today. Tonight we were at John Slabaughs' for supper. Then Sarah, Susie, and I went to singing at Mahlon Yoders'. I came home with Dan Yoder's boys."

The days following have notes about where I worked and how much money I made, as well as how much money I spent, without any indication of what I was going through emotionally. I didn't mention David in that diary again.

~ 18 ~

Family Immersion

We are linked by blood, and blood is memory without language.
—Joyce Carol Oates

During those months after returning from Vermont, I corresponded with many people in the Amish community: my cousins, uncles, and aunts who lived in Cashton, Wisconsin, and Conewango Valley, New York, and friends from several other communities as well as from Geauga County. The letters that reveal most about how I was trying to fit in were those to and from my uncle John. He was a minister in a community stricter than ours. I discovered that he was open to answering many of my questions, which most other Amish people avoided.

In one of my first letters from him, he wrote about the drama of his son-in-law being injured while using a buzz saw and an elderly man in his community dying. Uncle John had preached his funeral sermon. He also wrote about how they had divided a church district into two districts the year before and that they ordained a new deacon in the new district, and the lot fell on his nephew, my cousin Uria. Then he wrote,

> In regards to your picking a different place to live. I will leave it up to you but don't get discouraged too quick. Wish I could help you in some way. Don't know if you knew it or not but my mother after she was of age she started traveling with intentions of going to Indiana to see her birthplace. She had a stepmother and didn't have it too nice at home in Holmes Co. She came to

Geauga and never any further till after the death of her second husband she went to Indiana on a visit.

Uncle John gave his mother, my grandmother, a human face. I knew her after she'd been widowed twice. It seemed to me that she always wore dark clothing, as though she were forever in mourning. I knew her as the strict grandmother who thought it was wrong to have a mirror in the house unless you could hide it in a drawer or the closet when not using it. She thought people would bring sorrow on themselves if they laughed, and she believed it was wrong to have dolls with plastic faces; consequently, she burned my favorite doll when I was eight years old.

I knew that Grandmother had had a horrible childhood, with a cruel father and stepmother. Her father had tried to prevent his children from learning to read. My grandmother had rebelled against this tyranny and taught herself to read with an old *McGuffey Reader*. This book was in our library when I was growing up, an artifact to go with the family story.

Perhaps the best time of her life was when she was married and became a mother. But that, too, came to an abrupt end when her husband died of appendicitis during the Great Depression, when they had five children and another one on the way. To feed her children, she harvested potatoes for a dollar a day.

I knew all this. But never before had anyone given me a glimpse of her as someone who had aspirations of her own. I realized from this letter that, at least in some ways, I was not so different from Grandmother. She too had escaped a repressive home life and chose to live a different life than that of her childhood. The one thing I hoped was that if I ever had to endure the sorrows she did, I would not become embittered. I had never seen or heard her laugh. And she had a way of squashing everyone else's laughter and fun, too. I vowed that I would learn how to become a better person through my hardships, rather than let myself become bitter.

Then John got back to advising me about moving to a different community.

I don't want to tell you what to do but if you have a desire to visit some of the other places that don't dene with your church and your mother doesn't object, I would not stop just because they don't dene with you and I think if you get started once you would enjoy yourself a lot better than where you are.[8] And here's a hearty invitation to come to NY and visit your uncle and aunt and cousins. We sure would all be glad to see you and hope you feel welcome to go with us to church and with young folks to singing. That has often happened with people from other churches here and I'm sure Lydia E. Miller would be glad to see you too. She is teaching school. We almost expected her to marry this spring but spose she'll wait until fall.

I'm sorry your dad is not getting better. Had hoped if he would go to the Dr. regular he would at least get some better, although we realize he has never quite had the mental capacity and age would have some bearing on it too. Am wondering if your mother has told you lately what she has in mind if we can convince him. Let's all pray that we can do something that will help him and us all.

I longed for fatherly guidance. It seemed to me that Uncle John, who was just two years younger than my father, had ended up with the wisdom, the ability to care and communicate that he cared, and the everyday common sense that *Datt* lacked.

Another surprise from Uncle John was that even though he was a preacher in a stricter community than Geauga, he was actually encouraging me to find a different Amish community to live in. I certainly didn't want to join his community, though, because I didn't want to live in a stricter community than I was in. I didn't think that John was going to encourage me to join a more liberal community, either. But that door was at least cracked open, and it gave me hope that I could be Amish, even if I chose not to stay in Geauga County, Ohio.

---

8. To "dene" is to associate with other churches in ways such as preaching in one another's services, sharing communion, etc.

Uncle John's next letter is postmarked July 20, 1978, five days after I had told David I didn't want him in my life. John wrote about a visit to my parents' house:

> We found out the Dr and other people don't advise putting him (your dad) in a mental hospital but may try a little medication soon. I feel sorry for him and youns all. We talked and talked with him till way past midnite and again quite a while next AM.

> Was sorry we could not talk with you girls more as we talked with some people that said we should talk with "the girls" and tell them not to do things just to aggravate Dad but I don't know as you are involved in it yourself. But I can say that different people told us you are doing good yourself and even try to talk your sisters into doing better which we were so glad to hear and hope and feel the day will come when you will be glad you did. Often think of the chorus we used to have when I went to the singings in Geauga "Cheer up my brother, Live in the sunshine, you'll understand it all by and by." More words to it.

That John believed my father had mental problems and attempted to help was so different from the way the people in my community had dealt with this issue. It didn't surprise me that "others" had told John that he should talk to us girls about not "aggravating" *Datt*. That was how Bishop Dan in my home district had dealt with the issue: claiming that *Datt* wouldn't have this problem if the wife and children weren't so rebellious. I wondered how it could be that someone from the community in Conewango Valley, New York, which had a reputation for being stricter than us, was more understanding about my family situation and more willing to facilitate treatment for *Datt* than the people in my own community. I hoped that Uncle John would convince *Datt* to get the help he needed.

I felt very gratified that my behavior was acceptable to Uncle John, who was a pillar in his community. I had always felt that I didn't measure up to the people in my own. Getting understanding letters from other Amish people helped me to resolve to fit into an Amish community—someplace and somehow. Maybe teaching school would help.

~❀~

Exactly a week after my afternoon on the reservoir, I moved to the Troyers' property, into a little house adjacent to theirs. Someone else had moved out not long before. It would be only a ten-minute walk to the schoolhouse. I had six weeks to settle in to my new house and prepare to teach.

Setting up my own house was fun. I never thought I would be so fortunate as to live by myself. It was a nice little house, complete with a cupboard in the kitchen that had glass doors on it. I bought a set of "good" dishes with a rose pattern to display in the cupboard, and then I added the glassware that I had bought several years before when I went to the Fenton Glass Factory in West Virginia with a load of other Amish women.

One surprise that came from having my own place is that my relationship with my family members improved. They all seemed to like to come and visit me, and they usually came at different times. *Mem* would often help me bake. I was selling baked goods down at the sale barn in Middlefield on Mondays. I was not allowed to start baking until after midnight on Sunday nights because Sunday was our sabbath. *Mem* slept at my house on Sunday nights so she could help me bake. And so I would set my alarm and we'd get up and bake the rest of the night. I described our activities in a letter to Barbara Lalancette:

Mom and I got up about 12:30 Monday morning. We baked 10 elderberry pies, 8 peach pies, 15 dozen buttermilk cookies, 12 loaves bread. I didn't get to the sale until 'bout 9:30, so most of the spaces were taken. I had to take what was left, and the customers were up front asking for me. So I guess they might have liked our stuff. Mom helps me bake. Then in return I'd sell her extra vegetables. Once Katherine and I picked 40 dozen ears of corn and sold it for them.

My sisters also liked to visit me. It was as if Sarah and Susan had switched places with me: I was trying to adhere to the Amish ways while they were sowing their wild oats. They rebelled against the extra rules for women and took up smoking. At the time, the church leaders would look the other way as young unmarried men smoked cigarettes, but the young women were not allowed to smoke. I thought smoking was a dirty, nasty habit, and so I advised them to pick more carefully which issues to fight, such as the one that disallowed bicycles.

Even though Sarah and Susan had gone in a different direction than I had, we still enjoyed getting together. We often played board games in the evenings, or we would play Frisbee out in the field.

And then a miracle happened. The treatment that Uncle John had mentioned in his letter actually worked. Medication made all the difference in the world for *Datt*. I described this in a letter to Barbara:

> *Dad is so different. He doesn't seem like the same man. He's on medication, which must be the explanation for it. For a while his medication was too strong. He was so tired all the time, he could've slept 24 hours a day. Also he lost his appetite. Now they changed his medication and there is a happy medium. He's not listless, but he isn't violent either. But I'm not moving home. I like it too well where I am. There isn't enough room at home without sharing a bedroom. I'm already spoiled. I can come and go as I please.*

Datt would also visit me in my new home. He would do things for me, like bring me firewood, and he would stay and visit. I would often make him a meal when he did. His countenance was so different than it had ever been. I soon stopped being afraid of him or cringing when he came to visit.

Once I was settled into my little house, I turned my attention to the schoolhouse. The other teacher, Erma, and I got help from the women in the school community to clean the schoolhouse from top to bottom several weeks before school was to start. Then we prepared for the upcoming school year by making lesson plans, ordering workbooks and school supplies, and ensuring that all the reading and textbooks were counted out for each student. We also attended several teachers' meetings with the other Amish teachers in the area.

Every time I thought about the first day of school coming up, I'd have second thoughts about being a teacher. I wished I could get training before being thrust into my first day of teaching thirty-three pupils. Sometimes I wished I could push the day off into some future date. But it was fast approaching, whether I was ready or not.

∼ 19 ∼

On the Other Side of
the Desk

You can tell when you're on the right track.
It's usually uphill.
—Amish Proverb

The first day started the way many of my school days had. All
the pupils were looking to their teachers for direction as they
sat in their desks all in rows, facing the front of the schoolroom.
In all my other school days, however, I'd been sitting on the other
side of the teacher's desk. I wished I could be there now.

Erma, the head teacher, asked the pupils to get their song-
books out of their desks, both the English and German ones.
Starting with the eighth grader sitting in the front, she asked
that he choose and lead a song, this one in German. He chose
the most-sung song in the German book, "*Es Sind Zwein Weg*"
("There Are Two Roads"). Erma asked two more pupils to choose
and lead songs. After the third song, she asked them to stand and
bow their heads. Everyone recited the Lord's Prayer in German.
Then they took their seats. Erma walked to the front of the room
where there was a heavy canvas curtain, which she pulled toward
the middle of the room. Then she went to the back of the room
and pulled the other half of the curtain to the middle and snapped
the two together.

Suddenly I found thirty-three pairs of eyes trained on me.
The children's expressions revealed curiosity and openness to

learning. But I also saw an anxious anticipation there, as if they were just waiting to find out what kind of a teacher I was going to be. I wondered if they could see that I felt like running from the classroom. No amount of training could have prepared me for the overwhelming responsibility I felt at that moment. Certainly the training I did have was inadequate.

There was one kind of training I'd gotten: that of taking on more responsibility than I—or anyone—could handle. This training came from taking on the role I'd been assigned as I was growing up: the person who would fix things. The problem with that was that I'd been given responsibility for the well-being of the family without the power to change anything.

Now here I was, standing before a group of Amish pupils in four different grades, wishing I could crawl into a woodchuck hole.

I had been told it was important to let the children know the rules of the classroom right from the start and also the consequences of what would happen if they didn't obey those rules. I could hear Erma doing that on the other side of the curtain. And so I did. I let the children know that I expected good conduct. Whispering in class was not acceptable, and it was important to be honest and do their own work, rather than copy someone else's work, which is cheating. Even as I went down the list of dos and don'ts, I felt I was starting off on the wrong foot. Then again, it was hard to know, since I didn't know which was the right foot.

I passed out pictures for the second graders to color, and I asked the third and fourth graders to read the first chapter in their reading books. I asked the fifth graders to get out their math books, and I began teaching their first math lesson and assigned the math work that they were expected to have done by the next morning. Then I moved on to the fourth graders, the third, and so on. Before I knew it, I heard the little bell on Erma's desk dinging, signaling first recess.

In this manner, I managed to put one foot in front of the other. By the end of the day, I had given arithmetic and reading assignments in all four grades. All their work had to be done at school, because Amish parents do not accept homework, except in the case of illness. So as I gave each grade their lessons, the children set about completing them to be turned in the next day.

At the end of the day, after the children had been dismissed, I sat at my desk and stared out across the field beyond the barn. I wanted to think I was up for this task. Yet I felt so humbled with the thought that the well-being of all these pupils was now my responsibility each day. Whether they received a good education would depend on whether I was a good teacher. I knew that I could not back out, but I was not sure whether I could rise to that challenge.

~❀~

I wrote a letter to Barbara in which I shared my first impressions of teaching. It is tempting now to try to excuse the language I used to describe some of the situations I was dealing with, but at the time I wrote it, I had no idea I was being insensitive. I was speaking in the direct (sometimes inappropriate) manner of my culture.

I taught at Meadow Glow School, which I also attended for several years as a student.

At first I had my doubts that I could handle 33 of them. (Still do as a matter of fact.) I have about 8 slow learners in the bunch. I think I have a bad start. This is only my first year and I have one of the biggest classes in Geauga County. (There are about 20 schools with two teachers in each.) Then on top of that, I have a retarded girl in the class. She's also crippled. She's seventeen years old, and in my opinion she has learned everything she is capable of. On the other hand she likes to go to school too. She is my co-teacher Erma's sister. She disturbs the class. She can't help it of course, but if she starts laughing, she can't stop. Well naturally this is a disturbance to the other pupils. And the pupils know how easily she starts laughing, and I think some of my mischievous fourth-grade boys are making faces at her while I'm not looking. But I never can catch them. Every time I look around they're all innocently doing their lessons. Today she wasn't there and I must say it was quieter. I'm going to talk to Erma and see if she wouldn't teach her in her class, because I'm not any good to her, being I don't have the time.

I also have a very temperamental girl. She's big for her age, almost twice the size of some of the other third graders. She can do her lessons well, but sometimes she gets a stubborn streak, then does nothing but pout. When she raises her hand and I go to her desk she sticks out her lips into a "piggy snout," and points toward something in an angry way. That's when my patience wears thin. So I try to kindly tell her she has to tell [me] what she wants, because I can't tell when she just points. Then she looks at me real mad and just makes her lips go. I don't think last year's teacher was of any help. She used to try to spank her all the time. One time when she was trying to spank her, she was rolling around on the floor, she was fighting back so much. What do you do with someone like this? Use psychology on her?

I wrote more school news, and then I signed off, "A friend, Saloma or Linda."

I was trying to be my Amish self, Saloma, by settling into my own little house and my new role as schoolteacher. Yet I didn't want to give up on Linda either.

I thought that once I was a schoolteacher, my questions about the culture would finally settle down and I would feel more a part of the community. But the letter I wrote to Raymond a week after I wrote the letter to Barbara indicates that my wanderlust had not gone away. The letter conveys a restlessness that I could not express to anyone except my Vermont friends.

I heard from Barbara last week. She tells me she and Rick are going back to school. I think that's great. I sometimes wish I had sought means of higher education while I was still in Burlington. It would come in handy now.

Hope you enjoyed your vacation. In a way I envy you that you can go to the Northeast Kingdom anytime you want with your own boat. Here I'm stuck in Ohio with no such nice places to visit. Oh well, I don't mean to complain. Here is really where I belong, within the group of people with whom I grew up with. But still I can't picture myself living in Geauga County all my life. I'm looking forward to traveling and finding a future home. I had a chance to go to Rexford, Montana in August to a wedding. I would've except I was just buying things for my new home right at that time and couldn't afford it. I would've loved to though. There is an Amish settlement up there in Rexford located right in the Rocky Mountains. From what I've heard it is breathtakingly beautiful. Well you would know—you've been out West. I don't remember though whether you were in Montana or not. The family that started the settlement up there used to live in our area. I used to go to school with the girl that just got married. She is also a Saloma Miller.

My dilemma was whether to content myself with what I knew and the close-knit community where I'd grown up, or follow my desire to see the bigger world and live a life not dictated by the elders of the community. I could not have both and so I teetered on the fence.

Things sure have changed since I've given myself up to doing what I believe is the Lord's Will. It seems since then I have been showered with blessings. Of course the skies are not always blue and the sun doesn't always shine, but when I take my troubles to the Lord in prayer, it certainly makes my load lighter.

I certainly plan on coming to the New England States next summer sometime, Lord Willing. It didn't work out this summer like I'd planned and next summer seems like a long way off, but I'll manage.

An old friend,
Linda Miller

❧

Erma, the other teacher, and I would occasionally get together, sometimes at her house, sometimes at mine. On the night of the school board meetings, she would come and eat with me, and then we'd walk to the school together for the meeting.

One of the afternoons when she came to visit, my mail was lying on the kitchen table. I realized, too late to hide it, that one of the letters was from David. For reasons I could not explain, I continued to get letters from him. I didn't know what to make of them. I opened the letter and read it. I folded it and said, "That young man I met does not know how to take no for an answer."

I read judgment coming from Erma's big, dark eyes. She was, after all, the daughter of Bishop Jake of the Burton Station church district. He was a strict bishop with a loud voice who preached fire and brimstone more effectively than any preacher I knew. When I said David would not take no for an answer, she just stared straight ahead and was quiet for a long moment. Then she shook her head and said, "Oh Saloma, if I were you, I would stay as *faaarr* away from that man as I possibly could." And then she fell silent.

Then I went to the drawer where I kept my letters and pulled out the little brown cross that David had given me the day I was leaving Burlington. Opening the top of my woodstove, I dropped David's letter and the cross into the fire and watched the flames devour the sheets of paper. I felt a pit in my stomach, just as I had the day I'd burned the photos. It was a feeling of instant regret. On some level, however, I knew that I would regret it even more later.

~⁓ ❀ ⁓~

When I started teaching, Erma's half of the schoolroom was about the same size as my half. She kept saying she needed more room for a project table for her first graders, and we discussed having the canvas curtain moved over toward my part of the room to give her more space. We looked at the places where the curtain rod had been in the past. One set of holes showed that the curtain used to hang over a good three feet toward my room, which would make my room that much smaller. There was another set of holes in the other direction, which would have made her room three feet smaller. I let Erma know that I was not in favor of moving the curtain all the way over into my classroom, where it had been in the past. She suggested that we ask the men to make another hole halfway between where the curtain was and the other hole. We left it at that.

I offered to be there on the weekend when the men were planning on moving the curtain, but Erma said it wasn't necessary and that she would take care of it.

On the following Monday morning, when I walked into the classroom, I stopped short. My side of the classroom had the desks all pushed together in a jumble. I couldn't see how I was going to find room to have aisles between the desks. Erma's side of the schoolroom had the desks all neatly in a row, with wide aisles and a project table in one corner of the room.

My face must have betrayed my anger. Erma explained that the men hadn't wanted to make another hole and that she had had to choose between having them move it to where it is or not at all.

I don't remember what I said to her. Whatever it was, Erma turned her back and attended to something else. It was clear that she was in charge and that I would have to make do with the space I had. I barely managed to get my rage under control at the injustice of it all. I started moving desks around and then showed Erma that it was impossible to fit all the desks into my space. She made an indifferent remark about perhaps pushing two rows of desks together, and then she ignored me. I wanted to scream, I have to push two rows together while you have all that space? What gives you that right? But I already knew what gave her that right. Erma was the head teacher. Erma was older than me. Erma had been a teacher for years, and this was my first year. And most importantly, Erma was not one of Sim's girls.

Somehow I managed to teach thirty-three students in that crowded little schoolroom. Most of the time I managed good cheer, but there were times when my frustrations would build up and I had nowhere for them to go. Then I'd feel this frustration coming out at the children in the form of impatience. I didn't like myself when that happened.

My teaching, like all other Amish teaching, was textbook-based. I was using the same textbooks that had been used when I was going to school. Routine is the only way I could fit all the subjects into each grade.

Routine is also what would threaten to make mind-numbing boredom become the mood in the classroom. Only once in a while did we break that routine.

～❀～

The Troyers' two adult daughters, Lena and Rhoda, came home to live with their parents when they developed "nerve trouble." This was code for mental illness. At times Lena and Rhoda were functional, and at other times they would spiral back into psychotic episodes. Sometimes one of them would be in and the other out of these episodes. It seemed to me that mental illness was everywhere. I had left home to avoid *Datt*'s violent episodes caused by his mental illness. Then I experienced living with Janie at the Y. And now Lena and Rhoda.

The Troyer sisters sought help at the same mental health clinic where *Datt* had been treated. Other Amish people, including my sister, Lizzie, were also seeking counseling there. Eventually I decided that I, too, could use a counselor. I had not been able to cure my bulimia. I naïvely thought I could go to a few sessions with a counselor and become cured of the problem once and for all.

I started counseling with Rachael, who was soft-spoken and had a caring approach. After several sessions with her, I was expecting her to tell me what my problem was and how to fix it. But Rachael, in her wisdom, steered the conversation to other areas of my life, knowing that my problem was not as straightforward as what diet I followed or whether I lost or gained weight. We talked about the Amish faith, but there were aspects of the Amish ways that I was not allowed to tell her, such as what it means to make a public confession. Church members had an understanding that anything discussed in a members-only meeting at the end of a church service should "go no further." We were not allowed to discuss what happened in these meetings even among ourselves, and for sure not with Yankee people. I realize now these were the very aspects of the culture I was grappling with.

Rachael believed it was important to see people in their "natural" setting. So she observed in my classroom one day, and I introduced her to the pupils as "my friend Rachael." Afterward, when we talked about it, she seemed impressed with how well-ordered the classroom was. She also remarked about the great amount of responsibility I carried. It was good to get Rachael's perspective on that. I felt it was a huge responsibility, too, but people in my community didn't see it that way—or if they did, they did not share these feelings with me.

After working with Rachael, I came to understand that my disordered eating had a psychological root. She pointed out that I would often try to accept or "digest" the church dogma, and then I wouldn't be able to. She thought that my bulimia was symbolic of this desire to "swallow it" while my body and mind kept rejecting it.

Rachael suggested I keep a journal to record my feelings—taking note of exactly what I was feeling in my body when I started eating, what it felt like when I was gorging myself, and what I was thinking and feeling just before I purged. I discovered that I felt nothing—quite literally, inside I felt *nothingness*—when I headed into one of my bulimic episodes. If I was supposed to record my feelings, and there weren't any to record, I wondered why I was seeking treatment if I couldn't even follow my counselor's advice. That would lead to feeling worthless, which led to more bulimia. Sometimes I felt like there was no help for me.

∽ ❀ ∾

My journal in my first year of teaching conveys frustration about the number of students I was teaching, how I wasn't patient enough with the pupils, how I felt I had to punish the children too often, how hard it was to keep the parents happy, and my perception of Erma's condescending and dominating attitude. I asked her numerous times about moving her sister into her class instead of keeping her in mine. Erma kept evading the question until one day she said that she would ask her mother. She reported back to me that her mother said she would leave it up to Erma and me. And then Erma wouldn't tell me whether she would teach her or not. Finally, when I suggested we ask the school board who should be teaching Erma's sister, Erma reluctantly agreed to take her on. It was a visible relief in my classroom.

I spent my evenings grading papers and making lesson plans in the light of the Coleman gas lantern. In their good times, the Troyers' daughters, Lena and Rhoda, would come over and offer to help grade papers and we'd have pleasant conversations. They often visited when I had other young women friends over. We'd play Boggle or Dictionary, and in the summer we'd play Frisbee in the field next to the Troyers' driveway.

I was living the prescribed, predictable, and cyclical life of an Amish woman. One week was like the next, passing slowly—in Amish time.

~ 20 ~

Trip to Vermont

*Many of us will have to pass through the valley of the
shadow of death again and again before we reach the
mountaintop of our desires.*
—Nelson Mandela

O ne of the problems I dealt with as a teacher was discipline.
Now, these many years later, I often feel deeply ashamed for
the way I punished my pupils with the school strap. The Amish
in my community believed in the saying "Spare the rod and spoil
the child," and I had no understanding of alternative methods of
discipline. Even my mentors at the time did not teach any alter-
natives to keeping order and ethics in the classroom. The incidents in which I resorted to using the school strap on students
still haunt me to this day.

I am surprised now that I was not the least bit ashamed to
write to Barbara about the way I disciplined the pupils.

*This last while I've been having [school] parent problems. I try
to take it as constructive criticism, but somehow it's not done
with the right attitude, so it's hard to take. They were talking
about me behind my back, long before I knew it. So I talked with
the parents. It was about spankings. They think there's been too
much of it. I told them I agree there has been too much, but I feel
I don't spank unnecessarily. I have often gone to Erma asking her
what to do next. I have tried other punishments, but then the
children have the idea they'll get away with things. Ida says she
thinks they're trying me out, to see how far they can go.*

I was having doubts whether I would teach another year, until Friday night at the teacher's meeting. There's one person I can confide in about school troubles who understands—Urie Byler. He was one of the first Amish teachers in Geauga County. Matter of fact he opened Meadow Glow School in 1965 (my school). I was in the third grade at the time. He wasn't my teacher, but of course it was that school. Now he tells me I was his pet. He said, "You were the sweetest little thing." I remember one day he asked me to help him drill a hole in the floor for the rope for the fire drill. When he was done, he threw a tootsie roll in my lap. This last fall when I was getting ready for school and I was alone in the schoolhouse, I noticed the hole and I stopped dead in my tracks as the memory of this came back. At the time Urie was lying in the hospital in a coma. He had been in an accident when a car hit his buggy. They didn't think he was going to make it. But now he is as active as ever. Urie also understands other things, like my leaving home. He printed a story in our young people's magazine of the struggles he had when he was a young lad. He almost left the Amish, but he had a vision about his mother whom he had very fond memories of. She had passed away when he was eight years old.

As I was saying, I do go to Urie with my troubles and always get much encouragement from him. Friday night he said it doesn't matter how many times I spanked the pupils, so long as they deserved it. He said, "You're teaching another year too!" I said I was having my doubts and boy did he tell me! He said the school board expects it, and so does he.

Teaching was a full-time job. After the school day was over, I would come home and grade papers and make lesson plans. This was not a joyful time in my life, though I kept telling myself that I should be grateful and happy and that I should not have the desire to go back to Vermont. Here I was—living in a house by myself with more independence than I had ever had before. I was getting along with my family—even *Datt*. I had several close young women friends who visited me regularly. The Troyers were a good family to live next to. I was finding my way as a schoolteacher. And yet the pull back to Vermont was perhaps stronger than when I had been living at Joe and Emma's house and not enjoying my Amish life at all. I could not understand why this was so.

Writing letters to Barbara was a very important outlet at this time in my life. She was my confidante. I wrote details about my life that I didn't even write in my journal, because I knew that there was a chance someone would snoop and read what I'd written. Though she lived six hundred miles away, she was my closest friend. Without these letters, I would have forgotten about the spiritual search I was on at the time. This is evident in the openings of my letters to her.

Most people in my community did not quote Scripture, debate spiritual beliefs, or even invoke Jesus' name in everyday conversations. The "place" for renewing their spiritual beliefs was in church. Their everyday lives then became a deeply rooted lived faith that was largely unspoken. Even their prayers before and after meals were quiet, invoked with a bowed head.

And yet in letters to one another, it was common to start with the line "Greetings in Jesus' Name." This was true for all the Amish people with whom I exchanged letters, whether they were from the more conservative Amish communities or the more "mission-minded" ones.[9] The more conservative Amish would then go on to write their news, while the more mission-minded would include a verse from the Bible.

At some point along the way, I began writing letters with a Bible verse in the beginning. This occurred around the time I began reading Scripture in English, so I could understand it, rather than pronouncing the words in German and not knowing what they meant. I would sometimes get together with Lena and Rhoda to read chapters of the Bible. The beginnings of my letters

---

9. *Mission-minded* is a term the more conservative Amish use for those communities in which people adopt a more spiritually overt lifestyle. This can vary from saying prayers out loud at the dinner table without a prayer book, to getting together in groups outside of church to discuss Scripture, to offering Sunday school for their children.

to Barbara reflect this new piety, such as the one dated March 4, 1979. I then went on to share with her a healthy slice of my life at the time.

Dearest Friend Barb,

"The eyes of the Lord are in every place, beholding the evil and the good." ~ Proverbs 15:3. Greetings to you in our Savior's Name!

You don't know how overjoyed I was on Friday. I had come home on my lunch hour. As I was making a fire and eating my lunch, I kept thinking of how much I miss you. (Not that this is unusual.) On the way back to school, I thought I'd check my mailbox. When I saw the return address, I could have leaped for joy! On my way to school I was reading it (very intently) when Sam Fisher (neighbor) stuck his head out the door and yelled, "Hey, is that a letter from your boyfriend? It sure looks interesting!" I hollered back, "It is!"

I think I know why you've been on my mind more lately. Do you realize what today is? Last year at this time we were on our way to Ohio. So this morning at around 9 or 10 o'clock a year ago we said goodbye to each other. I think if I were alone right now I'd be crying. Sis Lizzie is sitting here reading.

The Geauga County teachers are planning a trip to Mio, Michigan, and Mackinac Island. That's in late May, so I really don't know if I'll go. I want to visit so many places, like Wisconsin and New York to visit relatives. Remember when you read a letter from Uncle John? I still write to him for advice and go to him for problems that normally you'd ask your father's advice about. Things like church matters. I'd like to visit him and his family for sure. But somewhere along the line I'm going to have to have more income, one kind or another. I was thinking of possibly getting a job waitressing or maybe cashier somewhere, but I don't want to be tied down, so I can go traveling.

Change of subject. Last Monday was the only day of school we missed because of the weather. So I took the day and went skiing.

*It sure did me good. I used the back road down behind the folks'
house. It doesn't get plowed out. It was like a winter wonderland
with snow and ice hanging on the trees, a fresh white blanket of
snow on the ground, except where wild animals had crossed the
trail. It was so quiet and peaceful.*

I wrote about my family and other happenings before I wrote
about my desire for love in my life and the lack of it:

*I remember an Amish minister saying at a wedding ceremony
that difficulties tend to bring two people, who really love each
other and want what is right, closer together. Of course I might
not know what I'm talking about as I've never had this experience. How I sometimes long for someone to love while he loves
me back! But it's still the same, no such luck. But then I also
think if I deserve someone like that God will lead me to that
person. Since I stopped going with the big crowd there really is
no one who is eligible.*

*I'll remember you in my prayers tonight. (Please do the same
for me.) I miss you all so very much. Thank you for those kind
words, Barbara. They were an inspiration right when I needed
it. It's a struggle to keep my head above water when it comes to
feeling inferior. Today I wrote a whole sheet in my diary. I just
wrote down my feelings. One sentence goes something like this:
"So asking for daily guidance and much encouragement from
Erma, my co-teacher, Urie Byler, and Barbara Lalancette, the
person who was first to make me feel like a worthwhile person,
I'm trying to win the battle of that awful inferiority complex."
So you see I feel you are more to me than I can ever be to you.
Thank you for just being you.*

Love 'n Prayers,
Saloma Miller

I felt so affirmed when Barbara wrote things that conveyed she
understood where I was coming from.

Your letter was so newsy. I'm especially glad your family situation is looking up in terms of your father feeling more mellow. So you're not going to move back because you like your independence, huh? Well let me tell you that I know how you feel. I tried to move back home after I had lived in an apartment one time and it was unbelievably difficult for me. After being able to plan my time and come and go as I pleased, it was very confining. It's funny because being married now, it's different. I still feel a certain freedom that I never felt at home. I guess I feel like my own person.

I hung on to every word Barbara wrote to me. Having someone say "I know how you feel" showed an understanding that I didn't get in my community life. Being Amish was about being part of a group, and that required self-sacrifice. Part of this sacrifice seemed to require giving up not only an understanding of my feelings, but also the *need* for the understanding of my feelings. Having a friendship with Barbara, with whom I could confide my innermost feelings, allowed me to have a foot in both worlds. It allowed me to live my community life as Saloma without completely forsaking the Linda in me. I did not yet recognize that by trying to have it both ways, I was splitting my soul in two.

～❀～

As the school year drew to a close, Erma and I handed out tests to our pupils. The classroom became unusually quiet, with only the sound of the children's pencils writing on their papers, or a sudden rubbing out with an eraser and then the stroking of a hand across the paper. Occasionally pupils shifted their weight in their seats, and then all would become quiet again.

I busied myself averaging grades from the semester to record on the report cards. Averaging scores had become a lot easier with my calculator. I had to think about the day I received it. We were visiting the Troyers' Yankee neighbors, the Groths, across the field, who had bought an old farmhouse and renovated it. Then Mr. Groth had taken ill. The Troyers would visit and they sometimes invited me to go along.

One day the Groths had other visitors. One of them, John Anderson, worked for a company that made calculators, and he showed me how to use one. I immediately thought about how that would come in handy for averaging grades. I asked how I could get one of them, and he offered it to me. "No, that's okay," I said. Then I thought about it for a moment and asked, "Can I see that again?" He showed it to me again, and I was amazed at what it could do. "Are you sure it's okay for me to have this?" John, being the kind man that he was, said, "Sure."

I was oblivious to the fact that I had the prototype calculator from Monroe, the company John worked for. Not that I even would have known what a prototype was. All I knew was how much easier my life as a schoolteacher had become with the generous gift from John Anderson.

The students had been asked to hand in their test papers when they were done, and then they exited the classroom quietly, so as not to disturb the students who were still working. They went out into the schoolyard for recess, and I began grading the tests.

Then came the last day of school, and the pupils were dismissed for the summer. After everyone had left, even Erma, I sat with my head propped in my hands and stared out the windows at the field beyond the barn. It was hard to believe I had made it through a year of teaching.

There had been many times when I had wanted to quit, but I had formed a bond with the pupils. Now I imagined that when fall came around, I would want to be their teacher again. I vowed I would find a better way to discipline them, though. I did not want them to be afraid of me. Somehow I would find a way to get the children to want to do the right thing on their own, not because they were afraid I would use the school strap on them.

I cleared my desk, stuck the pencils into the holder on the corner of the desk, walked to the back of the classroom and closed all the windows, and locked up the schoolhouse, closing my first year of teaching.

I wasted no time in planning a trip to Vermont after the school year ended. I knew I had to find someone to go with me. I certainly would not be trusted to go alone, lest I might not return. So I asked Sarah if she would go with me. She said she couldn't afford it, so we worked out a deal: she would help me bake on Monday mornings, and I would pay her way.

I sold the baked goods at the sale barn in Middlefield on Monday mornings. This limited my sales to one day a week. I also took on cleaning jobs. I would do anything to visit Vermont.

Sarah and I planned the trip for June. We took a bus to Burlington, where Barbara met us and took us to her in-laws, where we stayed for part of our trip.

We spent our first few days taking buses from the Lalancettes' to places such as the Shelburne Museum and downtown Burlington. I purposely spent time on Church Street, because I had a secret desire to find David there, peddling his wares. I was still embarrassed about rejecting him on the Akron Reservoir the summer before. I imagined he would call out to me from behind his display train and want to talk with me. But during all the hours I spent there, I did not see him. I did not know that he had moved on to other venues to sell his wares.

Raymond came to visit while Sarah and I were staying at his aunt's house. We talked with him about possibly climbing Mt. Mansfield, and he said he would be happy to take us to Underhill State Park and help us set up camp. He also took us to get fishing licenses, and we made plans to go fishing when we came back from hiking the mountain.

And that is how, a year after my birthday party at Joe's house, I climbed to the top of Mt. Mansfield in Vermont with Sarah. I wrote in my journal:

We started up the mountain at 9 o'clock and got to the "chin" at 12:15. It was quite a climb. I've been to the top of Mt. Mansfield, the highest point in Vermont. We could see into Canada, New Hampshire, New York, and Vermont. I hope I'll never forget that view! God's creation is really some sight to see! All we have to do is put in a little effort.

Some people take on Mt. Everest so they can say they did it. Mt. Mansfield was my Mt. Everest. I could not believe Sarah and I had done it. I wondered if any other Amish women had ever climbed Mt. Mansfield before.

The night before we were going fishing, Raymond Culligan stayed with the Lalancettes. We started out at four o'clock in the morning. First, we went to Norton Pond. In one of the photos of Sarah and me from that day, we are holding a string of fish between the two of us. In another, I am sitting on a rock out in the water of Norton Pond, looking at the mountains around me. Then Raymond took us sightseeing to eight other lakes in the Northeast Kingdom. He took a photo of Sarah and me sitting next to a waterfall by Lake Willoughby.

Sarah and I packed so much into our two weeks in Vermont. We saw sunsets over Lake Champlain. Barbara had a birthday party for me at her house and invited the Lalancettes and her neighbors.

On my visit to Vermont, I wore my Amish clothes but with a kerchief instead of a *kopp* on my head.

When we camped in Underhill State Park, we played cards with a young couple there in their campsite, and they climbed the mountain with us. We took a ferry across Lake Champlain and walked several miles to Ausable Chasm in the Adirondacks.

Even though Sarah had come along to keep me from "defecting," she did things I considered wild. I wondered several times who was really the other's keeper. She followed me everywhere. When I decided to do some shopping on Church Street, so did she.

While Sarah and I were staying at Barbara's house, we went running with her on the trail of the campus of UVM, twice in the early morning, and once after dinner in the evening. Little did I know at the time that I was more apt to run into David there than on Church Street. At that time he and his brother Dan were taking daily runs on that trail.

The only time I was away from Sarah was when I visited Maureen and Patti. They had gotten an apartment together in Winooski. They wanted to talk about old times and filled me in about David. He had been dating a woman at the Y who was from England. They had gone out often until the woman went back to England. Then David didn't visit the Y for a while.

They told me that one night, when Patti was working in a bar downtown, David came in and had a drink with her. Then he asked her out. She said no, and then no again when he came to their apartment to ask her out.

Maureen got a huge kick out of the story of David following me out on the reservoir in a rowboat. She said he was really hurt when he came back. I remarked about how he was still writing to me, so he couldn't have been too hurt.

Maureen asked me if I was going to be seeing David while I was in Vermont. When I said I wasn't planning on it, she said, "If he finds out you're here and you didn't see him, he is going to be really upset. He really cared about you, Linda." Maureen had never gotten used to calling me Saloma. I could understand why. Here I was, visiting with her in my Amish dress, but with a kerchief on my head instead of an Amish covering. My changing identities were bound to be confusing to my friends.

I told Maureen that, with Sarah along on the trip, I wouldn't really have a chance to call David or to see him. I didn't tell her that I hoped that I would see David "accidentally." I knew that calling him up was another matter. I wasn't sure he would even want to see me. A rejection would be crushing. What if he had found someone else by now? And even if he hadn't—what about the fact that I was Amish and he was not?

So when Sarah and I said our goodbyes to the Lalancettes and boarded the bus for our return trip, I had not gotten even a glimpse of David.

As the bus traveled south on Shelburne Road that day, Sarah and I saw the Shelburne Museum again. Had we been looking east instead of west at that intersection, I would have seen the back of the little white Cape Cod–style house that would be my future home with David, and the home where we would raise our two sons.

I had visited my future in another way during the trip. Sarah and I shopped in a little bookstore on Church Street called Hopkins Bookshop. That store was owned and run by a couple, William Cleary and Roddy O'Neill, who would later take me into their home and become my mentors. William was a former Jesuit priest and Roddy was a former Maryknoll nun; they had left their respective orders so they could marry.

The bus trip through Vermont was breathtakingly beautiful, with the sun sparkling on Lake Champlain and clouds in a blue sky above the Green Mountains to the east and the Adirondacks to the west. I felt like I needed to drink in enough of the beauty to sustain me when I returned to the community. I knew I could not afford to come to Vermont often. I had been paid only 250 dollars a month for teaching school. I had to clean houses on Saturdays to make up for the low teaching wages. In the summer, I had to find my own income. So far, I'd been cleaning houses and baking, but I was thinking of applying to become a tour guide at the Geauga County Historical Society.

Sarah was sitting by my side. Though she seemed unobtrusive, I felt like I needed to be farther away from her so that I could think my private thoughts. It often felt as though Sarah could read my moods and thoughts all too well. I told her that I felt like having a double seat by myself, so I moved farther back on the bus. I had to make a mental transition from my Vermont world to my Amish one, and I wanted to do that alone.

Not much had happened since my return to my Amish life. I loved adventure and discovering new things about the world, which was hard to do in a culture in which life is so predictable and self-reflection and an inquisitive nature are considered wrong. There were so many parts of my personality that did not fit into that culture.

I longed for my Vermont life almost constantly, though there were some distractions. I had taken a trip to Wisconsin by train for a cousin's wedding not long before traveling to Vermont. I enjoyed having young women friends over for visits. Without this camaraderie, I would not have been able to sustain myself in the community.

Spending time with Barbara had been such a boost to my self-confidence. She had a way of making me see things from a different point of view. I often put myself down. It was almost as though I was playing a psychological game with people. I wanted them to say, "What do you mean you're ugly?" "No you're *not* stupid!" So, by putting myself down, I was fishing for compliments. Barbara didn't buy into that. She'd say, "Saloma, why do you put yourself down like that?" She would admonish me for thinking so poorly of myself. I began to examine my motives for these self put-downs and soon learned not to do this in front of her. Once I stopped putting myself down in front of Barbara, I realized I shouldn't do it with anyone else.

Spending time with Raymond had been fun. As usual, he was comfortable around both Sarah and me. I sensed that would have changed had he and I spent any time with just the two of us. But Sarah didn't let that happen. In fact, she often scrambled up into his truck before I could, so she could sit next to him on that day we were traveling around Vermont to fish and see the lakes. I would have a flash of anger at what I saw as a lack of appreciation for the fact that I had been her ticket to traveling to Vermont and meeting the Lalancettes. She knew as well as I did that she wouldn't have made it there under her own steam. Our sibling rivalry had followed us to Vermont.

And now we were on our way back to Ohio to take up our expected places in the community. This trip had been another attempt at bringing together my two worlds. Sarah and I had gotten stares from people when we were out in public. We had especially noticed it when we were on Church Street in Burlington. It was a strange feeling, given I'd been Yankee when I lived there.

I tried to visualize my future. Would I stay Amish or leave again? If I stayed Amish, I was heading for a life I did not want. Because the Amish men were not asking me for dates, I would likely end up single. In fact, Joe had already dubbed me a "premature old maid." I could turn out like Erma. I groaned inwardly at the thought. Ten years down the road, I did not see myself as a single teacher in an Amish school. I knew I wanted to be married—life would be too lonely as a single person. And if that wasn't going to happen among the Amish, what was I still doing there?

What about David? Would I want to be in a relationship with him? Would he even want to get together again? His letters were becoming fewer and farther between. I received a card from him at Christmas, but I had not answered. I had to be sure that I wanted to be in relationship with him if I ever did get back in touch—it wouldn't be fair to him otherwise.

When Sarah came and sat next to me, I sat up straight and looked out at the landscape. We were now in New York. The day was clear and bright and there were lots of hills, but they were not the mountains of Vermont. I missed them already.

~ **21** ~

The Silent Beauty of a Moonlit Night

I love you with so much of my heart that none is left to protest.
—William Shakespeare

After my trip to Vermont, I continued to jog a mile every morning just as Barbara did.

But that routine came to an abrupt end when a Yankee neighbor observed me and remarked about it to the bishop's son, who told his father. I wrote to Barbara:

> *The bishop thought something should be done, so instead of talking to me personally, guess what he did? He talked to the whole congregation in church about it! He said that's not for an Amish person and there are other ways of losing weight. He added, "Seems to me you could go to the garden, or go out and work the yard." Of course everyone knew who does the jogging. It was so humiliating! Why oh why couldn't he have talked with me? So I had a very hard time getting over that, and going on with my life.*

I had not shared all the details of the incident with Barbara. Bishop Dan waited for his chance to make his public proclamation when I was not sitting in the service. I had left to help prepare *Mittag* (midday meal) for everyone after the service was dismissed. I was oblivious to the fact that there had been discussion of my jogging until later that day.

The Troyers' daughter, Lena, was the designated messenger. She and I were upstairs in the house where I lived, looking for something in the storage area behind the knee wall. She started out slowly by saying that Dan had asked for a members' meeting that day in church.

I asked what it was about.

"Jogging," Lena answered.

I was shocked into silence. I didn't dare ask. Lena told me the rest of the story—except she didn't tell me what the Yankee neighbor had said. So I asked—and then wished I hadn't.

He had said, "There she goes with her fat ass sticking out behind."

I was dumbfounded. I knew that the bishop hadn't repeated those words in the church service, so that meant that this story was all over town. I couldn't decide which was worse in terms of losing my dignity—the talk around town, or the fact that I had just lost yet another one of my liberties. I didn't know any other Amish bishops who forbade his parishioners to run.

Lena must have noticed my uncharacteristic silence and asked if I wanted to be alone. I nodded. When she left, I lay down on the floor of the upstairs bedroom in an almost comatose state. My mind could not bear the level of humiliation I felt. I have no idea how long I stayed there, and I don't remember getting up from the floor.

In the days that followed, I threw myself into my work. I baked up a storm for the Labor Day weekend; I harvested the vegetables from my garden and put food by; and I prepared for the beginning of the school year. I did anything to avoid thinking about the humiliation the bishop had served up to me as "humble pie."

I confided my feelings to Barbara:

You know Barbara, if I look back over my life, those four months I spent in Vermont were the happiest months of my life. I had no one to tell me right from wrong. I had to make those choices. They weren't always right, but it still made me feel good to be making my own decisions. Now to answer to what other people think and say . . . it's hard.

I look back to our trip to Vermont, and I have such happy memories. That party you had for me was very nice. When I look back to that and how you took us in, it makes me feel ever closer to you as a friend, Barbara. I meant that when I said to you that night that you were the first person who made me feel like I ever amounted to anything. Now I'm beginning to wonder about that. Sometimes I feel like I'm the worst person around. Why oh why can't I be satisfied with what comes along in church with no one finding out how I feel or do things? Why can't I be one of those quiet little girls standing around with nothing to say? Then I wouldn't stir things up all the time. Any criticism adds to my inferiority complex, and of late there seems to be plenty. This letter must be awful confusing to you. I'm just pouring out my troubles on my good old friend, Barbara.

Working hard effectively kept my despair at bay for about two weeks. Then one night, as I was sitting in the Troyers' kitchen, talking to Lena and Rhoda. I could no longer squelch my feelings. In a dispassionate voice, I said, "In the Amish community when someone makes a mistake, there are plenty of people who can correct that person—the other people in the church, the deacon, the ministers, and the bishop. If a deacon makes a mistake, the ministers and the bishop can correct him. If a minister makes a mistake, then the bishop can correct him. What if the bishop makes a mistake? Who is there to correct him?"

The silence in the room was so loud it was palpable. Slowly, tears started falling down my cheeks. I kept wiping them away, but more came. Then Lena spoke. She said, "Saloma, you have been working really hard lately. You must be really stressed. I think you need to take good care of yourself and get a good night's rest."

I left then to go back to my own house. I tried to follow Lena's advice, but I had a restless night. Then I had to get up early to go to school, which started the next day.

It would not be the last time the bishop would treat me that way. He did it again, this time when the church service was held in the basement of my house, where the Troyers held the service when it was their turn to host it.

I had gone upstairs to help with preparing the meal. This time while I was gone, the bishop talked about how there was a young woman who had been "swooping her hair" and that, because she was a schoolteacher, this was not a good example to the school-girls. Since Erma lived in the Burton Station district, there was only one schoolteacher in the district, and everyone knew that. Dan had been very effective in singling me out once again.

And he left it up to the Troyers to tell me.

What makes this incident so absurd is that I wasn't "swooping" my hair. This was a term used for the fashionable way some girls were combing their hair. Most of our hair was covered by a *kopp*, but the fashion at the time was to swoop the hair down and then back (instead of straight back), showing more of the hair.

I have no recollection of my reaction to this incident, although I must have told my sisters. Years later, they recounted what I did. I apparently marched up to the bishop's house. When his wife came to the door, I said to her, "I am *not* swooping my hair. My hair grows close to my eyes, and I can't help that." For good mea-sure, I pulled at the hair on my temple and said, "See! What am I supposed to do—pull it all out?" Then I turned on my heel and walked away.

Reading my journal from the months following these incidents reminds me how much I struggled with depression, disordered eating, and downright despair. There are numerous references to wanting the struggle to be over or wanting to just lie down and die.

In December of 1979, I started taping my Christmas cards on the wall in my living room. It was the only decoration the people in my community were allowed during the holiday season. My collection was slowly growing.

One day I found a package in the mail. My heart skipped a beat when I saw the return address; it was from David. I opened the flat package and found a *Vermont Life* calendar. I flipped through the calendar, savoring every image of Vermont and wishing I were there. I thought, here it is, a year and a half after I told him I didn't want to see him, and he still remembers me. I was touched that he remembered that I liked *Vermont Life* magazines. The calendar was a thoughtful gift.

I opened the card. It was handcrafted, with a drawing of three deer on the front. They had stopped in a pine woods outside a cottage. He also remembered that I love deer, I thought.

Then I opened the card and read,

Dear Saloma,

All living things respond
to the warmth of love.

May you share a warm
and joyful holiday season
with the ones you love.

Sincerely,
David

I was glad I was alone. The card, so thoughtfully chosen, with such a simple and clear message, conveyed David's feelings. In a flash, I remembered what I had been denying myself for eighteen months: those winter nights when David and I sat in the parlor at the Y and held one another, with my head on his chest. I recalled his smell of linseed oil and fresh air, and I could hear the sound of his voice, deep and resonant, coming up from his chest. I took his card and gift to the sofa and sat down. As I examined the address, the envelope, and the card, I wondered why David hadn't written a letter with the card. And yet the card had conveyed everything.

Could it be that David still had feelings for me? Did this mean that David hadn't found anyone else? God only knew that I hadn't.

I looked through the calendar again and wondered what 1980 would bring. Would I still be here, or would I be in Vermont a year from now?

I pulled open the drawer to the bureau in the living room where I kept my letters. I found the bundle from David and started from the beginning, with David's first letter to me when I was living at the Benders'. I read them slowly, sometimes staring off into the middle distance, as I recalled particular moments with him. I let the tears come at the bitter regret of knowing I would never fit into my community. And I have tried so hard, I thought; so why am I still here in this community where I don't belong?

I was reading the third letter from David when I heard foot-steps outside the kitchen door. When I first moved to the little house on the Troyers' property, I wanted to be a good Amish person, so I insisted they should "come right on in" instead of knocking at my door. Little did I know how much I would wish I hadn't. It seemed Lena and Rhoda both had a barometer for my depressed moods and often came walking in on them.

The kitchen door opened. I grabbed all the letters, shoved them into the drawer, closed it, and then said, "Hello!"

Lena said, "I can come back later if you want."

"Come on in," I said, as I dabbed at my tears.

Lena walked tentatively into the living room. I sat back on the sofa and invited her to have a seat.

I knew that Lena could see I was crying, but she didn't ask and I didn't tell. That was the way things went—pretend nothing was wrong, and then there wasn't.

By the time Lena left, my sorrow was adequately dispersed, so the tears were no longer reachable.

I must have had mixed feelings after my initial reaction to David's card. I hung it up with the rest of them on the wall. I don't know why I did that. Perhaps I wanted people to know that David was still waiting in the wings. Or was he? Why didn't he write a letter with the card? Instantly, as I remembered how I had rejected him at the reservoir, I knew the answer. I felt so deeply ashamed for having done that, and I felt I didn't deserve a second chance. Why didn't David just move on and find someone else when he had a world of possibilities open to him?

In the end, I decided to send David a card—a hideous, gaudy card, yellowed with age, with an image of a Christmas tree by a fireplace on the front. I had acquired the card when the Gingerich sisters and I had gone into an abandoned house down near the golf course. I found a box of Christmas cards next to the chimney on the second floor and took them. I told myself that they would likely get thrown out if I didn't take them, so I wasn't really stealing them. Then I couldn't get myself to send them to anyone because they were so ugly. Now I was sending one of them to David. On the inside, I wrote, "David" at the top and "Saloma" at the bottom.

I have no idea what possessed me to send such a thing, and in such a cold and heartless manner. Was this conveying my "come hither and stop right there" message again? Was I thinking that he deserved to get a card in return but I felt too ashamed to be genuine about it? Or was I testing him to see what he would do if he got a card from me? Likely I didn't even know what response I wanted.

~ ❀ ~

I made a New Year's resolution to stop bingeing and purging. I did stop purging, and then I started gaining more weight. It seemed that I loathed myself either way, whether it was for bingeing and purging or for gaining weight. To help combat the weight gain, I became active by skating, skiing, and walking.

One starlit night in January, I found myself on the Benders' pond, skating alone. I was babysitting on the farm for Urie's brother's children that night. I remembered another night when the stars were bright and I was standing in that same yard with David when he had asked for a kiss and a hug and I had only allowed a handshake. There was something about the snappy cold air and the beauty of the vast sky full of stars that evoked longing in me. I had an overwhelming desire to have him skating by my side. I wished David were here now, offering that hug. This time I would hug him and I would never let him go. My heart started beating fast in my chest, as if it were really happening. I could just feel his arms around me.

In that moment, I knew I would one day feel his arms around me again. I also knew who I wanted to spend my life with. Tears spilled down my cheeks and into the scarf I had tied around my neck. I looked up into the starlit sky and prayed, "God, if it's meant to be, then help me find my way back to David. I cannot bear to go through life alone, not having given our love another chance."

I must have expressed my feelings for David in a letter to Maureen that elicited her response in a letter dated February 2, 1980:

> I almost died when you told me you had feelings for David. I haven't seen him since before Christmas. I'm sure if he ever knew you felt that way he would take the next plane out. I can't believe he sent you a card and gift. He'll never give up on you! The thing is tho, if you ever wrote or called him you better be sure of it because he'd certainly take you seriously. Why the sudden change in feelings? You actually hated him at one point. Have you seen anyone else?

I knew that Maureen was right. I had to be sure. It just would not be fair to David otherwise. I had confused Maureen about my feelings for David. I had confused Sarah on the Akron Reservoir. Until David's card and the night I was skating on the pond, I had confused even myself. Now the only confusing part was how to find my way back to him.

The longing persisted. Some clear wintery nights I would stand by my window, looking out at the silent beauty of a moonlit night, and the longing would become so strong, it became an ache in my chest. I would imagine David standing next to me, with his arm across my shoulder, both of us looking out at the shadows of the trees on the glistening snow.

Little did I know that on one of those moonlit nights, David was driving slowly by my house—not once, but several times—trying to summon the courage to knock on my door. He, too, felt the longing that the silence of the moonlit night evoked.

When I could no longer stand the ache in my chest, I would turn away from the window. I'd pull the curtain to one side, so my bed would be bathed by the moonlight. I'd curl up under the covers and let the moon shine on me. I would think things like: I've denied my feelings for a year and a half—for what? To live in this community where I will never fit in? But if I decide to leave again, how will I do it? What if David is in a relationship with someone else? Then where will I go? And now I'm gaining so much weight . . .

Ultimately despair would set in, and I would lose confidence in my ability to make the drastic changes required to leave the Amish.

When I shared my feelings with my counselor, Rachael, our sessions took a different turn. Instead of focusing on my bulimia, I was open to talking about possibilities for my future. She pointed out that I was dealing with two different issues: whether or not to stay in my community and whether David and I pursue a relationship. I said I didn't know where I would go or how I would leave without David.

Rachael knew that I dreamed of going to college. I had described to her how I had been handed my eighth-grade diploma, signaling the end of school for the rest of my life. Ever since that time, I had dreamed of continuing my education. It was impossible back then, because at fourteen years old, I was just too young to make it on my own. I could not be Amish and earn a high school or college education.

Rachael encouraged me to consider my options. I was concerned about how I would pay for college. She told me that I could work my way through many of the colleges in the South, because tuition there was a fraction of what it was in the North. I had no idea where to begin to look for colleges, but I liked the possibility of earning a degree. Now that I was twenty-two years old, I could make this choice. Not that it was an easy one, but the dream of going to school still persisted.

At the end of the school year, when the school board president asked me to teach again, I declined. I had secured a job as a tour guide at the Geauga County Historical Society's Century Village in Burton, starting the following week. I would work Tuesday through Saturday, leaving Mondays open to continue my baking.

I had found my two years of teaching rewarding in some ways, but I realized how much I wanted to be a student instead of a teacher. I was seriously thinking about my options for attending college. But before I would look at colleges in the South, I needed to know whether a romance with David was still an option. I decided to take another trip to Vermont.

This time, I would go in the fall, and this time, I would go to see David.

A Little Faith in Plain Country

David Furlong

Where understanding and longing end, it is dark,
but God shines there.
—Meister Eckhart

When I visited "Linda" in her Amish world the first time, I had the opportunity to experience her as Saloma. This was the beginning of a deeper, more profound understanding of her. I was introduced to a complex person in the austere world of the Amish. I felt a stirring in me—like an awakening—and she was in the center of it. Saloma and her Amish grace pulled my heart in deeper than it had been before, yet she was only willing to offer me her friendship. I wanted more. We parted with a handshake, though I had asked for a hug and a kiss.

I had been encouraged by my first visit and thought that I could reconstruct my relationship with Saloma by joining the Amish. I was disillusioned by the dehumanizing nature of industry and its fragmenting effect on communities. The human touch was being replaced by a quick-paced economy based on profit. In my world, time to contemplate was vanishing—replaced by a multitude of distractions, such as the images on television and the bombardment of advertisements for buying yet more material goods. The pace of the modern world seemed manic and scattered.

This life lacked meaning for me, and I longed for something beyond what I could find in a shopping mall. This longing seemed beyond all my perceptions and beyond me. Saloma and her world among the Amish were, for me, a new way of being in the world, where the distractions were stripped away, leaving something more honest about humanity.

Why not move my toy business to Middlefield and live a simpler life? After all, I was making wooden toys because I wanted an honest, creative, and satisfying way to make a living with my hands. The Amish could offer community, peace of mind, and most of all, Saloma.

Except that Saloma had not replied to my last letter. I had to go directly to Joe's place to find her. During the long trip to Ohio, I created my own Amish romance story. Saloma would fall into my arms with joy when I announced that I would join the Amish, and we could live happily ever after. This was the perfect solution!

But then, when I finally found her at the reservoir, Saloma delivered a crushing blow to my Amish fantasy in good order. Gone was the promise of a new life with the Amish. I was too shocked to comprehend the words she was hurling at me.

"So I'll have to spell it out!" she exclaimed.

I wanted to start over, but it was too late. It seemed I had stepped over some line. My heart was beating fast for the wrong reason—every word hitting home with a dread that something was broken and could not be fixed.

"If you can't accept being my friend, then I can't have anything to do with you!" she said.

Shock and then panic set in, quickening my breath.

"Even if you were Amish, I wouldn't want you!"

I tried to control my emotions by slowing my words so I wouldn't blather; other Amish women were watching this spectacle. The hope and joy I had arrived with was replaced by despair. The door was closing, and I tried one last time to save something of our drowning relationship.

"Before I go, may I give you this autograph?" I asked.

When she dropped Bill Monroe's autograph into the water of the reservoir, I felt the door close and the light of her radiance go out.

As I rowed across the reservoir, I was crushed by Saloma's rejection. This was far more painful than the day the Amish contingent came to Vermont to take her back. This time she delivered the rejection herself.

I looked up, and I saw Saloma standing up in the canoe. That's odd—canoes are not meant for standing in, I thought. She was such a mystery—an exquisite mystery. But my mind was too numb to fully comprehend the danger of her situation.

I felt hollowed out, as if I had opened myself up wide to let the light of her fill my being only to be rejected, leaving a void—an emptiness that could not be filled. I felt selfish, having pushed for more than a friendship, though that is what Saloma had offered. This rejection was my fault because of my insensitivity to her situation.

On the way back to Vermont, I pondered Saloma's mystery with the song "One More Night" by Bob Dylan. I could not stop the tears. Even though I had been undone by Linda, I knew I could not forget her. Deep down I just could not believe that she felt nothing for me. I did not let myself believe it.

Saloma had suggested that I could join some other Amish group "if my conviction was real." I wondered about that now. Was my interest that strong without her? Maybe she was right. Maybe I wanted to be Amish to get close to her. I was too hurt to think about it.

Upon my return to Vermont, I buried myself in my work in my basement toy shop. I occasionally visited the YWCA to talk to Maureen, who was corresponding with Saloma. Maureen told me Saloma had her own place, was teaching at an Amish school, attending singings, and was planning a trip to see the Lalancettes sometime the following summer. I was happy for her.

Maureen encouraged me to write. "It couldn't hurt," she said as she gave me Saloma's address.

"You're probably right," I said, although I knew it could hurt. But I sent a Christmas card anyway, thinking I could at least salvage a friendship. I did not get a response.

About a year after the reservoir rejection, I was trying to fix the water pump on my pickup truck and had removed a part when the mail arrived. I read a card from Edith, whom I'd met when I was dating Linda at the Y. The short note informed me that my Amish friend had been visiting for two weeks, and she was leaving to go back to Ohio on the bus on Tuesday at two o'clock in the afternoon. But this was Tuesday, and Saloma was leaving in half an hour!

I quickly put the part back in my truck, slammed down the hood, and drove to downtown Burlington as fast as I dared. I arrived just in time to see the bus pull out of the station. I followed it as it headed south on Shelburne Road. Then I looked at the gauge in my truck and realized it was overheating. I had to give up the chase. What am I going to do if I catch up to the bus? I thought. Saloma hadn't even called me, so she might not want to see me anyway.

Saloma's mystery deepened. I was still under her spell and I couldn't help it.

My interest in the Amish spiritual path lingered as I traveled to sell toys along the East Coast. Several months after Saloma's return to her community, I visited Lancaster, Pennsylvania, on the way home from the Baltimore Winter Market. In those years before the tourist industry boomed, Lancaster was still tranquil, and I could sense that there was a divine quality in the lifestyle of Amish and other plain-living folks there. Yet I told myself that without Saloma, I could never approach it. I felt a deep longing for the relationship she and I once had.

My business in those days dominated my life. I was now working with my brothers, and I had hired neighbors to assemble the toys. I was committed to the business sixty hours a week. Still, I continued to write to Saloma.

Finally, one winter evening after a craft show in Pittsburgh, Pennsylvania, I decided to take a side trip through Burton, Ohio, a slight diversion of 130 miles before heading back to Vermont. Saloma had been on my mind all throughout the show, and 130 miles was as close to her as I had been in two years. With the address Maureen had given me and knowing Saloma was living in her own house, I couldn't avoid the temptation to just drive by her place. As I circled the little town square of Burton, I began to feel her presence. Just another mile now—I was close. The night was clear and cold, like so many nights when Saloma and I sat in the parlor of the Y.

All was quiet in Plain country, and it felt to me that the solitude and silence were beckoning me. Where would Saloma be at nine o'clock on a Sunday night? Home in her little place most likely. Suddenly, I was there. I saw the number on the mailbox and a small house attached to a larger one. This was it! A hundred butterflies fluttered within. I passed by in my Datsun pickup truck, pulling a trailer with my display train engine on it. I thought I saw a light in the window. I turned the truck around and passed by again. The longing to see Saloma was so powerful that it became an ache in my chest. She was not even fifty feet away.

There was no way to pull into the driveway without the people in the big house noticing. Saloma would hate me if I made yet another scene. I was thinking there was no way to see her alone and that I could not take another rejection. Hadn't she told me on the reservoir that I was "not even a friend"? I felt that hollowness creeping in and wondered what I was doing here. I slowly accelerated the truck and kept on going. The fields along the Burton Windsor Road were bathed by the moonlight that reflected off the freshly fallen snow.

It was a long trip back to Vermont, but I did not despair. I resolved to send Saloma another Christmas card and gift and let her know I'd not forgotten her. The outcome of our relationship was not up to me but in the hands of a higher power. I needed a little faith.

Part 3

~ 23 ~

A Birthday Gift

At times our own light goes out and is rekindled by a spark from another person. Each of us has cause to think with deep gratitude of those who have lighted the flame within us.
—Albert Schweitzer

My birthday in 1980 was a summer day like many others. I had just walked back home from my job as a tour guide at the Century Village in Burton. When I walked into my kitchen, I saw mail on the table. Gertie Troyer would have brought it over from our shared mailbox.

As I put my purse on a chair, I noticed birthday cards from several cousins: two from Wisconsin; one from Conewango Valley, New York; and several from cousins living in the area. I flipped through them, recognizing the return addresses. Then my heart skipped a beat when I saw familiar handwriting, with capital letters printed on a bright green envelope. My heart quickened as I opened the envelope and saw the carefully chosen card. There was a photo of a dirt road, curving through a green field with a wooded hillside beyond it. Some trees had a tinge of autumn colors, hinting the end of summer. It was unmistakably a Vermont scene. At the top of the card, there was a single line, "Wishing Life's Best For You."

I opened it and read in David's handwriting,

Dear Saloma,

Happy Birthday! It is not hard to remember your birthday since it is the day after mine. Whenever June comes around I find myself thinking of you.

Are you coming to Vermont this summer? If you do manage a visit, you are welcome to stop over and see me. Bring along anyone you may be traveling with. It would be nice to see you again and I have so much to talk about.

I often gave tours to school groups when I worked at the Century Village in Burton.

Saloma, if you are unable to visit Burlington this summer, then you must write and tell me how things are going in Ohio. I do enjoy hearing from you.

Your friend,
David

I was thrilled! How does he find these cards, anyway? I thought. And this time he wrote something personal, so he must still be thinking of me. Does that mean he doesn't have another girlfriend?

I pulled out a chair and sat down. I read the card again, this time savoring every word. It was clear and to the point. David still wants to hear from me, I thought. This time I will respond with a nice card. What do I have to lose? I have one foot out of the community already. It is only a matter of when and how. Why not leave for David?

Then I chided myself for not taking this one step at a time. Just because David was writing to me did not mean he was still interested in me. The rejection I had meted out to him two years before now seemed eons ago. I wondered if it felt that way to David.

I heard someone coming down the steps into the washhouse in the house next door. I quickly stuffed the card into my purse and picked up another card off the table. I was opening it when Rhoda Troyer walked through the kitchen door.

"Wow, you've gotten lots of cards for your birthday," she said.

"One of these is a circle letter."

"Still, you've been getting lots of cards."

"Yes, I have. I feel blessed to have so many friends who remember to send me cards."

I sensed that Rhoda had seen the bright green envelope with David's return address on it and was hoping I'd bring it up. Instead, I asked what she was up to and would she want to play Frisbee out in the field after supper.

~◦⁂◦~

That evening in my bedroom, I thought about the implications of hearing from David. I couldn't believe he would want me back after the way I rejected him. I allowed myself to drift into that place between dreaming and wakefulness and recalled what it was like to cook the first meal for David at the Burlington YWCA.

That February night in 1978, he had arrived with his cheeks red from the cold and he smelled of fresh air. As I smiled and took his coat, he smiled back. Our hands touched when I took his coat, though he did not kiss me. I guessed he was waiting until later that night, when we would most likely sit in the parlor.

When we sat at the table with steaming bowls of food, there was an awkward moment. David asked, "Do the Amish say a prayer before meals?"

"Yes, we had silent prayer before and after meals."

"Do you want to say a prayer?"

"No, just dig in," I said.

David looked amused. "Okay."

As David and I served ourselves healthy portions of Amish wedding-style oven-baked chicken, mashed potatoes and gravy, fried carrots, and salad, David remarked that he'd never had apples in salad before.

"It's called Waldorf salad. We used to make it quite a bit in the fall when my father worked at an orchard. He used to bring home bushels of apples, and this was one way of using them."

David and I talked about gardening, home canning, and other family activities.

As we talked, I was glad he had worn his contact lenses; the lenses on his glasses were thick, which obscured his beautiful, expressive blue eyes. He had a high forehead with hair that was neither blond nor dark but somewhere in-between, and he wore sideburns. That Friday night, he wore a blue shirt over a black turtleneck. I loved his wide, prominent shoulders and his broad chest. He was clearly in good physical shape.

After dessert and mint tea, David helped me with the dishes. It felt like we were already a married couple, with him drying the dishes as I washed. After we were done, I invited him to go sit in the parlor with me. I closed all the doors and sat down next to him on the couch. He looked at me and said, "That was a nice meal you made. Thanks."

"You're welcome."

David moved closer to me and put his arm around me. With his other hand, he took my glasses off and put them on the end table. Then he traced my nose with his fingertip. He said he loved my nose. My family members had always teased me about my "pug nose," and now it seemed that was one of the things David liked about my looks. I looked into the depth of his ocean blue eyes and felt lost. Our lips came together, and we started another blissful evening of *schmunzling* in the parlor.

David considered joining the Amish at several points in our relationship.

I loved the way his voice sounded with my ear on his chest: deep and resonant, like I could hear the source of his voice. We also enjoyed one another's company in silence. When he wasn't talking, I could hear his heart beating in his chest. We were in this relaxed position when David said, "If you went back to the Amish, I would follow you."

I sat bolt upright and said, "Oh, no! You can't do that! They would never let you!"

David looked surprised. Then he said quietly, "If you didn't let me know you were going back, I would follow you."

"You don't understand. If I go back, everything changes—I mean everything! How I dress, who I date, what I do for work . . ."

"That sounds hard. Can you be yourself?"

"Not really. That's what makes my decision so hard."

"I can understand that." David fell silent, and so did I. Then I settled back into that comfortable place underneath his arm, where time stood still.

Now, as I lay in bed more than two years later, my arms ached with longing to embrace David again. After all this time, he was still writing to me. It dawned on me that this could be an answer to my prayer for God to show me the way if David and I were meant to be together. Yet all my life I've been told that I have to stay Amish because I was born Amish, I thought. Now I'm bound by the vows I made when I was baptized—that I will stay with the church the rest of my days. Do I dare to believe that God is show-ing me the way out of the Amish? David seems to be willing to join the Amish, but do I even want him to?

Even before I asked the question, I knew the answer. I was already thinking of leaving the Amish, so why would I want David to join the Amish? Before I drifted under the comfortable blanket of sleep, I prayed for the courage to change the course of my life. I did not yet know the details, but David's card gave me the conviction and the clarity that I would not be confined by Amish strictures my whole life long.

⁓❀⁓

The next day, I walked to the drugstore during my lunch hour and browsed the card section. I was wishing I had David's knack for finding the right card for the occasion. I finally chose a Helen Steiner Rice card, and wrote a short message:

Dear David,

Happy Birthday! Sorry I'm late, but to be truthful, I forgot. This has got to be short, but I want to write a long letter soon.

Last summer I spent my birthday on top of Mt. Mansfield. Sis Sarah and I were in Vermont for two weeks.

Yes, I do plan on coming to Vermont, but in the fall this time. I might see you then.

A friend,
Saloma Miller

P.S. Hope you had a nice birthday! I did. Loved your beautiful card!

I am embarrassed now that I was so blunt. I not only confessed to forgetting David's birthday but also mentioned that I had been in Vermont. But David's faithfulness did not waver. The longer letter I wrote to David a week later has been lost, but David's response to it, dated in late July, survived and was full of affirming comments.

I'm glad you have a new job that allows you to meet people. You are good with people so the job seems right and you probably needed a change. Your letter was very informative.

Things sound good with your family and your living situation. I'm sorry to hear about your weight problem and the pain it causes you. However I know you have the willpower to do what you want. I could stand to lose some weight myself. The trick for me is to stay occupied with activities one right after the other. Saloma, I believe in you and your ability to do things. Good luck!

I wondered if David would still believe in me if he knew about my disordered eating. I wouldn't dare tell him. I was too deeply ashamed. He had no way of knowing that my weight gain came from my pact with myself to digest the food I was eating rather than purging myself. Now I had to establish healthy eating habits and stay active, as David had suggested.

How are your plans going with your visit? The foliage peaks at different times in different areas around New England. I believe it peaks in Vermont in early October.

This summer I hope to do a little traveling on my own. I would like to visit Nova Scotia. On the East Coast of Canada. People tell me it reminds them of Scotland and parts of the British Isles. Later this year or next I would like to visit England. I have a friend in London who has invited me over for a visit.

I worried as I read the letter that the woman David had been seeing at the Y was the friend in London he wanted to visit. Why hadn't he pursued that relationship instead of writing to me? But if we were meant to be together, then the woman in England was not an issue. The conversational tone of David's letter gave me a longing to sit and talk with him for a long time. I missed his presence, his smell, his voice, his laughter, and his eyes searching mine. Most of all, I missed his touch.

~24~

Linda's Day in the Sun

To dare is to lose one's footing momentarily.
To not dare is to lose oneself.
—Søren Kierkegaard

There were several times in my young adult life when I seemed to tempt fate. It happened when I stood up and rocked the canoe on the Akron Reservoir. Another was when I rode the snowmobile with Maureen in Peacham, Vermont. Now, as I began corresponding with David, I began a new phase of reckless behavior. And I began taunting the bishop by finding loopholes in the *Ordnung*.

In my home community, people would often take trips to other places. When they were away, they could get away with doing things that weren't allowed at home, such as bicycling, posing for photos, or watching television.

Ever since living on my own, I wanted in the worst way to own and use a bicycle. I thought it was crazy that I could hire van drivers to take me places but that I couldn't get there under my own steam. I had never learned to ride a bicycle as a child, but I sure would have liked to learn.

I must have mentioned this to my colleague Ann at the museum. She offered me the use of the bike she'd had since she was ten. Though I knew that the bishop's family lived just up the road, I decided to accept. Lena and Rhoda Troyer were allowed to ride bicycles when they lived in Michigan, and Gertie and Will didn't seem to care.

So for several evenings in a row, I practiced on the paved driveway, starting at the top where there was a slight downhill grade. I scraped my knees several times, but I did not quit. On the fourth night, I started at the top of the driveway, got some momentum, and the bike picked up speed. I forgot the bike had the kind of brakes in which I had to reverse the pedals. I realized I was going to crash somewhere and I started crying out, "Wooooooooooouuuu!" I didn't want to crash into the barn at the bottom of the driveway, so I steered left, into the cornfield. The cornstalks broke my fall, and I landed in the dirt between the rows.

I picked myself up and then my bike and steered it out of the cornfield. There stood Will, Gertie, and Rhoda, all laughing heartily. Will had a ready laugh, but in all the time I'd known him, I'd never heard him laughing so hard. I stood at the edge of the cornfield looking at them and said grumpily, "What's so funny?" That brought more gales of laughter so contagious that I had no choice other than to join in.

Once I learned to stay on those two wheels, using the bike to go places was too much of a temptation and I couldn't resist. I would ride most of the way to my parents' house and then leave the bike just up the road in the woods. To ride back from Burton was a dilemma. I could either coast down a big hill on my bike, right past the bishop's house, or I could ride three or four extra miles to go the roundabout way. What a thrill it was to coast down hills on the bike, with the wind rushing past my ears and butterflies in my stomach.

One day I dared to take the more direct route. I hoped that no one in the bishop's house was looking toward the road when I went by. After all, they lived up a long lane, behind the schoolhouse. But the bishop's oldest daughter lived close to the road with her family. So I started at the top of the hill and let myself pick up momentum. It was a miracle my dress didn't get caught in the wheels as I skimmed down the hill. As I sped past the bishop's daughter's house, I saw her walk up to the window with a towel and pretend she was cleaning the window. She's not very good at pretending, I thought to myself, chuckling. She may as well have stood by the door and gaped.

~❀~

I was planning a trip to Cook Forest in Pennsylvania in August along with six other young women, including my sister Lizzie and the Troyer sisters. All the others, except for Lizzie, knew how to ride a bicycle, and I didn't want to be left out of that activity. We had hired a van driver to take us to a cabin in Clarion, Pennsylvania. Joe, the driver, kept us entertained all the way. He was many of the young women's favorite driver. Ever since he had tried to make a secret rendezvous with me, however, I made sure I was never alone with him. But for now, it was about vacation and fun, and there was no harm in joking our way to Cook Forest.

We settled into our rooms, two per bed, for the next eight days. We had a honeymoon phase of the trip, when all seven of us got along well. One young woman, Carol, assumed the leadership role. And as Amish women, we were programmed to follow the leader. I was developing an independent streak, and I didn't always want to play that game, either as the follower or the leader.

One day we were all on a bike ride when we came to a crossroads. Carol wanted to take a dirt trail that led through the woods, and I wanted to stay with the gravel roads. All seven of us sat at the crossroads, debating. Carol kept saying we should all stay together. She also kept saying she wanted to take a left. I stated clearly that I didn't want to go that way. I suggested we go in two separate directions, with each one choosing the way she wanted to go. The decision no longer had to do with which direction we were going to go; it had to do with popularity. By choosing left, some would be choosing Carol. By choosing to go the other way, people would be choosing me. We were at a standoff.

All of a sudden, Linda, who was usually the quiet one, said, "Let's just go!" and she took off on her bike in the direction I had advocated. I followed, not caring a hoot which way the others chose. They ended up all following Linda and me. Later, I had to deal with the undercurrent of resentment from Carol and her friend Miriam. They were used to being treated as the popular girls—the ones we should all want to follow. I was tired of playing the game.

I was rebelling against what I *didn't* want, but I didn't yet know what I did want.

~∙❁∙~

One day during our stay at the cabin in Pennsylvania, I found a private space, sitting by a waterfall, with time to answer a letter from David. I described several recent events including our adventures in Pennsylvania, my sister's relationship with the Yankee man she was dating, and my upcoming plans for my New England trip. Then I changed the subject and wrote what was on my mind:

> *David, have you ever wondered why I wouldn't have anything to do with you at one time? I've asked myself many times, why? I've been seeing a counselor about my weight and I talked to her about our relationship. She helped me understand my feelings. Remember how I became angry when you came out to see me on the Akron Reservoir? I think that stemmed back to when I was still in Vermont. Do you remember how I said I don't like us to be together so much? So you said you would call from then on. A few times when you called I didn't feel like seeing you, frankly, but I didn't tell you because I didn't want to hurt your feelings. I have since learned that doesn't work, because you end up getting angry. That's what happened when you came out to see me without me having anything to say about it. Besides all that, I was under much pressure as I was adjusting to things back home. I knew I had to make a decision about our relationship, but I felt pushed from both sides. All of a sudden I felt like I had no control over that when you showed up. Also, when we were together, I felt something for you, I'll admit. Some of it, I'm convinced, was infatuation. Now, when I think of you, it's more on a level-headed basis. I appreciate the person you are, and I am glad I knew your friendship. It took me a while to get over that feeling*

I had when you came here. I couldn't yet face you last summer, but my feelings started changing some time ago. Now, when I come to visit, I'll be ready to see you. I appreciate your patience and the fact that you didn't push anything for so long.

Before I signed off, I mentioned that we would probably go canoeing on the Clarion River and that there was a doe with two fawns grazing outside our cabin. I wrote that I looked forward to hearing back from David and signed it, "Your friend, Saloma."

I walked to the gift shop and bought postcards to send in the letter to David and mailed it at the post office. When I joined the others back at the cabin for supper, I felt like I had stepped out and had a visit with David. It was my own little secret.

❧❀❧

Before leaving home for the trip, I had borrowed a bathing suit from my sister Susan. It was homemade and very utilitarian. One day, when the sun finally came out, I decided I would use it.

One of the activities in the area was inner tubing. I hired someone to drive me several miles upriver, paid for the ride and the inner tube, and then walked down by the water, ready to go in. But first I took the pins out of my dress and stripped down to my bathing suit. I floated down the Clarion River toward the center of town. As the sun bathed my bare skin, I felt daring. Since I knew that bathing suits were not allowed in the community, I wondered what had gotten into me. A year ago I was trying so hard to fit in to the community. I knew the girls on the trip would go back to the community and talk about me behind my back, but I didn't care anymore. It was as if the person I had become in Vermont was emerging again. As I slowly floated down the Clarion, I felt more like Linda in Vermont than Saloma in Ohio. Like the kingfishers along the way, I felt at peace with myself and the natural world.

I saw Amish dresses go by on bicycles and I wondered which of the girls they belonged to. I hoped they didn't see me, but there was no hiding from them, so I continued on my merry way, floating along on the current.

Lena and another one of the women, Miriam, had gone down the Clarion in tubes the day before. They did it the "proper" way by wearing their Amish dresses, but that didn't help them when they got themselves into trouble. Just when they were trying to steer toward shore, they were swept away by the current. They floated under the bridge toward the rapids before they got their bearings and found their way back to shore. When I neared the place where I was to get off, I hugged the shore and used my arms to paddle to where I wanted to be. I quickly got dressed and hauled the inner tube back to where it needed to go.

That night Rhoda began crying and couldn't stop. After some discussion with the group, Lena called her parents, Gertie and Will, who hired a van driver to bring them to Pennsylvania and take Rhoda home. When they arrived at the cabin, Gertie was stiff-backed and seemed miffed, only saying a few curt words. Will walked up to Rhoda and laid his arm across her shoulders in a caring way. I rarely saw anyone showing affection in the community, so I was surprised. Rhoda continued crying as she gathered her things to return home.

On one of our last days in Cook Forest, Lizzie decided she wanted to go down the river in an inner tube and that she wanted me to come with her. I had done it the day before without too much effort, so I accompanied her. We were wearing our Amish dresses, and all was well until we neared the landing place. Lizzie was ahead of me, and she was headed in the right direction. Then a current caught her inner tube, and she started heading toward the bridge. I was just about to touch shore, when Lizzie panicked and started yelling, "Saloma, you have to *help me*! I'm going to DROWN!"

I tried reasoning with her, "But how am I going to help you? I can't catch you!"

Lizzie was swiftly moving toward the bridge, all the while screaming, "Saloma, you have to HELP ME!"

I paddled out into the river and got caught by the same current. I looked down and realized how deep the water was. Neither Lizzie nor I could swim. We saw several people up on a hill near a house, and Lizzie called out to them, "HELP, WE CAN'T SWIM! HELP US!" In my desperation, I also called for help.

Someone on shore called back, "GET OUT OF YOUR INNER TUBES!"

"BUT WE CAN'T SWIM!"

"YOU CAN TOUCH BOTTOM!"

In my panic, I didn't check to determine if the person was right. But as soon as I was in the water, I knew I was in trouble. The bottom was far below my feet, and my dress was acting as a sail in the current. In my panic, my arms grabbed upward, and they circled right around the inner tube. I hung on for dear life, even as I floated under the bridge and toward the rocks down the river. I kept trying to use my legs to paddle toward the shore, but my dress was the sail that determined the direction—right into the middle of the river into the swiftest part of the current.

I called out to Lizzie, and she called back. At least she was alive! Now how would we find our way to shore?

As I struggled in the water, I kept thinking, *As long as I hang on to this inner tube, sooner or later my legs will hit bottom.* But I also didn't want to get dashed against the rocks.

I kept calling out to Lizzie, and she kept calling back. Then all at once she got quiet. I screamed and screamed her name, at the same time that my feet were hitting something down below. Finally, I found my way up onto a big rock and pulled the inner tube with me. I stood up and yelled, "LIZZIE, CAN YOU HEAR ME???!!!"

"I'm right here," she said, stepping from behind bushes on the shore, right close by.

"You scared me! Why didn't you answer me?"

"Oh, Saloma, I just couldn't," she said in her most dramatic and put-upon voice.

"How long have you been on shore? Do you think you could have told me how you made it?" I asked incredulously.

She just repeated what she had said before. I felt like pushing Lizzie really hard, just when we should have been hugging one another for the joy of having survived. We were both sopping wet and shaking. I felt like my legs couldn't hold me, so I sat down on the big rock and cried out of sheer relief. I did not want to think about what could have happened. Instead I wanted to kiss the rock I was sitting on.

Eventually Lizzie and I found our way to the shore of the Clarion River and walked back to the place where we meant to get off, dropped off the inner tubes, and then sloshed back to the cabin for a hot shower.

⁓⸎❀⸎⁓

On Saturday morning, back in my little house in Ohio, with my windows open to catch the summer breezes, I overheard an argument between Will and Gertie. I heard Will saying, "You can't blame that on her."

"Well, floating down the river in a bathing suit is not fit for an Amish person! How is Rhoda supposed to react to something like that?"

Then it dawned on me that Rhoda must have caught sight of me on the river. Perhaps it had triggered something to start her downward spiral into an episode of anxiety, related to her mental illness. I thought I should feel shame. If I had overheard that conversation a year ago, I would have been crushed. But for some reason, I did not feel shame or hurt. Later that day, Lena confirmed that Rhoda became disturbed when she caught sight of me in my swimsuit.

The Amish way to look at what happened in Cook Forest when I nearly drowned was to believe God had punished me to remind me that he could end my life at any time. I could just hear someone ask in a grave voice, "Do you think you would have been ready?" This implied that the only way to "be ready" for death is to be at peace with one's Amish life and be ready to face God with a clear conscience.

My honest answer would have been, "No, I am not ready to die," but not because I wore a bathing suit or for any of the other reasons inferred in such a question. My brush with death made me realize that I had not yet fulfilled the purpose for having been born on this earth. There were so many ways in which I had to choose between who I was by nature and conforming to the Amish ways. Had I died, my twenty-three years of life would have had no meaning—except for the four months I was free to be myself. Now I had to find my way back to that person. I had a hunch that it had something to do with reconnecting with David.

~ 25 ~

A Rendezvous

Good night, good night! Parting is such sweet sorrow,
That I shall say good night till it be morrow.
—William Shakespeare, *Romeo and Juliet*

At work, my supervisor came and told me that there was someone on the phone for me. My heart skipped a beat when I heard David's voice. "Hi Saloma," he said. "I'm at my grandmother's house, picking up furniture, so I thought I'd give you a call."

My heart fluttered when I realized that could mean David was close by. I asked, "Where does your grandmother live?"

"Cleveland. I told you that, didn't I?"

"Oh, yes, I remember now. So are you coming out this way?"

"If you'd like me to."

"I'd have to sneak out, otherwise someone might find out."

"Should we meet somewhere?"

We decided to meet at Belle's Restaurant in Burton, at seven o'clock. Then I said, "David, I have to warn you that I look different than last time we saw one another. I've gained thirty-five pounds."

"That's okay," David said in a way that sounded like he was trying to convince both of us. "So, I'll see you at seven," David said, excitement in his voice.

Back home that evening, I told the Troyers that I was going to go across the street to visit Ada, a widow, and then walk to my parents' house and stay overnight for church the next day. I did go visit Ada, but instead of walking to my parents' house, I headed in the opposite direction up the hill toward Burton for the second time that day. I arrived at Belle's early and sat at a table right inside the door. I was uncomfortable in my own skin. I wished I could shed all thirty-five pounds right then and there. I wanted to look like the person David used to know. But I had changed, and that was all there was to it.

There were several Amish men in the restaurant. I worried that they would notice me meeting with David. I would ask David to go over to the Century Inn across the street as soon as he arrived.

I was trying to remember what David looked like when I saw him come around the corner. He was wearing a white shirt with the sleeves rolled up and a pair of light-colored pants. I shook his hand and said, "Let's go across the street." As I led the way, I told David that I didn't want the Amish men seeing us together.

At Century Inn, we kept looking at each other from across the table. David had a pleased smile on his face. He ordered a bowl of soup and I talked with him while he ate. I was famished, but I was determined to start now to reverse the weight gain. So I stayed famished. We talked about his grandmother's transition into a nursing home. He and his father had come to take furniture to Vermont with them. They were staying with his sister, Bernadette.

David said, "What about you? Did you just get back from Cook Forest?"

"Just this morning, as a matter of fact."

"So I almost missed seeing you."

"But here we are," I said cheerily.

David laughed, his blue eyes dancing. "How was your trip?"

"Pretty good, mostly. Until yesterday, when my sister Lizzie and I almost drowned."

David interrupted a swallow of soup. "What do you mean you almost drowned?"

As I told David the whole story, he stopped eating to listen. His face clouded over with concern several times and then looked relieved when I described what it was like to finally have solid rock underneath me.

"So you never learned to swim?"

"No. Amish girls aren't allowed to wear bathing suits. A lot of Amish boys swim, but we can't swim too well in dresses."

David thought for a moment. Then he said, "You know that day on the reservoir when you were canoeing?"

"Oh, David, I feel so bad about that now. I was so mean to you that day. I can't believe you ever wrote to me again after that."

"I got over it. But that's not what I was going to say."

"Oh. What were you going to say?"

"Did you stand up in your canoe that day?"

I could feel my face turning red with shame. "Yes, I did."

"Why?"

"I felt so bad when I saw you rowing away. I thought I might never see you again. My feelings were all mixed up inside, and I think I was beside myself."

David's eyes searched mine. "I know I put you in a hard place that day, and I'm sorry."

"It wasn't just you. I was living at Joe's place at the time, and I was getting a lot of pressure to end the relationship with you. I was so confused that I didn't know what I wanted. And then you showed up."

"I appreciated the letter I got from you just the other day. You described your feelings in such a way that I could understand where you were coming from. There was one word I would have changed, though. I don't think *infatuation* is what I felt when we were together. I would say *attraction*, but not *infatuation*."

"You're right. *Attraction* is a better word."

"You said your feelings started changing some time ago. Was there something in particular that caused the change?"

I told David about the night on the pond under the stars and the moonlit nights the winter before, and the longing I felt whenever I looked out at the moonlight.

"I know the feeling you're talking about," David said.

Our waitress came to take David's money, and we realized that the restaurant was about to close. Neither of us was done talking—we were just getting started. David suggested we take a ride in his truck.

Outside, David said, "Speaking of moonlit nights!" A full moon had come over the horizon and now seemed caught in the branches of one of the maple trees across the street. He unlocked the door of his truck, got in, and unlocked the door on the passenger side. I got in and noticed that there was a pile of papers on the seat between us. Maybe it's just as well, I thought.

We drove around the area and talked for hours. I told David my Amish woes: about the tensions between the bishop and me; about how I just could not fit into the community, no matter how hard I tried; that I'd had only a few dates since my return to the community; and how I had come to recognize that it just didn't matter to me anymore that I couldn't fit in.

This photograph represents the era of my life when I was Amish and David was not.

We left David's truck at the legion hall about a mile from my house and walked down the hill to the house. We walked in companionable silence. I pointed out the schoolhouse where I had taught, visible in the clear moonlight. I whispered that the bishop lived right behind the schoolhouse and that his daughter lived in the house we were passing. We became quiet near my house as I showed David where I lived.

I decided I wanted to walk barefoot, so I took my shoes off and put them into the ditch across the street from my house. Then we walked back up the hill to the truck.

We were still not ready to say goodbye, and so we decided to go for another ride. David drove around the area, and then he stopped the truck on a dirt road, with the moon bathing the fields around us. We rolled down the windows and heard the crickets, but otherwise the night was quiet. We sat there a long time, talking—about old times, about developments in our lives since we'd last seen one another, and about my weight problem. All the suggestions David made I'd already tried. I didn't tell him that I was trying to kick my bulimia habit. I was too deeply ashamed.

Several times I had the urge to move over into the middle of the seat, but that pile of papers was there. Around two o'clock in the morning, David said he should get back to Bernadette's, and I said I had to go to church the next day. So David drove toward my house—and then kept on going. He pulled over to the side of the road and said, "Before I go, I'm going to steal something from you." Before I had time to react, he leaned over and kissed me—a soft and sweet David kiss.

David moved the gearshift, turned the pickup around, took off up the hill with a pleased grin on his face, and said, "And they drove off into the moonlit night!" I laughed out of sheer delight of the kiss and David's romantic streak. I knew no matter what happened in our relationship, it was a night we would both remember.

Just before David dropped me off, I said that I hoped we could see one another in New England. "When are you coming?" David asked.

"I'll be traveling between October fifth and nineteenth."

"My sister Claire is getting married on October eleventh. You should come to her wedding."

"Really?"

"Sure. I'll ask her to invite you. It would mean a lot to me."

David had stopped the truck to let me out. I hopped out and then reached over and touched David's arm. He leaned over and kissed me again—a lingering one. Then I closed the door of the truck, and he drove up the hill toward Burton. I waited until his truck disappeared up over the hill and I could no longer hear the tires on the pavement. Then I found my shoes and quietly entered my house through the back door.

I was walking on air. My feelings for David were real. After this night, I would never be able to deny them again. I undressed, pulled back the curtain to let the moon shine onto my bed, and slid between the fresh-smelling sheets. I curled up into my comfortable sleeping position and remembered the kiss David had "stolen" from me. Lying there in the bright moonlight, I wondered whether it was possible to fall asleep with a smile on my face.

~ 26 ~

Moonlight in Vermont

*Your vision will become clear only when you can look into
your own heart.*
—Carl Jung

The next morning, church was being held at my parents' house.
I heard hardly a word of either of the sermons. My mind
drifted to the night before and I relived the evening, one exquisite
moment at a time. I could no longer discount the feelings I had
for David. And here I was, attending an Amish church service—at
least in body. My mind was somewhere else completely. My life
felt like a lie.

After the service, several people asked me about our trip to
Cook Forest. I said we had fun, and I focused on the deer that
grazed near the cabin and what it was like to walk through a virgin pine forest. I knew they wanted me to talk about getting swept
down the river and admit to having done "unseemly" things. But I
felt completely removed from the power these kinds of questions
used to have on me.

❖

My life after David's visit became focused on one thing: my trip
to New England. I had to be careful about who I talked to among
the Amish, because I was getting resistance about traveling alone.
Rumors that I wouldn't return abounded. But that did not stop me
from talking with Yankee people. One day the Andersons, whom
I had met while visiting the Groths, were visiting the Troyers, and

I brought them over to show them my quilt project. Pat oohed and aahed over my tiny quilt stitches, which made me feel proud.

Then, partly because I liked John and Pat and partly because they were a new audience, I told them about my plans for traveling to New England. I voiced my reservations about going through New York City on the bus. "You should come and visit us!" John said. "We live in Short Hills, New Jersey, right outside New York City. I can meet you at the bus station, and you can stay with us for a few days."

"Really? I wouldn't want to be a bother."

"You would not be a bother at all. We'd love to have you visit us!" Pat joined in and added her welcome, and so I decided to accept their offer. Perhaps they were just the guardian angels I had been praying for to watch over me as I traveled.

~ ❀ ~

I wrote out my plans for my trip to Barbara in detail, explaining that David had invited me to his sister's wedding. But in this letter, I also told about trouble brewing in my family.

A few months ago, Sarah and Susan moved to an apartment with a friend, Marie. Susan had just turned twenty, so she started keeping her own money. That's the age most young people start to keep their money, but not so in our family. Through the church, Dad has managed to have Susan move back, so he could have her money again. I think that's pretty sneaky, because he didn't make this a money issue until he was sure she was moving home.

Sarah has gotten herself into something too. She had a landscaping job and used to ride back and forth with this Yankee guy. They fell in love with each other and he is planning on joining the Amish. I am not too fond of him or their relationship, to be honest. He is very possessive of Sarah, even to the extent of Sarah not being able to spend time with the family when he's around, without him feeling jealous. He is a childish person. Sarah doesn't seem like my sister anymore. She seems to be living in a dream world and seldom the happy Sarah.

At the same time I was writing this to Barbara, I was holding my secret rendezvous with David on the moonlit August night close to my heart. Whenever I would feel particularly judgmental of Sarah and her boyfriend's relationship, I would examine my relationship with David and wonder if theirs should be a cautionary tale for me. Then I would remind myself that there was a world of difference between Sarah's boyfriend and David. The fact that they were both Yankees didn't mean anything.

⁓⚜⁓

In a letter to David dated September 5, 1980, I laid out my plans for my trip, and then I went into great detail about the resistance I was getting from people in the community for me taking the trip alone. Then I wrote about our relationship:

So far I've been safe about your visit. It almost doesn't seem possible that it happened. It seems as if I dreamed it. I did enjoy talking with you again, and believe me you were an encouragement to me. Not only about my weight, but about life. Sometimes I feel life has no meaning. I haven't been feeling that way since your visit. My trip has plenty to do with that too. I enjoyed your visit and thanks for a nice time. The night was beautiful.

We've been having gorgeous sunsets this last while. Last night I went down to the pasture in the back to get a better view. I wish you could have seen it. I feel so close to our Maker whenever I see something so awesome. I also hope to see some beautiful sunsets over the mountains when I come to Vermont. In the fall they are always more so. I think this trip is about the most important thing to me. It'll be the best thing that has happened to me in a long time.

I don't know whether to say I'm doing well or not as far as losing weight is concerned. I've lost a few more pounds since you were here, but somehow it doesn't seem as important to me. Maybe there are more important things in my life right now.

I ended the letter with a poem I found inspirational and then signed off as "Your friend, Saloma."

Then things began to unravel in my family. My assigned role had always been to "fix" things. Like the spring before, when someone had cheated *Mem* and *Datt* out of money for their maple syrup. Every spring they sold their syrup to a place called the Burton Log Cabin, which was a retail outlet for maple products. One day when I had gone home to help with sugaring, I found *Mem* in the sugarhouse, stewing about how they'd been wronged. She said that the head honcho at the Log Cabin had claimed that the first syrup *Datt* had brought in to sell was "number one" grade rather than "fancy" grade. *Mem* and *Datt* both knew better. Their syrup was always the lightest around, and this was the first syrup of the season. In fact, it was some of the lightest they'd ever made. The difference in price was substantial, especially because *Datt* had brought in quite a bit of it.

Mem was so angry, she said, "Oh, I could just!" and she gave two hard yanks with her hand. I got the picture. "A lot of good that would do," I said. "Why don't you say something? Take a sample of syrup in and tell them you know it was fancy!"

"No, *Datt* would never do that."

"Then why don't *you*? Both of you work hard at this. Why should he get away with slighting you out of what you deserve?"

Mem said she wouldn't say anything.

That's where I should have left it. But it went against every grain in my body, and I couldn't resist. I asked, "Do you want me to say something?"

Mem looked hopeful. "Let's ask *Datt* when he comes in with a load of sap."

Datt got a pleased grin on his face when we asked him. So I asked for details. When did *Datt* deliver the syrup, and how many pounds were there?

Then I did call the manager. He said we should bring in a sample and he would take a look at it.

I reported back to *Mem* and *Datt* what they had to do. As soon as the run of syrup was over, *Datt* and I drove up to Burton in the horse and buggy. When we arrived at the Log Cabin, I asked *Datt* if he was coming in with me, and he said he didn't think so. So I walked into the Log Cabin by myself. The manager looked at me. I'd known him since I was a little girl; he and his wife used to buy eggs from us. I held out the sample and started telling him that I was here for Katie and Simon Miller.

"We already know. You're right, it was fancy."

I wanted to throw the bottle at him. It seemed to me that he had asked us to go through the trouble of bringing in the sample—thinking we wouldn't—so he would get away with the cheat.

"So, are you going to pay the difference?" I asked bluntly.

"Yes, we'll include it in their next check," he said.

I looked at him straight in the eye. I thought about saying I didn't trust he would and that he should pay up right now, but I figured my look conveyed that. So I put the sample in my pocket.

"Okay, make sure you do," I said. I turned and left.

Datt was waiting eagerly to find out what happened. When I told him, he got a toothless grin from ear to ear and said, *"Lomie, ich bin so froh es du epas tzott hosht. Denke!"* (Saloma, I am so glad that you said something. Thank you!) He said he should pay for what I'd done as he untied the horse's head and climbed onto the buggy. I told him he didn't need to pay me. It never seemed to occur to *Datt* that he could learn how to speak up for himself and that you don't get what you need unless you ask.

I knew *Datt* appreciated what I'd done, because I never heard him thank anyone as much as he thanked me that day. On the ride home, he was happier than I'd seen him in a long time. Over the years to come, he would continue to bring it up by saying, "I'll never forget what you did for me at the Log Cabin in Burton."

At least I had been able to effect a change in the case of the maple syrup. The family troubles that were cropping up as I was thinking of leaving were a whole different story.

My family members often showed up at my house when they had a problem they didn't know how to handle. Except for Joe. He and I had our differences, and it was most comfortable for both of us to keep our distance from one another. One night, Susan and Sarah asked me to go for a walk with them because they had something to tell me. They said they didn't want the Troyers coming over in the middle of it.

Once we were out of hearing distance of the Troyers, they announced to me that Sarah was pregnant. I was quiet for a long moment. I had seen this one coming. Sarah's boyfriend was making a great show of becoming Amish. That meant that he could date Sarah in bed. Not having been taught proper bed courtship etiquette, as most Amish men had been, I thought he was likely having his way with Sarah. That this resulted in a pregnancy came as no surprise to me.

"We knew you would find out sooner or later," Sarah said, "so we thought we'd tell you." This was a put-down. In the past, they had accused me of not being able to keep a secret. I realized it didn't matter anyway; eventually the secret of a pregnancy would be found out. I was wondering why they had bothered telling me at all.

"What are you going to do about it?" I asked. I hadn't yet clarified exactly what I meant by that—that is, are you putting the baby up for adoption? If not, are you going to raise the baby at home in *Mem* and *Datt*'s house? Before I could clarify any of this, Sarah snapped, "Well, I'm certainly not going to have an abortion!"

I walked on in silence. Now I knew why they had told me. They wanted me to fix it. Except I couldn't. No one could. As I walked alongside Susan and Sarah, I felt like I was being handed a responsibility that I had no control over. I felt myself detach. I wished I could escape from my life.

Over the next several weeks, the relationship between Sarah and her boyfriend unraveled, and they broke up. I didn't know whether she planned on giving the baby up for adoption or raising the child herself. Being a single mother among the Amish would be hard enough; raising a child in *Mem* and *Datt*'s house would be daunting, if not impossible. Then again, this was a choice Sarah would have to make.

~❀~

Right around this same time, *Mem* voiced her concern about Katherine. Apparently Katherine had been missing her periods since spring. The idea that she might be pregnant came as a shock to us, because we had no idea that she knew anything about sex. At sixteen, Katherine had the mentality of a nine- or ten-year-old, which made her seem innocent, untouched, and untouchable. But *Mem* decided to take her to the doctor and have her checked out.

My sisters and *Mem* got together at my house after the doctor visit. *Mem* came up next to me and whispered, "Seven months pregnant!" She was trying to hold back tears.

I was so shocked that all I could say was, "But who would *do* such a thing?" It felt like a defiling of the worst kind. I felt stunned by the knowledge that Katherine had been violated right under our noses and that we hadn't been aware of it.

Sarah took Katherine into my bedroom and explained to her how someone becomes pregnant. She told Katherine the reason we need to know is because the father of this baby needed to take responsibility for what he did. Katherine finally burst out, "Jerry Boscoe!"

Because we didn't think Katherine would make up such a thing, we believed her.[10] Jerry was a Yankee man who had been coming to our house for years. When we were young, my sisters and I hid when he came because we felt he was a creepy old man. I always wondered why my parents allowed him to visit. There were times he would visit five times in one week.

Now *Mem* had a tough decision to make. Katherine would not be able to raise a child, which meant that either *Mem* would have to raise the child or else she would have to give the baby up for adoption.

I had several sleepless nights worrying about what would happen to Katherine. Then I felt myself detaching, much the way I had about Sarah's pregnancy. I knew that if I allowed my family troubles to prevent me from living my own life, I would never find my way out.

I had learned my lesson on the Clarion River. I could not save my family from its troubles any more than I could save Lizzie

---

10. Some time later, Katherine claimed that it was actually our brother Joe who did this to her and that he had told Katherine to say it was Jerry Boscoe.

from the waters of the river. I would not allow myself to get pulled into the current this time to chase after trouble. I decided to continue my plans to travel to New England.

~⚜~

I had been living under the illusion that my battle with disordered eating would stay my private affair—at least until *Ordnungs* church came around. This daylong church service took place every spring and fall and was a chance for everyone to renew their commitment to the church rules before communion services, which came two weeks later. Women were supposed to wear black dresses for both these services. On the morning of *Ordnungs* church, I realized that my black baptismal dress no longer fit me. So I wore my navy blue dress instead. I'd seen other women wear a dark color other than black to *Ordnungs* church, and I told myself I would have to make a new dress before the next church service.

That morning at *Ordnungs* church, I took my assigned place on the bench between the girl just older than me and the one just younger than me. I listened to all the sermons, starting from the Adam and Eve story to the end of the New Testament, with the warnings of what it would be like at the end of the world. The fire-and-brimstone sermons always made me squirm.

After the service, when I was helping with the dishes, the deacon's wife pulled me aside. She asked me if I didn't know I should be wearing a black dress today.

I was flabbergasted and said, "I thought it was okay to wear dark for *Ordnungs* church."

"You know better than that," Mary chided.

"Well, my black dress doesn't fit," I said.

"Well, why not?" Mary asked, as she looked pointedly at my front.

"Because I've gained too much weight."

"Well, why?" she asked, again looking at my belly.

"The same reason we all gain weight," I said, looking pointedly at Mary's wide hips.

"Well, is it?" Mary retorted.

I felt my cheeks burning with indignation at the inference.

When Lena, Rhoda, and I were walking back from church, I wondered aloud why Mary had asked me all those questions, and then I found out that there was a rumor going around that I was pregnant. I was stunned. "But that's impossible. Who do they think the father is? I've not dated anyone in ages! And besides that, I'm a virgin!"

"They think it's the taxi driver for the school children."

We had arrived home at that point. I went straight to my little house without inviting Lena and Rhoda over, closed the bathroom door, and threw up into the toilet. The baloney sandwiches and the cookies I'd eaten at church came up as easily as if I'd never stopped purging. I was shocked with this realization. Then I brushed my teeth to rid myself of the bitter taste in my mouth. It didn't do any good.

I sat on my sofa and I thought about my predicament. Of course people wondered. Since keeping my New Year's pact with myself not to purge anymore, I'd gained thirty-five pounds in the past nine months. Thirty-five pounds is about the amount of weight a woman will gain when she's pregnant.

There were moments when I knew that a man had lusted after my body. The driver who took us to Cook Forest was not the only one. The father of one of the families I worked for had made inappropriate remarks. There was a moment when I thought he was going to make a pass, so I moved away from him. I quit the job soon thereafter. How would the people in the community know that I had not succumbed to any of these flirtations?

I decided to ignore the rumors in the community. I knew the commitment I'd made to myself. Deep down, I didn't feel I was being completely honest when I told Lena and Rhoda that I was a virgin, because I had been sexually abused when I was younger. Yet I didn't feel that should count because it was a violation. I believed that sex should be something sacred, shared by two people who love one another deeply and had made their marriage vows to be faithful to one another the rest of their lives. I wanted to offer this to the person I would eventually marry.

～❀～

David's letter of September 24 came as a welcome reminder that joy still existed. As if to validate the line in his Christmas card the year before, I felt warm circles emanating from my heart as I read,

> *The sunrise this morning was clear and colorful with the sun slowly making its way over the mountains. Some trees are beginning to change as autumn takes over. The trees should peak about the time you arrive, give or take a week.*

> *Your letters are always a joy for me. You do a good job keeping me informed about the news in your life.*

> *My visit seemed like a dream to me too! A nice dream. I didn't know whether I would see you again and suddenly you were there. Good thing you didn't get into trouble with that visit. I'm happy I could be encouraging. This is a real compliment. I found our talk to be truly meaningful. You have a good mind and a good attitude about life. I thought that evening was beautiful and I'm glad we could share it. Did you ever find your shoes?*

> *It is now evening and tonight the harvest moon is out over the mountains. The sky is clear and the air is chilly. The moon is amazingly bright. You would like it. (Did you ever hear the song "Moonlight in Vermont"?)*

I felt I was there with David, enjoying the bright full moon over the mountains of Vermont. I had never heard the song, but I hoped I would someday—maybe in David's company. The tranquility of the scene David had described was like a bridge over troubled waters. My trip was only days away. My stomach fluttered whenever I thought about it. Now it was more important to me than ever. It was like I was grabbing for the inner tube and hanging on for dear life.

~ 27 ~

Trip to New England

Your sacred space is where you can find yourself over and over again.
—Joseph Campbell

The day of my trip finally arrived. I awoke before the sun came up and could not go back to sleep. I drifted into that place between awake and dreaming. In less than a week, I would see David. It was so freeing to allow the memories to drift by, as if I were watching them on a screen.

The first time I saw David, I didn't take any interest in him because I thought he was Janie's boyfriend. But then, several weeks later, on a Saturday afternoon, David and I talked in the kitchen of the Y for hours. As the daylight waned, I switched the light on in the kitchen. We both blinked in the bright light. I told David that I still took delight in flicking the switch to turn on a light instead of having to fill the gas lanterns and the oil lamps for the evening. I recalled David's youthful face as his chin rested in the palm of his hand, and how he regarded me with interest in his blue eyes.

I relived the feelings I had when he first asked me for a date. It was as if my body knew this was not a casual date long before my mind comprehended it.

I remembered the exquisite date at the Tiki Garden, when we talked again for hours. When I first met David, he seemed shy, but there was nothing shy about him when he started to talk. I had always wanted to be acknowledged for who I was, and here was

264 • Bonnet Strings

David doing exactly that. And his sense of humor was so contagious. He made me laugh when the fortune cookies arrived after we had discovered we are both Gemini. I asked David to read his, and he read, "Gemini are irresistible."

"You're kidding me!"

"Yes, I am."

"So, are you trying to say I'm irresistible, or that you are?" I teased.

"Both," he said. Then we laughed, and I noticed how his grin spread all across his face.

My mind drifted to the first time we were alone in the parlor, just before our first kiss. The intrigue of kissing a Yankee man added to the thrill of kissing someone I liked so much.

Now, as I anticipated my trip to Burlington, I wondered what it would be like when David and I were together again. Would it be like getting a whole new start? Or would it be like taking up where we left off?

I looked at the clock and realized the van driver would be here in an hour. I had packed my suitcase the night before, so I only had to shower, get dressed, and have a quick breakfast.

❧

Sarah and Susan accompanied me to Parkman and waited until I had boarded the Greyhound bus. They stood out on the sidewalk and waved. I waved back as the bus took off with a roar, heading west toward Cleveland. Suddenly I was on my own!

Upon arrival in New York City, I realized how hard it would have been to try to navigate it myself. I was so relieved and happy to see John Anderson that I gave him a big hug. He seemed surprised, but also delighted. We got into his car and he whisked me off to his house in Short Hills, where I had dinner with the Anderson family.

During dinner, Pat said she'd arranged for me to go visit her daughter's sixth-grade class, if I wanted to go. I agreed that I would.

Pat showed me to my room and gave me clean towels for showering. And then I was alone, on my first night away from home.

The next morning I went to school with the Andersons' daughter. I was her "show and tell" in her social studies class. I talked about the Amish way of life and answered the questions the students asked. Afterward, I felt like I was living a double life. On the one hand, I was educating students about Amish life. On the other, I was thinking about leaving it.

At midday, John dropped me off at the train station, bound for Stamford, Connecticut. He insisted on paying for the train fare and wished me well for the rest of my trip. Then I visited with a family for whom I had cleaned house back in Ohio before they moved to New Canaan, Connecticut. I stayed overnight and then boarded a bus to Boston. It turned out there were no vacancies in any of the Boston hotels, so I took a bus to Sturbridge, but there were no vacancies at the inn or at any of the other hotels in the area. The woman at the desk asked, "Did you just get off that bus?"

"Yes, I did." I was trying to hold back the panic that was threatening to set in. She said she could put a cot in a meeting room but that I had to be out of there by eight o'clock in the morning. I gratefully accepted the offer. That night, lying on the little cot in the middle of the cavernous room, I again thanked God for kind people and angels watching over me.

In my Amish clothes, I felt like a pioneer at the living history museum in Sturbridge. One of my colleagues at Century Village had a brother who worked there, and she had told me I should look him up. I asked around until I found the person I was looking for. We had a long conversation out in a field, next to a flock of sheep. In his costume, he looked like he'd stepped out of the past. I probably looked the same to him.

If I felt like a pioneer in Sturbridge, I felt like a Pilgrim the next day when I arrived in Plymouth. I stood at Plymouth Rock and walked onto the Mayflower II. Suddenly the history I'd read in grade school came alive. I toured Pilgrim Hall and walked through the graveyard where many of the Pilgrims were buried. Even though these things had happened four hundred years ago, the idea that I was walking on the same ground the Pilgrims had walked, and seeing the graves where they were buried, made me realize these were real people. History was no longer so abstract. I also thought of stories I'd heard about our Anabaptist ancestors migrating from Europe and the dangerous crossings they made. Even though most of them had landed in Philadelphia, I felt a connection to them.

The seagulls fascinated me. I had never seen even one seagull in Ohio, so I found them to be exotic. I loved hearing their calls as I walked along the beach and collected shells and rocks. Then I decided I would like to have some seafood. I ordered fresh haddock "fish and chips" by the seashore and found a place to eat outside. After the first bite, I decided I wanted to get some ketchup and salt. As I stood up to get some, a dozen gulls, with loud screams and much fluttering, swooped down onto my table and destroyed my lunch instantly. I tried shooing them away, but it was too late. Suddenly, they didn't seem so exotic at all. I wanted to hit them.

The people at the Lobster Hut replaced my lunch at no charge. I was so grateful. It was the best fish I'd ever eaten.

Back in Boston, I had to wait until the middle of the night to board the bus to Burlington. So I rode the elevator to the top of the Prudential Building. Looking out over Boston from that far up gave me a perspective I'd never had before. The lights of the city shone far below. As I looked around at the couples who were enjoying the sights together, I felt so alone and lonely that I wanted to sit down and cry. I had never experienced feeling lonely in a crowd before. I felt like my Amish clothes set me apart from other people. Seeing new horizons from this perspective was like seeing my loneliness stretched out before me. I longed to be with David. I tried to shake off the feeling and walked around, looking at the plaques that described what I was looking at. After all, what did I expect, traveling by myself? I wondered.

Greyhound buses were becoming like home to me. I had bought a bus ticket that would take me anywhere in the United States in fifteen days. I boarded the bus from Boston, bound for

Burlington, Vermont, in the middle of the night. I thought I would sleep along the way. Instead, I befriended a young woman who lived in Providence, Rhode Island, and we talked most of the way to Burlington. We exchanged addresses and promised to write one another before parting.

Barbara met me at the station. I was so happy to see her. She was cheery, as always, and her lively eyes reminded me of what I missed about her. We hugged and then Barbara took me to their new house and showed me to the guest bedroom. She asked me if I wanted to take a nap; I said I would do that later.

I confessed to Barbara that I didn't know what to wear to Claire's wedding. I felt uncomfortable in my Amish clothes, and yet I had nothing else to wear. So Barbara pulled out some of her clothes and I tried them on. They either didn't fit me or just looked wrong on me. So, in the end, I wore my brown dress and I combed out my hair and braided it into two pigtails. I still felt self-conscious, but I wasn't going to allow that to stop me from attending the wedding.

A Yankee Wedding

*And now faith, hope, and love abide, these three; and the
greatest of these is love.*
—1 Corinthians 13:13

David came to pick me up around one o'clock. He was dressed
in gray dress pants, a white shirt with a tie, a sweater over
that, and a jacket over the sweater. He looked dapper. Best of all,
he was wearing his contact lenses, which showed his blue eyes. He
drove me to his home. I remembered the terrain from our ride to
Richmond on that Sunday morning, which now seemed long ago,
and I told David so.

"We had a good time that day, didn't we?" he said.

When we arrived at the house, there were people everywhere. I
met David's mother right away. She smiled as she shook my hand
and said, "I thought I was going to meet you a long time ago."

"Yes, I remember! And then I ended up going back to Ohio the
day before I was going to visit you," I said.

"Right. I'm glad you came," she said. From her friendly smile,
I believed her.

I said hi to Bernadette and I met her new boyfriend, Maurice.
And then I met the bride and groom, Claire and John. A photographer with a German accent was telling them where they should
stand, how they should stand, and snapping lots of photos once
he was satisfied with the result.

I also met David's father and his brothers, Dan and Bob. I was
just being introduced to several of David's cousins when there

was a sudden flurry of people taking off in cars to go to church for the ceremony.

When we arrived at the church, I saw David's parents in the front pews. I was keenly aware of my plain clothes inside such an ornate church. David said he had to sit with the family up front and asked if I wanted to join him. "No, I will just sit right here," I said, as I sat in a pew near the back of the church. I wanted to melt into the woodwork and not have anyone notice me.

John, dressed in a white tuxedo, emerged from a door at the side of the sanctuary. A few minutes later, the organ music started. Much to my chagrin, everyone turned around and looked to the back of the church. I felt my face turn red. Then I realized people weren't even looking at me. The bridesmaids and groomsmen were walking slowly up the aisle. Then Claire, in her white gown and with a crown of daisies on her head, followed on the arm of her father. She looked beautiful with her long blond hair, clear skin, and blue eyes. She looked happy as she walked slowly up toward the priest and John, who were standing by the altar. I would later learn that the priest was Claire and David's uncle Gerard. The organ music stopped. They were bathed in bright white lights. Claire's father took his seat with the rest of the family, and Father Gerard began speaking. First he said that if anyone had any objections to this marriage, they should "speak now or forever hold your peace." That surprised me. The Amish did that too. I had heard so much about the Catholics and how they had persecuted our Anabaptist ancestors that I had no idea there was any resemblance between our sacraments.

There was silence in the church for a long moment, and then Father Gerard continued on with the ceremony.

It seemed to me the service was over shortly after it began. The organ music started up again, and everyone stood up. Then the bridesmaids and groomsmen preceded Claire and John in walking down the aisle toward the door of the church. David's parents and then another couple, most likely John's parents, followed them. Claire's and John's siblings came next. When David came near the pew where I was sitting, he motioned that I should come with him, so I did.

The wedding party was standing outside the church, greeting people with hugs and handshakes as they went slowly by. I shook hands and congratulated Claire and John and then stood off to the side with David. His brothers, Bob and Dan, came and stood with us. Soon we were surrounded by David's cousins, and David introduced me to many of his relatives. I was beginning to wonder who had more cousins, David or me.

There was movement in the crowd. Claire and John were heading for their car, and people were snapping photos. The photographer with a German accent was telling John to hold Claire's arm in a certain way, and then they were off down the sidewalk, toward their car.

On the way to the reception, David asked me how I was doing.

"I feel a little out of place in my Amish dress, but other than that, I'm fine."

"You look fine," David said. He looked at me with that soft expression that I used to see in the parlor of the Y, the one that made me feel so cherished.

I decided that was enough for me. I was not here to please the whole crowd. I was here for David.

I sat with David during the reception. His brothers and several of his cousins sat at the same table. Bernadette was a bridesmaid, so she was with the wedding party most of the time, but she and Maurice came over to visit with us at one point.

After several toasts, the dancing started. John and Claire looked each other in the eyes as they turned slow circles to the music. It was so romantic. I wished I could dance. I yearned for David to hold me in his arms and dance like that.

Several songs later, after Claire had danced with her father and more couples were up on the dance floor, David came and said, "My mother asked if we're going to dance. Would you like to?"

"I don't feel comfortable doing that," I said.

"Then we won't. I'm not that good at it anyway."

"Boy, that couple is!" I said.

"Oh, yes. That's my mother's best friend, Skip, and her husband, John. When my mother was young, she and Skip would go dancing at night. They loved it. Skip and John got really good at it."

As Claire and John were about to leave the reception, people started throwing rice at the couple. I wondered why they did that, but I didn't ask.

People slowly began leaving. David said that relatives were going to be gathering at his house and asked whether I would like to come. I said I would but that I wouldn't want to stay too long. Having spent the previous night on a bus and experiencing the culture shock of a Yankee wedding, I was getting tired.

"I'll take you back to Barb's as soon as you're ready," David promised.

When we arrived back at David's house, it was as if we walked into the same scene we'd left before the wedding, but this time it was dark. David's mother was still wearing her corsage and looking very serene. Bernadette was laughing her lusty laugh. David's aunts were bustling about, putting out plates of food. People were standing and sitting around with little plates of food, visiting in groups.

David took me downstairs to show me his toy shop. Then other people wanted to see it, so David and Dan took turns taking groups of people downstairs.

As people started leaving, I whispered to David that I was ready to go. It took some time saying goodbye to people before we could get out the door.

On the way over to the Lalancettes, David asked me what I wanted to do the next day. He said that Claire had given him permission to use her car while she was away, and that she had a tape deck in her car so we could listen to music. He said we could go someplace together if I wanted to. I said I'd like that. We decided to drive to Fairfax to visit his potter friend, Bill.

When we arrived at the Lalancettes' house, I asked David if he wanted to come in.

Sitting down on the sofa in the living room, David moved over and, without a word, embraced me and kissed me passionately.

I kissed him back, and then all of a sudden I felt like the bridge I had been trying to build between my two worlds completely collapsed.

There was no having it both ways: I would have to choose one world or the other. How could I go on exploring the world with David in it, not knowing if I would stay in it or go back to the Amish world? From his advances, I could tell he expected us to take up where we had left off.

I felt my body go limp, and then I pulled away from David. I felt tears well up, and I couldn't stop them. Soon I was sobbing.

"What's the matter?" David asked.

"Nothing is resolved," I said. "I don't think it's fair to you to keep going like we were before if I'm not even sure whether I'm leaving the Amish again or not."

With that, David's body sprang into action. He got up, grabbed his coat, and said, "I know you're tired. I shouldn't have just assumed like that. I'll just leave. Why don't you get a good night's rest. I'll see you in the morning."

"Well, you don't have to leave . . ." I started.

"I think it's best if I do," David said. And then he went out the door.

I was grateful that Rick and Barbara were both in bed. I kept wiping my eyes as I prepared for the night. Collapsing into bed, I sobbed out of exhaustion, confusion, and fear.

~29~

By the Waterfalls

From this day forward,
You shall not walk alone.
My heart will be your shelter,
And my arms will be your home.
—Anonymous

Sunday morning dawned clear and cool with an autumn snap in the air. Barbara invited me to have breakfast with her. As she prepared oatmeal and fresh fruit, she asked me about the wedding. I gave her several details, and then she asked what it was like to see David again. I stammered and became teary-eyed.

She looked at me sideways as she was getting something out of a cupboard. "Are you falling in love with David?" she asked directly.

Until Barbara asked it that way, I could not have put those words to it. "Yes, I'm afraid I am," I said.

Barbara said in her cheeriest voice, "Saloma, I think that's the best thing that could happen to you. I know from your letters that you've been unhappy back in your Amish community. If those Amish guys are not smart enough to snatch you up, why shouldn't you fall in love with David? He has been waiting for you for more than two years! How romantic is that?"

With a talking-to like that, I didn't feel like crying anymore. "But that means I have to leave the Amish altogether," I said. "It's all or nothing."

"Are you happy with the Amish life?"

"Not exactly. But there are some things I would miss, like the community. And I would miss my family."

"I know that's hard, but maybe someday you could go back and visit your family. I cannot believe you would go through life without ever seeing them again."

"You're probably right," I said.

"Anyway, kiddo, let's have some breakfast."

Barbara and I were still eating breakfast on the patio when David showed up. She greeted him cheerily, and David and I exchanged looks. I could tell David was trying to figure out if I was still upset.

Barbara said, "Have a seat. Have you had breakfast?"

I was still wearing my Amish clothes during the week I visited David in Vermont.

David answered, "I sure did. We had a bunch of guests this morning, and it was rather crazy. I was glad to get out of there."

Barbara and I laughed, and I went inside to get my sweater and my purse.

Before we left the driveway, David got a boyish grin on his face and stuck a cassette tape into the deck in the dashboard of Claire's car. It was the Eagles' *Desperado* album. Heading out of town, David took the ramp to Interstate 89 and went north. We drove along, listening to the music, but after the first song, David turned off the player and said, "Anyway, we can listen to that later. How are you doing?"

"Much better. It's amazing what a good night's rest can do."

"And a gorgeous day in Vermont."

"I know. Isn't this just the perfect autumn day? I love that fresh smell. And look at the beautiful colors!" I was looking at the hills, saturated in gold, red, orange, and brown, with the dark green of pine trees mixed in.

We drove on in silence for a long moment. Then we both began to speak at once. We looked at each other and laughed. I said, "What were you going to say?"

"I was just going to say that I should have been more considerate last night. I should not have assumed anything—now what were you going to say?"

"I was going to say I am really sorry for getting so upset last night. I probably ruined your evening."

"No, you did not ruin my evening. In fact, I meant to tell you how much I appreciate that you came to the wedding. That meant a lot to me, you know." David smiled at me. "My mother told me how much she enjoyed meeting you. She would like to have you come visit this week when there aren't as many people around."

"I'd like that."

When we arrived in Fairfax, we found that David's potter friend, Bill, and his wife, Barb, weren't home. When we walked back to the car, I said, "You know who else lives here in Fairfax?"

"Who?"

"Raymond Culligan."

"Oh yeah?"

"You wouldn't want to stop in and see if he's home, would you?"

"Sure, why not? Where does he live?"

I remembered Raymond's address from our correspondence. We soon found his house. With David by my side, I went to the door and knocked. Raymond came to the door and exclaimed, "Hey, what a surprise, come on in!"

So we sat in Raymond's kitchen, visiting for a time. I remarked on the placemats he had on the table. He chuckled and said he enjoyed them. My sister Sarah and I had made them for Raymond and sent them as a Christmas gift after our trip to Vermont.

I was surprised that David had so readily agreed to visit Raymond. It showed that he didn't feel threatened by him. I suddenly knew why I had asked to stop in to see Raymond. I needed to be sure about my feelings. And in that moment they became crystal clear. David was the one I wanted to be with.

Back in the car, on our way to Stowe, I saw that we were passing a huge waterfall. "David, can we stop?" I asked. "I love waterfalls!"

"Sure," David said, as he swung the car around. He crossed the bridge to the other side of the falls in Fairfax and found a place to park. As we got out of the car, we could hear the roar of the falls and see the mist rising from down below. I began hopping from one rock to another to get closer to the falls. "Saloma, be careful," David warned. "Here, hold on to my hand."

Hand in hand, we kept hopping from one rock to another. "See that rock right there?" I pointed. "I'm trying to get over there."

"I don't know if we should," David said.

"We'll be fine," I said.

Then we were standing on the flat rock. Looking up, we saw a thick sheet of water, coming over the side of the dam. Looking down, we saw the water tumbling over huge boulders into pools far below. There was a thick stream roaring down the rock right beside us. I sat down and looked up at David. He sat down next to me.

And there beside the water, seeing and hearing it flow down over the falls, everything fell into place. David talked in a calm and unassuming manner about how much he enjoyed those times in the parlor at the Y and how he longed for them after I returned to the community. "I just could not let go," he told me. "I've always known how I've felt about you, but I've never been sure how you felt about me."

There was a long moment of silence. Then I reached out and took David's hand and said, "Until now, I wasn't sure of my own feelings. But what I feel at this moment cannot be described any other way except that I love you." His hand was warm and loving. He looked at me with his blue eyes and I didn't think the mist in them came from the waterfalls. The roar of the water falling down over the rocks enveloped the moment.

30

Mull of Kintyre

Since love grows within you, so beauty grows. For love is the beauty of the soul.
—St. Augustine

On the way to the mountains to visit the lodge of the von Trapp family (the Austrian family of *Sound of Music* fame), David asked me about my trip so far. I talked about all the places I'd been and my feelings about each place. I even included my lonely feelings at the top of the Prudential Building in Boston. I said, "I kept wishing you could be there with me. It was like the feeling I had when I was on that pond back in February."

David was quiet for a moment and then said softly, "That's touching."

We rode on in silence for several moments. Then I thanked him for stopping to see Raymond.

"Oh, you're welcome. He seems like a nice guy."

"He is. I don't know why it's taken me this long. I had to go there to be sure, but it is clear to me that the most Raymond can ever be is a friend. And that's what he has always said he wanted. I had a hard time accepting that, but something settled in my mind this morning."

"Then I'm glad we stopped by to see him. Look what it got me," David said with a big smile.

The views from the Trapp Family Lodge took my breath away and reminded me of the day Sarah and I had climbed the mountain together. Standing on the hillside next to David and feeling the autumn breezes kiss my face, I knew if I had been alone at that moment, I would have cried. All I could say was, "It's so beautiful!"

David looked pleased. "Living in Vermont, do you take this kind of beauty for granted, or are you in awe of it every day?" I asked.

He was silent for a moment. "I think it's probably somewhere in-between. But seeing these views through your eyes is like seeing them for the first time."

"Then I guess you should always have me around," I joked.

"I'd like that," David said, so quietly I thought I might have imagined it.

The tearoom of the Trapp Family Lodge was open. David and I each had a bowl of soup and popovers while looking out at the views. It felt like I had entered my dream world. And there was David, sitting across from me, with those blue, blue eyes. I thought my chest might burst with joy.

Around every turn on Interstate 89 on our way back to Burlington, the views were exquisitely beautiful. Just when I thought I couldn't take in any more beauty, David said, "I want to share something with you." He popped a cassette into the player and the song "Mull of Kintyre" by Paul McCartney burst forth. I was mesmerized. Then the bagpipes started in, and I felt the hair on the back of my neck stand up. Being surrounded by the Vermont landscape, being with David, hearing that music: it was almost more than I could bear. When the song ended, I looked at David and said reverently, "Wow, that was beautiful!" David played it again.

The colorful trees skimmed by and the music enveloped me. It was one of the first times in my life when I felt the lines blurring between beauty and love.

⁓·❀·⁓

Back in the Lalancettes' living room that evening, David held me in his arms. We were quiet for a long moment. Then David shifted, and he pulled my glasses off. I laughed and said, "I was just remembering the other day that you used to do that."

"Really? You must have hated that."

"No, I didn't. I liked it."

"Do you remember when I used to do this?" David asked, as his finger traced the outline of my nose.

I closed my eyes. "How could I forget?"

I felt David kissing me softly. I opened my eyes. "I remember when you did that, too." David was looking at me intently. The dim light from the street lamp outside was just enough to make out his expression. "I love you," David said tenderly.

"I love you too," I said, as tears choked my words. I grabbed on to David and hugged him. He hugged me back. I wanted him to hold me forever.

⁓ ❀ ⁓

The next morning when I awoke, Barbara told me there was something in the mailbox for me. I went out to look, and there was a single red rose and a little card with David's handwriting, "Just for being you."

"Isn't that nice!" Barbara said when she saw my face. "Here's a vase—you should put it on the nightstand next to your bed."

Alone in the guest bedroom, I had to collect myself. Here was the problem again: being torn between my Amish world and my Vermont one. I hadn't been able to handle it when the Amish had come to Burlington to take me back, when David had visited me at the Benders' and later on at the Akron Reservoir, or last summer when I'd visited Vermont and decided not to contact him.

But this is different, I reflected. David and I had now verbalized our love for one another. We couldn't go back on that.

I decided I would talk with David about what we were going to do, now that we knew we wanted to be together.

David came later that morning and took me to his parents' house for lunch. The house looked bigger now that there were fewer people in it. His mother greeted me with her serene smile. She was wheeling around the kitchen in her wheelchair, preparing grilled cheese sandwiches and tomato soup. The table was already set with a blue tablecloth and blue plates and bowls.

As David hung up my coat, I asked his mother if there was anything I could do to help her.

"You're the guest; that's all right," she protested.

I looked at David, wondering if I should insist or step back.

"Mom, Saloma is used to helping wherever she goes," David said.

"Well, if you want to, you can watch the sandwiches."

David's father came in while I was flipping the sandwiches. He had come home for lunch from IBM, where he worked. Everyone gathered around the table. They said a blessing, then crossed themselves. I bowed my head in silence.

I was quieter than usual, observing the Furlong family. Even though this was my first meal with David's family, there was something vaguely familiar about it. It was as if I knew this was one of many meals I would eat with them in the future. Seeing David in his own surroundings gave him a whole new dimension.

After the meal was over, Mr. Furlong returned to work. Dan put the leftovers away and I washed the dishes; while David dried, his mother wiped the table and counters and swept the floor. She was capable of doing a lot from her wheelchair. I remembered one of the first things David had told me about her: "She doesn't let anything stop her."

❧❧❧

That night, back in the Lalancettes' living room, it felt like David and I were both making up for lost time. At some point David stopped kissing me and said, "Passionate, aren't we?" And then we kissed some more.

When we came up for air, I said that we had to be careful not to tempt one another. David held me tenderly and looked into my eyes. He said, "I know you want to save yourself for marriage. I promise I'll never have sex with you unless we are married."

I started crying.

"I didn't mean to upset you," David said.

"It's just that it brings up the question I've been avoiding for too long. If I want to be with you, then I have to leave the Amish again."

"Unless I join the Amish."

"But why would you do that, if I'm leaving?"

"What is it that you want?"

David asked the question in such a sincere way that it touched me deeply. It helped me clarify what I wanted from the deepest part of who I was. "All I want is to be where people understand me," I replied.

David held me as I cried. I got up and found tissues in the bathroom. Then I sat down next to David, and he waited for me to explain.

"Even though I have lived in a whole community of people all my life, there is not one person I feel really understands and accepts me for who I am. It seems they are trying to change me into someone I'm not—someone quiet and submissive who can just go along with the rules. I've tried being like that, but I cannot stop the questions that seem to come up from within me and I cannot seem to stop asking them."

I took a breath. "From the first time you and I talked, I felt you understood me and accepted me for who I am. Now you even love me for who I am. I cannot tell you how much that rose you left me this morning touched me. All my life I've been denying myself what I really want. I know if I turn away from the love we have for one another, I will regret it for the rest of my life."

I was sobbing now. David held me fast until I calmed down.

"Saloma, I am deeply touched." David said. His few words, simply put, were all I needed in that moment.

~❁~

After David left and I was in the bed next to the nightstand with the single red rose, I thought about the implications of the promise David had made. He had used the word *marriage*—was I ready to even think of that? I've been leading David on in thinking I'm saving myself for marriage, I thought, but I'm not really a virgin. I couldn't keep letting him think that I was. But how would

I tell him? Before I decided to leave the Amish, I had to know whether he still wanted to be in relationship with me. And I better tell him about my bulimia too, I thought; he has a right to know that I'm far from perfect.

Before falling asleep, I decided I would talk to David about these things. Just thinking about it made me want to shrink into myself, like a turtle hiding in its shell.

I awoke before dawn and was ready at the door when David drove up to the Lalancettes' house. We were planning to go to Woodstock for a day of bicycling.

As we drove toward Montpelier, the sun was coming up over the Green Mountains. Wisps of mist rose toward the tops of the mountains, but otherwise it was a clear day. The mist next to the colors of the trees was beautiful. "David, would you play that song again?" I asked.

David put on the "Mull of Kintyre" again. When the bagpipes started, I reached over and took David's hand and held it there between us. The beauty of nature, the music, and our young love felt like a perfect symphony. My heart was expanding to make room for it all.

When the last notes of the song died away, I looked out my window so David wouldn't see my tears. As soon as I faced forward, David looked over at me and said, "Do I see a tear in your eye?"

I quickly swiped at them and said, "Sometimes I just get overwhelmed."

"By what?"

"Everything points to one thing. This is where I want to be—with you, here in Vermont. That means I need to leave the Amish again. Now it's just a matter of when and how." I paused and then continued. "It will be devastating for my mother. She seemed heartbroken when I said goodbye. There are rumors that I will not be coming back, and I know she wondered if I would. So I have to go back and at least say proper goodbyes."

David reached over for my hand and held it in a long moment of silence before he spoke. "Have things gotten better for your mother since your father has improved?"

"As far as Dad is concerned, yes. But there are some other things happening in my family that are difficult. I feel like I would be abandoning her if I left now."

"Do you want to talk about it?"

"My sister Katherine is pregnant!" I blurted. Sobs heaved from my chest. "We didn't even know she knew anything about sex, and here she was being violated right under our very noses! She has the mentality of a nine- or ten-year-old!"

David seemed too stunned to speak. Finally he asked, "Does anyone know who the father is?"

"She said it was this guy who has been visiting us since before Katherine was born. I believe her. He always was a creepy old man. We girls would hide upstairs if we saw him coming when my parents weren't there."

David suddenly hit the steering wheel with a guttural "Ugghh!"

"I know, doesn't that just make you so angry? I cannot tell you the thoughts I've had of what I want to do to him!"

And then I told David the whole family saga, including Sarah's predicament. I ended by saying, "In a way, I feel like I'd be abandoning my family, but in another way, I'd be glad to get away. Why should I stay there and share in all the misery when I can be here in Vermont, building a whole new life for myself? But then I feel selfish when I think that way."

"But you didn't cause any of it to happen."

"I know. It's just that Mom has a hard decision ahead of her. She has to decide if she is going to raise Katherine's child or not. Katherine can't do it. And Sarah has to decide what *she's* going to do. She's thinking she'll raise her child while living at Mom and Dad's. I sure wouldn't do that."

"Then again, it sounds like you wouldn't have gotten pregnant by that guy in the first place."

"That's true. I didn't trust him from the start. I cannot believe I lent him any money at all."

"You lent him money?"

"Yes, in a weak moment. He and Sarah came to me with a sad-sack story about how much he needed it for a car payment, this and that, and blah, blah, blah. I thought I was helping Sarah out. As it turned out, I only made things worse. When it came time to break up with him, she kept hanging in there partly because they hadn't paid me back."

"How much did he borrow?"

"I'm embarrassed to tell you; it was 450 dollars."

"Four hundred and . . ." David's voice trailed off.

"I know. It took me since my trip to Vermont last summer to save it up, and now it's just gone."

"So, he never paid any of it back?"

"Nope."

As we were eating breakfast later in Montpelier, I brought up the topic of when I would be leaving Ohio to come back to Vermont. I said, "There are quite a few of my belongings I don't want to leave behind."

David said, "I'll come and pick you up if you'd like me to."

"Really?"

"Sure. I have my pickup truck. You can bring as many belongings as we can fit in the back of the truck."

"Well that would be a relief. That takes care of the how. Now it's a matter of when. Maybe I should stay through the holidays and then leave. Barbara has already said I could live with them for a while."

"That would actually work for me. I'll be pretty busy through the holidays with my business."

"Okay, let's do that. I cannot tell you how much of a relief this is to have a plan. Now we can have fun the rest of the day."

"I'm glad I have your permission," David said with a mischievous grin.

~ ❀ ~

Fun does not describe the day in Woodstock with David—exquisite, divine, and heavenly would be closer. We rented bicycles from the Woodstock Inn and biked the countryside together. Neither of us knew or cared how many miles we biked. The air was invigorating, the autumn colors were bright, and we were young and in love.

Toward the end of the day, we came down a long, steep hill. I let go of the brakes and let the bike pick up speed and followed the twists and turns of the road. I heard David calling me from way back somewhere, but I barely heard him as I skimmed down the hill so fast that it felt like I was flying—just like the flying dreams I'd had since I was a child. I felt the thrill from the top of my head down to the tips of my toes. I knew I would never forget that feeling as long as I lived.

31

Fairy Stones

*[P]erhaps . . . love unfolded naturally out of a beautiful
friendship, as a golden-hearted rose slipping from
its green sheath.*
—L. M. Montgomery, *Anne of Avonlea*

On the way back from Woodstock, David and I stopped to see Moss Glen Falls. It was right around twilight and the air had a night chill. We both realized we were tired from the day's activities, so we got back in the car and continued north on Route 100. Then all of a sudden, we came around a bend and saw the full moon coming up over the horizon—bright and huge.

David pushed the Eagles tape into the player, and the song "Saturday Night" blared through the speakers. I let the music wash over me as David navigated the curves on Route 100. The last line in the song, "Whatever happened to Saturday night?" was drawn out, and then the last notes of the song died away. David pushed the stop button and said, "I can't tell you how many times I've listened to that song. I would always be thinking of a particular Saturday night.

"The Saturday night when the Amish came and took me back?"

"The one before that, actually."

"Oh, the one at the Ira Allen Chapel!"

"Yup."

"I remember that night. A week later, I was back in the community—just like that! Did I ever tell you where I was when I discovered the cross you gave me?"

"No."

"Just about halfway between Vermont and Ohio. It was like a cross between my two worlds."

"Do you still have it?"

"No. It went the way of the photos I burned. And I have regretted it more than once." I described the circumstances.

"But it wouldn't have burned. It was a stone."

"Oh, it wasn't petrified wood?"

"No, it's called a fairy stone, and it was mined out of the ground in the perfect shape of a Maltese cross."

"It was a nice gift. When I saw it, I was feeling so torn between the Amish world and my Vermont one. I had such a longing to see you again, and I didn't know if I ever would."

"And now here we are," David said. We drove along in silence. We came around the bend, and there was the moon—suspended just above the trees right in front of us.

"Yes, here we are. It feels like a miracle."

※

In the next five days, David and I visited the Walls, a couple we met at Claire and John's wedding who owned two hundred acres on a mountaintop. Their vista included Mount Washington, more than seventy miles away. We also visited the potter, Bill, and his wife, Barb, in Fairfax. We took a walk with them and saw a flaming sunset over the mountains. We had lunch with Dan at Zachary's Pizza, sitting in the spot next to where David had asked me for my first date. I cooked a dinner that David, Barbara, and I ate out on Rick and Barbara's sun porch. I spent several quiet mornings sending postcards to people back home. David and I drove to Georgia, Vermont, and danced at the Cobweb. We drove to Norwich University to see David's neighbor who was a freshman there. We spent time by the lake and watched the sailboats and saw the ferry leaving for Port Kent. We ate brunch at the Shelburne Inn on Sunday morning, the day before it was time for me to leave. And we visited Maureen and Patti at their apartment.

It took me until Sunday night, when David and I were sitting in a restaurant called Déjà Vu in Burlington, to find the courage to broach the subject I had been avoiding all week. We had just finished our buckwheat crepes filled with chicken, mushrooms, and fresh vegetables when I said to David, "There is something I need to tell you."

He looked concerned.

"I feel like I've been giving you the idea that I'm a virgin. I would be, except for something that happened when I was eleven that I have never admitted to anyone before." I looked at David for encouragement.

"When you were eleven? You mean someone took advantage of you?"

"Yes."

"Was it that same creepy guy that got Katherine pregnant?"

I shook my head and whispered, "It was my brother Joe."

David bent his head down and said, "Did you say it was your brother Joe?"

I nodded my head. And then out of shame and the release of the secret I'd held inside for so long, I started crying—right there in the restaurant. I was glad it wasn't busy. I bowed my head and blew my nose.

David reached out and held my hand.

My resolve to hold it together collapsed and I started crying in earnest. "David, maybe we should go."

"Sure. Let me pay the bill, and we will."

Back in the truck, I covered my face with my hands and sobbed. My chest heaved, and I thought I would lose control of myself. David reached over and put his arm across my shoulder as he said, "Hey, it's okay. It doesn't change my feelings for you."

"Really?" I asked, still trying to control my sobs. "I feel like I've been living a lie by not telling you the truth."

"But it wasn't your fault," David said.

"I've always felt like it was."

"You were eleven years old."

"I know," I sobbed. "I didn't think I had a choice."

David moved over into the middle of the seat and gathered me up in his arms and held me. In the circle of his arms, I felt safe and cherished. Slowly my sobs subsided. I decided now was the time to come clean. "There is something else you need to know about me," I said.

David held me and listened.

"I've had an eating disorder. It's called bulimia—I hate that word. It means I would throw up after eating. I made a New Year's resolution that I wouldn't throw up anymore, and that is why I've gained so much weight since January. Now the Amish think I'm pregnant." I started laughing and crying at the same time. "Fat chance of that! I've not had a date in more than two years!"

"Who do they think is the father?" David asked. I wondered whether he believed I was pregnant.

"Some taxi driver. He drove the children to school in the mornings and back home in the afternoons. He used to visit me at my house, but he's married, and he never did anything inappropriate. There were others I wasn't comfortable being around because of the way they acted or things they said. But I removed myself from those situations and nothing ever happened."

David moved back into the driver's seat and started the truck. "Let's go and sit by the lake for a while," he said. He drove to a park where we sat on a bench, looking out over Lake Champlain. I sat next to David, absorbing his warmth. After a long moment of silence, he said, "None of this changes my feelings for you."

I felt such gratitude for David. I looked at him, awed by his acceptance of all parts of my past. He took my glasses off. Then he traced the tears with his finger and kissed my nose and then my wet cheeks. "If anything, I love you even more for being so honest. I've always liked that about you."

"Really?"

"Yes. The first time I noticed it was the night I came to Zachary's and I was talking about Janie. Do you remember what you said?"

"Remind me."

"You didn't come here to talk about Janie, did you?" David said with the intonation and accent I had used.

"Yes, I do remember that! And then you asked me for a date."

"Yup. And we went to the Tiki Garden. I should have taken you there this week."

"There will be plenty of time when I come back."

David and I sat for a long time, absorbing the promise of being together. My mind drifted to the inevitable. We were just getting used to being together, and now it was time to part—at least for a time.

"I cannot tell you how much I have enjoyed my week. It has been the best week of my life. It feels like much longer than a week. It almost feels like we stretched out time."

"It does feel longer than a week. It's also been the best week of my life."

"Really?"

"Yes. You seem surprised by that. It's not every week I fall in love with someone."

"I hope not. Unless it's with me," I laughed. Then I added, "Can I have my glasses back now?"

After making plans for him to drive me to the bus station, David suggested, "You probably want to get a good night's rest. I should take you back to the Lalancettes'."

"Only if you come in for a while."

"Sure. Are you kidding me? This is our last night of *schmunzling* for a while."

"You remembered that word!"

"And I remember how," David joked.

"And how!" I said.

"You're not so bad yourself."

"Yes, it's like riding a bicycle—it comes back to you, even after two years of no practice."

"So let's go," David said with a grin, as we headed for the truck.

❧ ✿ ☙

The next morning when David arrived at the Lalancettes', I had my suitcase packed and was ready to go. I had shared my plans with Barbara several days before, so she was aware that I was planning on returning to Vermont. She was generous in offering that I could live with them. My heart was filled with gratitude for such a good friend.

Barbara wrote a nice note in my autograph book before we left. As we hugged goodbye, she said she was looking forward to seeing me when I returned to Vermont.

David and I had lunch with Maureen, and then we drove to his house. His mother had a big smile for us, and I asked her to sign my autograph book. Before I went out the door, I gave her a hug. She looked very pleased and waved from the window as David and I left the driveway.

"I really like your mother," I said.

"She likes you too."

"Yeah, well that takes some effort. Liking your mother doesn't."

"What is this? Just because you're going back to the Amish doesn't mean you have to start putting yourself down, does it?"

"Sure it does. I'm just staying in practice."

"Remember, I like you just the way you are. That doesn't include putting yourself down."

"Fair enough." I smiled. David had a way of pointing out things about me that I would not have noticed.

"I bet it'll be good to see your family again."

"Yes, it will. And I have to fall-clean my house. Church is going to be held in the downstairs. The Troyers are hosting the church service. Will has his business down there where he refinishes furniture."

When we were standing next to the bus, I asked David what he wanted for Christmas. "A quilt," he told me.

"Okay," I said, with a big gulp. I was wondering how I was going to manage making a quilt with all the big changes coming up in my life.

We kissed, and I leaned in for one more hug. "Better get on the bus. You don't want to miss it."

"Maybe I do," I joked.

After I boarded the bus, I waved to David and he waved back. We threw kisses to one another as the bus started moving. And then he was out of sight.

~32~

Sister Talk

The course of true love never did run smooth.
—William Shakespeare

When I arrived back on my doorstep the following morning, I was exhausted. The overnight bus ride had been anything but restful. I went right to bed and slept for four hours. At some point I heard one of the Troyers come in and then leave again. When all was quiet again in my house, my mind had a chance to make the transition to my Amish life.

I got up in mid-afternoon and began the fall cleaning I needed to do for the church service that would be held in the downstairs of my house in less than two weeks. Since I was scheduled to return to the museum the next day for work, getting started now would be prudent, I reasoned. Starting with the pantry, a little room that had been built to keep things cool during three seasons of the year, I cleaned out all the cupboards, washed the ceiling and the walls, and cleaned the floor. Then I took down the curtains to wash, starch, and iron.

Lena came over after supper that evening, and we talked about my trip. I was glad Rhoda didn't come too because she had been dead-set against me traveling by myself. I would have felt self-conscious, because I sensed she felt envy for the freedom I had to take trips on my own. Likely she also didn't trust that I would "behave" myself after what had upset her in Cook Forest.

Lena eventually brought the subject around to whether I had seen David. Before I left on the trip, she had asked me if I was planning on seeing him, and I had said in a casual manner that if our paths crossed, I would probably see him. Now Lena was curious—had our paths crossed?

During my long bus ride home, I had rehearsed how much I would tell people about my trip and most specifically about David. I would confide in Sarah and Susan about my relationship with David and let them know of my plans to leave. To anyone else who asked, I would say that David and I had seen one another and we had traveled to different parts of Vermont together. But I would not talk about the relationship. I would leave that to their imaginations.

So that's what I did with Lena. I told her about biking around Woodstock, Vermont, and we even looked it up on the map. I talked about visiting the couple high on the mountaintop and visiting the Trapp Family Lodge, which she found intriguing, since she had also read Maria von Trapp's book.

When Lena left, I sensed she wasn't satisfied with the information she had, because she'd wanted to know more. The new self that was emerging from within me wanted more privacy than the Amish life allowed for. It would be hard to keep my secret for long.

One thing I had decided already. No matter how many people discovered my plans to leave, no one would be able to convince me to stay. If anything, they would only make me want to leave sooner than January.

~ ❀ ~

The Yankee neighbors who lived next to the Troyers had set up a phone out in their barn for the Amish to use. I found myself over in the barn frequently, dialing up David's number. He couldn't very well call me, because he might get someone else at the other end of the line.

At night when I went to bed, I would wonder what was keeping me from just leaving. Then I would remind myself that I had come back to say proper goodbyes.

Sarah was the first person I confided in. She invited me to stay with her at an overnight babysitting job, which I thought would be an appropriate place, away from an Amish setting, to broach the subject.

After the children were in bed, Sarah asked me questions about my trip and I told her about the time I'd spent with David and the things we did together. She was quiet and then asked me if I was "falling for him." I said that we had come to a place where we wanted to be together.

Sarah said bluntly, "So you're leaving."

"Yes, that's the plan."

"When?"

"I'm thinking after Christmas."

Sarah was quiet for a long moment. Then she said, "So you won't be here when my baby comes."

"Not unless you come with me."

Sarah's surprise filled her next question. "What do you mean?"

"What I mean is that there are probably organizations in Vermont that would help you with the birth, and possibly even raising your child."

"I wouldn't know anything about that or how to find those institutions."

"I could help you with that."

Sarah changed the subject. "Are you sure that you're not falling for David just because you're lonely?"

"It's true that I've been lonely, especially because the Amish men won't date me. They say, 'She left once; she could leave again!' I finally realized they're right. I *can* leave again."

Sarah didn't react to my joke. She asked, "What about your salvation? Don't you think you would be trading off your salvation for living the life you want while you're here on this earth?"

"You know Sarah, I don't believe I will go to hell for leaving the Amish." It felt good to say it out loud. "I made peace with that question even before I left the first time. Have I ever told you what it was like for me when *Mem* turned down the social worker's offer for help the second time?"

Sarah didn't answer.

"I think that was the lowest point of my life. I felt like I had only two options left—committing suicide or leaving the Amish. I felt like both of them were going to get me into hell. I knew if I committed suicide, I would go to hell right away. Then I thought that if I'm going to hell for leaving the Amish, I'd at least have a lifetime on earth before I go to hell. And as soon as I thought that, I realized that the Amish preachers have us believing that so we don't leave the Amish. They could be wrong!"

"But do you want to take that chance?" Sarah asked.

"Yes—because I have my conscience to go by. God gave each of us a conscience to know right from wrong, and it is our responsibility to listen to that inner voice."

"That can also lead us astray. Look at what happened with my relationship."

"Do you think you were listening to your inner voice at the time?"

Sarah paused. "I guess I was listening to someone's voice—not necessarily my own."

"You mean his?"

"Maybe I never told you how I was talked into accepting his advances. I had no feelings for him at first. In fact, I kept saying no to him. So he went to Susan and my friend Marie and confided in them. They sat me down one night and gave me a talking-to. They said I considered myself too good for him, and that if he were Amish I would accept him. They also said that he loves me. So the next time he made advances, I gave in."

"No, I didn't know this. Do you remember how you did that when Donny asked me to go steady?"

"Yes, and I've often wished I hadn't. Look how that turned out."

"Both of these are examples of how we did *not* listen to our inner voices—we listened to other people's voices instead." I thought for a moment about how much to say to Sarah but decided that my reflections might be helpful to her. "I think the same is true in matters of faith. How do I know that my best chance of salvation is to stay Amish just because I was born Amish? That reasoning doesn't wash, when you think about it. If that's true about

Amish, is it true for everyone? Then the Anabaptist faith wouldn't exist, and neither would the Amish! And what about people who are born into atheist families—are they supposed to stay atheist because their parents have those beliefs?"

Sarah didn't have an answer. We sat in silence for some time; then she asked, "Where are you going to live when you go to Vermont?"

"With Rick and Barbara for a while, and then I'll probably get a place of my own."

"I have no money saved up. And I don't want to be a burden on anyone."

"Just think about it," I told her. "I think if there's a will, there's a way."

"It's tempting. But I don't know if I agree with you about salvation if I leave the Amish. And now that I'm back in the church, I don't feel like I want to leave."

"I'm not saying you should do anything that is not right for you. No one can know what that is except you."

During most of our younger years, Susan and I had engaged in fierce sibling rivalry. That all changed when she took instructions for baptism that summer as I was slowly making my way out of the Amish. By then she was in love with the man she would marry, and she seemed at peace with her life. She and I often took walks and talked for hours in my little house.

In a journal entry the day before I left for my New England trip, I wrote,

> Susan and I walked to church at Eli Yoders for communion ser-
> vices. Church was very inspirational. Susan has become a dear
> sister to me. She and I have much in common and are much
> closer since she has started joining church. I cherish the time we
> spend together ever so much.

Susan was the second person I confided in after my Vermont trip. While on a walk together, I talked about my trip and how David and I had decided we wanted to be together.

Susan stayed quiet for a long time; then she asked if I was sure about my decision. She pointed out that I had a pretty good situation—living at the Troyers'—and that maybe I was not grateful enough for that.

I said that I was very grateful for the time I'd been living there and I would not have stayed as long as I did if it wasn't for that. Then I confided in Susan about feeling like a misfit, and she understood. She said that she had thought about leaving many times, but that she finally realized that she would be tempted to live a wild life if she left, and she was much happier now that she was a member of the church and was settling down. I told her how I could see the changes she had made since she joined the church, and I wished her well with her relationship with her boyfriend.

Susan asked me about my relationship with David. I described the times we had spent together, including the moment by the waterfall. She said she was happy for me and that she had noticed my loneliness. Then she said, "I just wouldn't want you to look back sometime in your life and realize this was the best time in your life and regret the decision you're making now."

"There's still no way for me to know for sure whether my relationship with David will work out, but I have a feeling if it does, I will remember this as the time I tried to fit into the Amish community and couldn't. I'll also remember this last year as a time when I wanted to be with David and could still not admit it."

"That long? Why didn't you let him know sooner?"

"My pride. I felt so bad about rejecting him—like I did on the reservoir—that I couldn't face him."

"He must really want you, after being rejected like that and then waiting another two years."

"Sometimes I almost don't feel worthy."

~◈~

My older sister, Lizzie, had been treated as the scapegoat within the family all her life. *Mem* passed her over and plugged me into the eldest daughter role at a young age. It was as if *Mem* had never accepted Lizzie for who she was—a person with more limitations than most. She had learning disabilities in school, especially in math. She was often labeled "just like *Datt*" and scapegoated. Consequently, Lizzie developed a bucket of need, which happened to have a big leak in it. Most people shied away from trying to help her because she would emotionally glom on until that person wanted to shake her off. I vacillated between feeling sorry for her and wanting to shake her out of sheer frustration.

I can only imagine what it was like to be the scapegoat within a family that was already a scapegoat in the community.

Lizzie used to come and visit me at the Troyers'. After she had asked if she could move in with me and the Troyers had said no, she hid in her room at *Mem* and *Datt*'s house. During the night when everyone else was sleeping, she would get up to find herself something to eat. This caused strife in the family, which made Lizzie even more of a recluse.

One night when I went home to visit, I dared to go up and knock on Lizzie's locked door and coax her into going for a walk with me. She finally agreed.

I told Lizzie of my plans. She did not respond. I thought she might become completely despondent, as she had in a few instances in the past.

I asked Lizzie if the counseling she was receiving was helpful to her. She said she didn't know. Then she started sobbing and said, "Sometimes I just feel like committing suicide!"

"Why? What is the issue?"

"Well, you know—being Amish!"

"If that's the issue, then why don't you just leave the Amish? You don't have to commit suicide. There are other things you can do with your life other than stay in the community if it's making you that unhappy."

"But if I leave the Amish, I'll go to hell."

"How do you know that?"

"Well, we've always been taught that."

I told Lizzie how I had come to terms with the question of salvation before I left the first time.

"But—where would I go?"

I knew this was the tricky part. It was going to be challenging enough to find my own way in Vermont. I couldn't have Lizzie dragging me down. I chose my words carefully. "You'd have to figure that out. Where would you want to live if you could live anywhere?"

"I would not want to live in Vermont—I know that."

"That's fine," I said, trying not to show my relief. "Can you talk with your counselor about it and have her help you figure out your options?"

"I probably could."

"That's what counselors are for."[11]

---

11. Lizzie was the first of my four sisters to leave after I did. I had nearly forgotten this conversation until many years later, when she reminded me of it. She claimed that I had saved her life. Ironically, she was battling cancer when she told me. She lost that battle on June 24, 2009.

~ 33 ~

Arm in Arm with the Future

The greatest force in the life of any child is the unlived lives of their parents.
—Carl Jung

One night I decided that it was time to break the news to *Mem*, so I walked over to have dinner with the family. After dinner and dishes, *Mem* and I took a walk up the road. I slipped my arm through *Mem*'s to support her walking.

We walked along for a while, and then I said, "I know you probably believed the rumors about me not coming back. I have come back, but partly because I wanted to talk to you. I am going to leave again."

We took several more steps, arm in arm. Then she spoke slowly, "This young man you met—does he have anything to do with your decision?"

I measured my words carefully. "If it wasn't for him, I would still be leaving. I would probably be moving somewhere down south to go to college. But because of David, I am planning on going back to Vermont."

If I had any expectations for the kind of reaction I would get from *Mem*, it would have been her playing the martyr and begging me not to go. That would certainly have come as no surprise. So I was not ready for her response.

"Well, I wouldn't want you to tell anyone this, but . . ." *Mem* paused. "I once had the chance of marrying someone outside the Amish."

I could barely comprehend what *Mem* was telling me. All my life, I had felt like I had two mothers—the one who was nurturing and understanding, and the one who was harsh and determined to break my will. Now I was discovering that she had held this secret inside for longer than I'd been alive. *Mem* added in a musing voice, "And I have always wondered what that would have been like."

I was so shocked that I wanted to sit down, right there on the ground. What *Mem* had just shared with me was too profound for me to fully comprehend. We kept walking on in silence. In that moment, walking arm in arm with *Mem*, I felt for the first time that she and I understood one another in a way that didn't require words. I understood the reason that she was torn in two. She had likely never reconciled her desire for a life different from the one she had. I felt like I was getting a look into my own future, should I decide to turn away from the love David was offering me.

I was still trying to comprehend all this, as well as the fact that she had pretty much given me her blessing to leave, when *Mem* said she was not looking forward to hearing from the bishop and his family about my leaving. She said, "And they are just the perfect family with their fifteen children who will most likely all stay Amish."

"*Mem*, it's not your fault that I'm leaving. This is my own decision. But the way Dan has picked on me in the church is part of what made me decide to leave."

Mem stopped in her tracks and looked at me under the starlight. She pulled herself up to her full height and said, "Then why don't you tell him that?"

"Do you want me to?"

Mem took a step forward and said with a sigh, "No, probably not. It would just make things worse for us."

"I'm sorry for that," I said. "I wish it weren't so. But I'm glad we talked. I decided I wanted you to hear this from me, rather than hearing it from someone else."

We walked toward the place *Mem* called home. There was no need for words.

~⚜~

The night after I talked with *Mem*, I wrote David another letter.

I feel so content right now, sitting here in my living room with the wood cracking merrily in the stove. I feel almost as if you were here. You are—in my soul.

Last night I spent time with the family. I took Mom for a walk and had a talk with her. I think she knew. I was very surprised how well she took it. She didn't seem heartbroken at all, like I thought she would be.

Later, Sarah and I were sitting in the kitchen doing artwork when she started questioning me. She asked if I talked to Mom about the same thing I talked to her about. I said, "Yes." She asked me what Mom said. I wasn't about to tell her, so I passed her off by asking her if she had told anyone. She said she had talked to Susan. She started giving me a hard time, saying things like, "It doesn't matter how you look at this, it can't be right, all you're doing is living for now, but what about eternity?" I asked her what had changed her attitude, probably talking to others, eh? She retorted, "Oh, you don't think I can form an opinion of my own?" She said I had smooth-talked her into believing the way I do. Finally she ended the conversation by saying, "Oh nobody can tell you what to do, you're too stubborn! I've never seen anyone quite so stubborn!" We cut off there and kept the rest of the art lesson friendly.

I bought material for your quilt today. I think you'll like it. Next I need to figure out what pattern to quilt onto it. I have several ideas that I might put together. I also need to figure out where to borrow a quilt frame. You might as well keep my frame until I come that way again. It's hardly worth it to bring it here and ship it back so soon. The truth is, David, I'll never make it for two months. I feel in a way it was ages ago that I last saw you,

*and I miss you more each day. I now have talked to my mother,
which was my main concern. My decision is made. I really don't
know what I'm waiting for, except that I still haven't figured out
the when and how. I'm putting an ad in the paper to sell my oil
and cook stoves. Money is a bit of a problem, so that'll give me
a couple hundred.*

*Along with cleaning for church, I've been cleaning out draw-
ers and sorting out my belongings. One thing I've decided—I'm
going to accept your help to get there, but how? I can't imagine
what a scene there would be if you came here and we started
loading my belongings up to move. And also this is not my place.
Oh my, what should I do? I'll talk to you Saturday, and we'll
figure something out. One thing certain—I'm asking for trouble
if I stay two months. Everybody would be on my back by then.*

*Once we plan something out I need to let Barbara know, and see
if her offer is still good for a place to stay—at least until I find a
place of my own, and a good job.*

Sincerely yours,
Saloma

The letter I received from David crossed in the mail with my
own. He started out by thanking me for the photos I'd sent him
and telling me I looked attractive and happy in the photo behind
his house. Then he referred to a conversation we'd had several
days before:

*I'm glad you and Sarah could talk about things. She said some
things about you that are true. She knows you are strong in char-
acter and it makes you a better person because of it. I respect you
for who you are and hope to be worthy of your respect.*

*Saloma, you have helped me find a part of me that was missing
for a long time. That part of me is my faith in God. Suddenly my
life has more meaning and I see the beauty around me in nature.*

Tonight the moon was out and very yellow. It was a three-quarter moon with bright stars filling the black sky. The moon in autumn is heavenly. It is cold tonight as I write this letter. I wish you were here to warm me up. I was out for a walk earlier tonight. It occurred to me during this walk that all the events in our lives for the past few years have brought us closer together despite distance, culture, and our own fears. It only makes me more sure of my feelings I have had for you since the days at the Y. I do not feel lonely anymore knowing the way you feel about me. I do miss you a hundred times a day. I have never felt so good about anyone before and I have never told anyone so much about myself. You are the one I love, Saloma. I have faith in God that He will bring us together and that our love will grow stronger.

Sincerely,
David

～◦ ✿ ◦～

On Saturday evening, as Will was setting up the church benches downstairs, I slipped away to the barn next door to call David. We made plans for me to leave November 7, exactly three years after I'd left the first time.

"I can come and get you if you'd like."

"Really? Isn't this a busy time of the year for you, though?"

"I'll manage. That's a Friday, which is good because it gives me the weekend to get back for work on Monday."

"I just cannot *wait* to see you. I don't know what I was thinking when I planned to stay through the holidays."

"That would be a long wait for me, too."

We finished our conversation. When I stepped out of the barn, two of the bishop's daughters were standing there, waiting to use the phone. I wondered for a quick moment how much of my conversation they had overheard. Then I decided I didn't really want to know.

~34~

Farewells

To love someone deeply gives you strength. Being loved by
someone deeply gives you courage.
—Lao Tzu

During the church service in the downstairs of my house, I
thought about how this would be the last Amish church service I would attend as a member in good standing. The last time
I left, I wasn't sure I would be staying away. I had left because of
the family situation. This time I knew that I was leaving for good.
Now that my living situation was much better and my relationship with my family members had improved, I was living a more
"normal" Amish life. I couldn't help but think: If I could only be
like the other girls and accept the ways of the Amish, I wouldn't
be leaving.

I looked sideways up the row of unmarried women. Nearly all of
them had their arms folded across their chests in the demure way
of Amish young women. Many of them were chewing gum, their
jaws moving slowly, as if they were even chewing gum in the Amish
way. Did any of them ever wish they could go to college? Did any of
them know what it's like to have questions boiling up from within,
with nowhere to go with those questions? Didn't any of them ever
feel restless? Did any of them wish they had the freedom to choose
their life's path? If so, what did they do with these feelings?

I said a silent prayer, or rather a plea, to God: Why did you
make me so different from the rest of them, if I am meant to stay
and be a part of this community my whole life long? I have tried

to be like them, but it's just not who I am. Please show me the way I am meant to go.

I wondered if people would surround me after the service, trying to talk me out of leaving. Then I wondered if anyone had found out yet. I tried not to fidget through the two sermons, but my mind was churning and it was hard to sit still. I was already imagining pulling all the curtains on the front porch and stashing my belongings there as I packed them for the journey to Vermont. The Troyers would have to actually snoop to find out what I was up to, considering I could also pull the curtains on the window of the door to the porch.

I thought about the belongings I wanted to take with me. I knew I was limited to what we could fit on the back of the pickup truck. I had sorted out the keepsakes I wanted from my teaching days. I had packed all my letters in bundles and stacked them neatly in a drawer. I would leave all my Amish clothes hanging in the closet, because I would have no use for them.

I would leave the sofa. I would take the maple bed frame I had bought at a yard sale, but the mattress set belonged to my parents, so I would leave that behind.

What about my treadle sewing machine? Would I take that with me or leave it behind? I decided to take it if I had room.

I would take my set of dishes with the rose pattern that I'd bought when I moved into the house. I'd wait to pack those until the last minute, given they were in a glass cupboard. Having them missing would be obvious to the Troyers. My kitchen items would fill several boxes.

I kept trying to imagine how to move my belongings. I saw no alternative other than David backing his truck into the driveway so we could load it up. I imagined people gathering around to try to talk me out of leaving. Then again, David would be there to support me. And they didn't usually overwhelm someone in the presence of a Yankee person.

I noticed several women heading up to the kitchen to make preparations for the meal that would be served after church. I followed them. The deacon's wife was ahead of me on the stairway.

When we got to the kitchen, she turned around and said, "*Gut fa dich!*" (Good for you!)

"What?" I asked.

"That you came back!" she said.

"I told you I would, didn't I?"

"But people didn't think you would."

I busied myself with putting baloney and cheese on plates. I felt like a liar. During the service, I had been planning my exodus out of the community, and here Mary wanted to credit me for coming back.

Mary was the one who had implied I was pregnant a month before. About a week before my trip, she had sent word for me to come and visit her. She took it upon herself to admonish me about going on the trip alone, saying, "It doesn't look good," and "People are talking."

If I looked at it from the Amish point of view, Mary was right. But I was looking through a whole different lens now, even though I was participating in an Amish church service.

When the service was over, most of the men gathered outside, though several helped Will set up the tables downstairs. Two rows of benches were lined up together for tables and covered with tablecloths. A row of benches was then set up on either side of the bench table.

The young women carried the plates of bread, baloney and cheese, pickles, butter, bowls of "Amish" peanut butter (in our community, it was peanut butter mixed with maple syrup and marshmallow cream), pots of coffee, and pitchers of water downstairs. Large bowls of cookies would be passed around after everyone had eaten sandwiches.

When the tables were set, the men and boys filed in and took their seats. Then the women filed in and sat at the other long table. Mothers restrained little children's hands from grabbing the food. When people were seated, the bishop asked everyone to bow their heads for a silent prayer.

I observed all this as if for the first time, even though I'd been experiencing church services much like this since before I could remember them. I realized I had taken them for granted and now this would be my last one. I wished it wasn't all or nothing. I would miss certain aspects of Amish life, especially community events like church services, weddings, and large extended family gatherings. But giving up everything Amish was required if I was going to have a life of freedom in Vermont—there was no having it both ways. The preachers were certainly right about that.

⚜

David called me at work on Monday. The sound of his voice made my heart beat faster. The longing to be with him was so strong that it felt tangible. We talked about our plans. David would drive all night on Thursday to get to Ohio by Friday. He'd sleep at Bernadette's house for a while before coming to see me. We planned to meet at the Century Inn on Friday.

Each day felt like it was a week. I worked at the museum during the day, and in the evenings I packed my belongings and stashed them in my bedroom closet until it became too full. Then I moved everything to the porch.

On Thursday afternoon, I met with my counselor, Rachael, in my living room. She knew of my plans to leave from a previous session after my New England trip and wanted to meet at my house to say goodbye. I shared with her my intimate moments with David, including the one when I realized how important it was for me to be with people who understand me. Rachael wiped tears from her own eyes as I spoke. Then she surprised me by telling me that she had something personal to share. She said that she used to be a nun and that there had come a time when she decided to leave the convent.

I was stunned. I made a remark about her knowing exactly what my struggle was about. She said that obviously there are differences between being Amish and being a nun. But leaving the convent had taken a lot of courage, just as it was taking a lot of courage for me to leave the Amish. Being Amish and being a nun are each a way of life and a belief system rolled into one, she said.

I told her I realized how much restraint it must have taken for her not to tell me.

She said she thought it might have affected my choice if she had told me before I made my decision.

I told Rachael that I would miss our conversations.

She assured me that I was moving toward the life I had been yearning and preparing for, and she wished me well.

"I am so grateful for all the sessions we've had together," I told her. "And here I thought I was coming to fix my eating disorder. I've dealt with a lot more than that." I told her that I had kept my New Year's resolution to stop purging until about a month ago, when I had found out about the rumor going around that I was pregnant. I told her that I had purged several times since then, but that it was different from before, somehow.

Rachael encouraged me to pay attention to my feelings and not to use food as a substitute for my other needs. She said that disordered eating is a reaction to oppression and that, if the source of the oppression is removed, the eating disorder will likely lose its power. Then it would be possible for me to develop a healthy relationship with food.

Rachael and I hugged when we said goodbye. It was one more farewell. There were so many.

I went to visit my family that evening and stayed overnight. I had a hard time sleeping. I kept thinking about David driving all night and prayed that he would travel safely.

In the morning, Susan and I took a walk over to my house as the sun was rising. The sunrise was so intensely beautiful that I felt I was getting a glimpse into the world beyond—that place we cannot know as long as we walk on this earth. I knew that *Datt* would tell me it was a bad sign: "Red sky in the morning is a sailor's warning." But I felt like it was God lighting my way.

Susan and I did last-minute packing, including my dishes from the cupboard with the glass doors. In the middle of it, Will came over and said he knew that I was planning to leave. I stopped what I was doing, and said, "Okay," as I wondered how many other people in the community knew. Usually once one person in the community knew, so did others.

"I just hope that you know what you're doing," Will said.

"I've certainly thought about it long and hard."

"Do you want to tell me why you're leaving?"

"It's just that I've tried really hard to fit into the community, and I'm just not happy."

"I know," Will said. We looked at one another. He said, "I didn't think I'd be doing my duty if I didn't warn you."

"I understand. I will certainly miss all of you. I really appreciate that you allowed me to live here. Without this, I would likely have left a lot sooner. About the rent—do you want me to pay you for this week?"

"No, don't worry about it," he said with a wave of his hand.

❈

I went to work at the museum for the last time that morning. All my colleagues knew that I was leaving. Several of them took me to lunch, and others gave me money to buy new clothes. I was minding the general store for B. J., who was in his eighties and came in to work at the store every day, when David walked in. It was two hours before we were scheduled to meet at Century Inn. It felt so good to be in his presence. The three weeks we hadn't seen one another seemed like three months.

David waited for me to finish work, and then we drove over to my parents' house.

We encountered *Datt* outside. "Lomie, you're not supposed to be hanging around an American," he said as we approached.

My first impulse was to correct him by saying we were Americans too, but I knew that wasn't the point. Instead, I said, "*Datt*, don't start in." I continued walking up the steps and into the house. *Datt* talked to David in an animated voice, and I heard David respond calmly. I wondered whether I should "rescue" David, but I decided to let them be. After all, *Datt* was entitled to his reaction. Although I hadn't told him I was leaving, I thought he probably knew more than he let on. He learned a lot from making as if he were a piece of furniture in the room.

Katherine met me at the door and started telling me all the latest goings-on in the community. When David came in, she offered us warm slices of homemade bread and elderberry jelly. I took that warm, earthy goodness for granted—*Mem* had been making bread for as long as I could remember. David's eyes lit up when he took a bite. He said, "Wow, Katherine, this is really good bread!"

"You like it?" she said, her blue eyes shining. Her curly hair was escaping the covering on her head. Her face had that radiant glow she'd get when someone praised her. That open, innocent, trusting expression on her face was what someone had taken advantage of. She had carried the shame of someone else's sin under her heart in secret for seven months. Now it was clear that she was pregnant, but that did not change her childlike openness.

David arrived in his pickup truck, shown here outside the house where I grew up, to take me back to Vermont.

Susan and David remembered one another from the first time they'd met during David's visit when I was living at the Benders'. They greeted one another with a handshake.

Mem was in the living room, observing us as she bent over to pick her next strand of wool for the rug she was braiding. I introduced David to *Mem*. I could feel her sizing him up, and I sensed that she liked who she saw.

Lizzie was also in the living room, talking to her parakeet, watching us out of the corner of her eye. David asked about her bird, and she told David what its name was and showed him how the bird would "kiss" her. The smile on Lizzie's face was refreshing after the depression she'd been suffering for weeks.

After visiting for a while, Susan offered to come with us to help load the truck. Grateful for her support, I accepted. On the way over, I asked her if she was concerned that she would get in trouble for helping me, and she said she'd deal with it.

A light rain was falling as David backed the truck into the driveway. We made several trips in and out, carrying out my belongings and loading them into the truck. No one came to stop us, though I could sense the eyes watching us from the Troyers' kitchen windows. After all the worrying I did about this part of my leaving, it felt anticlimactic now that it was finally happening.

When my belongings were all loaded onto the truck, David pulled a black tarp over the top of everything. As David and Susan were tying it down, I went back into the house to say goodbye to what I had called home for two and a half years. I stood briefly in each room as memories flashed by—conversations with friends in my little living room; meals with my family and others in the kitchen; and the lonely nights in the bedroom with the moon shining onto my bed. I was just about ready to allow myself to cry, when I heard David and Susan coming in. "Is that everything?" David asked.

"I think so. Susan, you can wear the dresses if you want to, or give them to someone else. Anything else I left behind, you can have."

Susan didn't answer. I could tell that she was trying not to show that she might miss me.

Then I turned off the lantern and took it down from the hook in the kitchen. I would take it with me so I could use it for camping trips. Then I locked the doors and left the keys on the kitchen table.

~❀~

David, Susan, and I drove to Middlefield and bought pizza for my whole family. When we got back to the homestead, we spent time visiting as *Mem*, Sarah, and Katherine were braiding rugs. We ate apples as we visited. I was putting off what I knew was inevitable—saying goodbye.

Finally, I said to David it was probably time to leave. I went and stood before *Datt*'s rocking chair. I said, "Bye, *Datt*. I'm going now." I offered a handshake, and he accepted. And David said, "It was nice to meet you," as he shook *Datt*'s hand. *Datt* looked up at David for a moment, and then he hung his head.

Susan gave me a brief hug and said, "Saloma, you know how much I hate goodbyes." She headed upstairs. Her reaction reminded me of Maureen's when I was leaving the Y that Saturday morning.

Sarah, Lizzie, and Katherine all shook hands with David and me.

When I turned to *Mem*, I saw that her eyes were wet. I put my arms out for a hug, and she grabbed on to me and squeezed. I heard her gulp a sob as I said, "*Mem*, I'm going to *miss* you."

"I'm going to miss you too," she said in the low voice she'd get when she was moved.

When I turned toward the door, I was also crying. I heard David say to *Mem*, "I promise to take good care of her."

"You do that," *Mem* said, her voice wavering.

~❀~

On the way to Bernadette's house, where we would be spending the night, David held my hand as we rode along in silence for a while. The enormity of the farewells settled into my chest, and David seemed to sense my need for silence. Eventually he asked, "Where was your brother Simon, by the way?"

"He works for Joe on the farm."

"Do they get along?"

"They didn't used to, but they do now. I'm glad Joe wasn't there. I wouldn't have wanted to face him. I don't even know if he knows I'm leaving. I sure wasn't going to tell him. I've not seen him since I came back from Vermont."

We were quiet for a moment. "It was so different from the first time I left. I can't believe I actually told my mother this time, and that I wasn't bombarded with the preachers coming to my door. And of course I didn't have you by my side last time." I looked at David and smiled.

David smiled back. "I wouldn't have missed it for the world."

When we arrived at Bernadette's, she showed us to our rooms. David's father was also staying there, visiting his mother, David's grandmother, who lived in a nursing home on Cleveland's West Side.

The next day Bernadette and I went to the mall to shop for clothes. That evening, we celebrated Mr. Furlong's birthday, and after the dishes were done, David and I took a walk to a nearby park. Alone for the first time since his arrival in Ohio, we sat on a park bench, hand in hand, just enjoying each other's company and talking about the days gone by and about our upcoming trip to Vermont.

─❦─

Around midmorning on November 9, 1980, David and I started our journey to Vermont. In the back of the little yellow Datsun pickup truck were the belongings I was bringing from my Amish world to my Vermont one. As we traveled Interstate 90 through a small portion of Pennsylvania, and then into New York State, David and I talked—about our family members, about our hopes and fears, and about me getting settled in Vermont. We also reminisced about the days at the Y.

David had brought along a tape player to listen to music. He remembered to bring Paul McCartney's *Wings*. When the "Mull of Kintyre" started, it evoked the feelings of loss I had been try-ing to avoid. When the bagpipes sounded, I could no longer hold back the tears. David noticed and asked, "You feeling homesick?"

I nodded. My head collapsed onto David's shoulder, and I cried in earnest. "It's just that I have to leave my whole life behind—my family, my community, my little house, my friends. And soon they'll have to shun me . . ."

David put his arm around my shoulder as I took my glasses off and blew my nose. Then David took his arm off my shoulder and waved to the car passing by.

"Who's that?" I asked.

"My father."

"Uh-oh. He probably sees me blubbering."

"Don't worry about it," David said. He put his arm around me again and said, "I can imagine it's hard to leave your family behind."

And then I knew that I was exactly where I wanted to be— driving toward Vermont with David. With the feelings we had for one another, I could make this necessary step of leaving home so we could be together.

Hours later, after getting off Interstate 90 in New York, when David was navigating the secondary roads, we saw the sign "Welcome to Vermont." He pulled just past the sign, onto the shoulder of the road, and stopped. "What are we doing?" I asked.

He said, "Welcome to Vermont," and leaned over and kissed me. Then he looked out his window, pulled back onto the road, and headed north. I knew that a new phase of our relationship was just beginning. With David's love and support, I could face the homesickness and the uncertainty of not knowing where I was going to live or how I was going to earn a living. Besides, he'd promised *Mem* he would take good care of me.

White Knight

David Furlong

Love is our true destiny. We do not find the meaning of life
by ourselves alone—we find it with another.
—Thomas Merton

Two years after the rejection on the reservoir, my vigil was coming to an end. I resolved to send one more card for Linda's birthday. I carefully selected a Vermont scene with a winding country road and wrote a few personal lines. I said to myself: This is my last try.

Then to my surprise, a card arrived from Ohio, complete with a big thank you for the beautiful Vermont birthday card. She even signed her name as "Linda."

"Hallelujah! Linda is back!" I proclaimed from my toy shop. I didn't care who heard me. I knew right away there was a change in "Linda." I felt my heart lighten. I dared to hope that maybe she was back for good.

I was thrilled every time another letter arrived that allowed me to imagine her sitting next to a waterfall, sitting in the light of the lantern in her little house, or out flinging a Frisbee across an open field. She signed her name as Saloma after a while. That was okay with me—she would be as sweet by any name.

That August evening when Saloma and I met in Burton, I knew she felt self-conscious about the weight she'd gained. Though it was noticeable, I wasn't going to let that stop me. I hadn't waited two years for her affections to reject her now. After stealing a kiss from Saloma under the light of the moon that night, I drove away with my spirit soaring. A romance with Saloma was still a possibility, and I knew it.

The week Saloma and I spent together in October when we talked about our feelings for one another was the best yet. Our romance was more than just a dream.

When Saloma needed help moving her belongings, I knew what to do. Playing the White Knight had always appealed to my ego. I fancied myself as one of the good guys in life's daily dramas: never selfish or greedy, just a guy ready to step in and save someone in a difficult situation. Like a White Knight, I had my faithful charger—a yellow Datsun pickup truck. When Saloma was ready to make her final exodus out of the Amish, it afforded me the once-in-a-lifetime chance to play out this role to its fullest. I had my faithful charger gassed up and ready to go.

Epilogue

Now join your hands, and with your hands your hearts.
—William Shakespeare

The first time I left the Amish, I didn't want to betray my Amish faith by attending "worldly" church services in case I decided to go back.

The second time I left was different. I knew this time I was not going back, and I needed to find a church community that would provide nourishment for my soul. David was interested in searching with me, so we began visiting various churches in the area.

David's parents wanted him to continue attending Catholic mass, so one Sunday evening, David took me to a large, ornate church near his home. I dressed up in my best clothing, because that is what I had been taught to do.

The church was packed. Many of the young people were dressed in faded jeans, and they looked bored and disengaged from what the priest was saying and the rituals he was performing. The organ music was loud and boomed into my inner reflections. People stood up at the indicated times and invoked prayers with the priest. And before the hour was up, people poured out of the church, nearly running to their cars in their haste to leave and go back to life outside the church.[12]

I thought David wanted me to like it, and I hated to disappoint him, but it was the antithesis of an Amish church service. Frankly, the service had made me feel the Amish preachers were

---

12. I have since attended services in the Catholic church that were very different, and hence my response to them was also quite different.

right about "worldly churches." I cried when David asked me how I felt about it.

David wasn't upset with me. He admitted that on the one hand, he was hoping that we could just continue the Catholic tradition and make no waves in his family. On the other hand, he said the Roman Catholic Church was not resonating for him, either.[13]

After visiting many churches, David and I landed in the one that was right for both of us. It was Christ Church Presbyterian. The first time we attended, I was sitting and listening to the minister giving his sermon when I realized I knew him. He was the Reverend William Hollister, with whom I had counseled when I was in my spiritual struggle during my first months in Burlington. I felt a strong sense of community, especially when people were asked if they had any joys and concerns to share and several people did. At the end of the service, we all gathered in a circle, and the reverend broke the bread and said, "And then Jesus broke the bread and said, 'When you eat this, remember me, for this is my body broken for you.'" Baskets of bread were passed around, and people held the basket for the person next to them and said, "Peace," as each person broke off a piece of bread and ate it. Then there were little cups of wine shared the same way. I knew I had just found the church community that was right for me.

When the service was over, I waited while the minister talked with another parishioner. When he turned toward me, I reminded him how we'd met several years earlier. He thought for a moment and then his face lit up and he said, "Yes, I remember! At my office at the Church Street Center!" I was surprised and delighted that Bill Hollister, as we soon came to know him, remembered me. I told him that I was back in Vermont after returning to the Amish for a few years, and I introduced him to David.

At the end of our conversation he said, "It feels better this time, doesn't it?"

Until Bill Hollister posed this question, I hadn't realized just how different it was. It did feel better. I was more settled in my

---

13. Of late, David has been digging deeply into the roots of Catholicism and is discovering the crossroads between mystical Catholicism and Anabaptist/Amish beliefs. He is finding meaning in the faith of his ancestors.

decision to leave the Amish and in my relationship with David. My community members may have sensed this, for no one showed up at my front door to take me back. I no longer wondered whether I should return to the Amish. I had had the chance to say goodbye to my parents and sisters, and I had received something at least close to a blessing from *Mem*.

When David and I began planning our wedding, his parents stated their strong preference that we be married in the Catholic church. They said to David, "Saloma left the Amish, and now she wants you to leave the Catholics." We knew the possible consequences if we didn't take their preferences into consideration. We had witnessed it when David's parents refused to go to Bernadette and Maurice's wedding in a Presbyterian church in Ohio.

We discussed this dilemma with Bill Hollister. He said he would be willing to share the wedding ceremony with a Catholic priest and suggested we go and talk with a local priest, which we did. The priest was not able to come to the wedding, but he said he would give us a dispensation if we promised to raise our children in the Catholic tradition. I was reticent to make such a promise until Bill Hollister explained that it depends on how we interpret "in the Catholic tradition." He said that *catholic* actually means "universal." He said we would likely not prevent our children from going to Catholic services with David's parents, and that we never know where our spiritual path might lead—it could include the Roman Catholic Church. And so when we signed the dispensation, we basically received a formal blessing for our marriage from the Roman Catholic Church.

It was through the community at Christ Church Presbyterian that I met William Cleary and Roddy O'Neill. They were a dynamic couple who understood my journey, with many similarities to their own. Bill was a former Jesuit priest, and Roddy was a former Maryknoll nun. They had left their respective orders to marry one another. Bill and Roddy became my surrogate parents. When they found out I was living in a run-down apartment in Burlington that was not in the safest part of town, they offered that I could come and live with them. They had two young sons,

Tom and Neil. I lived with them for eight months and started baking bread and pies for the neighborhood, which became part of my livelihood.

David and I planned a low-budget wedding. I bought several hams and baked oatmeal rolls, which I froze for the occasion. I asked the guests to each bring a dish for the wedding, which they did with good cheer. Two women from the church offered to coordinate the meal and serve the food.

On the morning of May 29, 1982, a soft spring rain began falling. I didn't fret because I thought my father's saying would likely be true: "Rain before seven, it'll stop before eleven." It was a year and a half since David had welcomed me to Vermont. Now we would be welcoming one another into our marriage. We had sent my family and several people in my Amish community invitations to our wedding. None of them came.

I went to Maureen's house early that morning to have my hair done. Then two of my friends helped me get dressed in a borrowed wedding gown that made me feel more elegant than I had ever felt in my life. Each time I thought about what I was about to do, I felt butterflies fluttering in my stomach.

On the morning of our wedding, David prepared in his living room.

From the moment I stepped inside the church, everything else became a backdrop. I walked into the sanctuary of Christ Church Presbyterian on the arm of Bill Cleary, and there awaiting me was David, standing next to the altar with blue forget-me-nots. It was my moment of blue: David with his blue blue eyes, dressed in a blue tuxedo, was observing me walking toward him. Everyone stood while Tom Cleary, who was ten years old at the time, played the Shaker tune "Simple Gifts" on the organ. I walked toward the altar, and the service and ceremony began.

I could not take my eyes off David, and my joy was boundless. I was dimly aware that we had rehearsed the service the night before. I also remembered that I had said with confidence that I would be able to memorize my lines. Bill cautioned that I might want to repeat them after him. That was a wise thing that he said—I was so moved now, I could barely repeat the lines after him, especially when David slid the ring on my finger and vowed to stay with me the rest of our lives.

The joy of having overcome the cultural barriers and impossibilities of our relationship was overwhelming. I was no longer torn between two worlds—this was my last step out of the Amish community and into my new one. This was what I had been moving toward when I had yearned for David on those moonlit nights but hadn't known how to find my way back to him. I barely managed to repeat my vows after Bill Hollister. And then he pronounced us husband and wife. It was my moment of glory—never had my heart and soul soared to that height.

The hymn that was sung afterward is barely a blip in my memory. When the last notes of the song died away, David and I greeted his parents. Then we were supposed to leave the church slowly arm in arm, while the music was playing, but David grabbed on to my arm and walked so fast that I felt I was running out of the church to stay up with him. His discomfort at being the center of attention showed.

Outside, it was a gorgeous spring day. The rain had indeed stopped before eleven, and now the sky was clear. The trees had new green leaves and the lilacs were blooming, which fit the occasion perfectly. It seemed to me that God was blessing our marriage and that nature was celebrating with us.

David and I felt loved and supported as our forty guests greeted us and wished us well. People told me I looked beautiful. I knew I was radiating the love and joy I felt within.

When everyone went to the community room, we found there a table laden with food. It was a wonderful bounty that showed how in the miracle of sharing there is enough for everyone. Not only was there enough food; there was also more than enough peace, support, love, and good cheer.

David and I celebrated our wedding on a lovely spring day in 1982.

The next morning, when we would usually have been attending church, David and I were just waking up in Calgary, Alberta, Canada. David rose first and went outside. When he came back in, he brought with him the smell of fresh air and said excitedly, "You have to come out and see this really cool bird! It's got this really long iridescent black tail!" We soon found out the bird with the long tail was a magpie—a bird that we would never see back East.

We spent several days traveling around Banff and then decided to take a train trip to Vancouver and back. Sleeping in a berth on the train, we awoke on Sunday morning, a week after seeing our first magpie. We opened up the shade next to our berth and looked out at the Canadian Rockies around us. We noticed it was seven o'clock, and we realized back in Vermont it was ten o'clock, the time when people would be gathering for church. We gave the

David and I were eager to embark on our honeymoon to the Canadian Rockies.

people in our church community a long-distance wave from the train.

Over breakfast in the dining car, we looked out at the passing terrain and kept wondering if there could be a place on earth more beautiful than this. We were traveling through the valleys of green. The mountains, sculpted by the Great Artist, had the spring green of new leaves. It was another moment when the lines blurred between beauty and love. All that David and I had endured in the past only intensified our joy. We were in the valley of love and delight.

Acknowledgments

I can point to the time when I first started thinking about writing my story. I was twenty-three years old, still wearing Amish clothes and working at the Century Village of the Geauga County Historical Society. My supervisor, Gloria Armstrong, witnessed the unfolding of the young romance that was happening in front of her eyes. She kept telling me that I needed to write my story. Besides still wearing Amish clothing, I was also wearing my Amish humility, so I felt unworthy. Who would want to read my story? I asked myself.

It did not take long after the second time I left that I discovered the answer to this question: many people. Unlike the first time I had left, this time, I kept my given name, Saloma. This often triggered a reaction: "What kind of a name is Saloma?" I soon learned to have two different responses at the ready. If I was inclined to tell my story and we had enough time, I would tell them I grew up in an Amish community. Sometimes I would try to take a shortcut and say that I was named after my maternal grandmother. The shortcut didn't always work. Almost invariably, as soon as I would mention that I was born and raised Amish, the person would ask me why I left. Because there wasn't just one reason, and because I wanted to include the nuances, it usually took a while to finish. The nearly universal response was "You have *got* to write your story!" Each time I told it, I would become more determined to someday write it down.

Once I had this determination, I needed to find my voice and hone the craft of writing. That began at the Adult Basic Education

Center in Winooski, Vermont, in 1981, when I was studying for my General Education Diploma. That is where I first saw my own words in print and it gave me a taste for more.

In the years that followed, I was part of several writing groups and classes. I appreciate all the suggestions, edits, and encouragement I received from my teachers and fellow writers. You know who you are—thank you!

I am blessed to have such a wonderful and warm group of friends. It is because of your encouragement that I've had the gumption to write about my life.

I am also thankful for those people who have challenged my way of being in the world. You are my best teachers, and you've helped me to define what my core values and beliefs are.

To the nearly eight thousand people who have attended my book talks: thank you. Your interest in reading the rest of the story that I started in *Why I Left the Amish* has become my muse and supported my purpose for writing this book.

I would like to thank all those who read at least one draft of what has become *Bonnet Strings: An Amish Woman's Ties to Two Worlds*: Callie Wiser, Jeanne Braham, Candelin Wahl, Corinne Urban, Lynnanne Dennison-Fager, Vanessa Ryder, Beth Berry, and Teri Wilhelms. Your perspectives were helpful in shaping the story.

In this digital age, when personal connections are becoming more rare, it seems they are still important when it comes to publishing books, at least if I go by how *Bonnet Strings* found its home. I am grateful to Shirley Hershey Showalter, author of *Blush: A Mennonite Girl Meets a Glittering World*, for suggesting I talk with Amy Gingerich at Herald Press about publishing my story. Amy and I soon decided Herald Press was a good match for *Bonnet Strings*. I'd like to thank Amy Gingerich for acquiring the manuscript and Russ Eanes for approving it.

How to best tell my story became a wonderfully collaborative effort with a capable editorial team. I am grateful to Byron Rempel-Burkholder and Valerie Weaver-Zercher for their expert edits and advice on several drafts of the manuscript. They were helpful in finding ways to frame certain parts of my story to be less provocative, while still staying true to the story. I would also like to thank the rest of the team at Herald Press, including the creative talents of Ben Penner, Wayne Gehman, Jerilyn Schrock, and Merrill Miller. I would also like to thank Dorothy Hartman, who coordinated so many details.

I appreciate that Leanna Mast was willing to model for the cover of *Bonnet Strings*. She took time out from her busy schedule as a nurse to "wear Amish." I am so grateful she is my niece. She is as beautiful inside as she is out.

I appreciate the talents of Kristin Hall, who helped me alter my original dress pattern and make the Amish dress for Leanna. Kristin did so with good humor. It was like stepping back in time, and I was surprised that the know-how to make an Amish dress has never really left me, even thirty-three years later.

My deepest gratitude goes to David, who has heard or read every draft of my manuscript and has become my inspiration to finish the story. I am especially grateful to him for agreeing to write his perspective on the crucial parts of the story of our romance. Our lives would not have turned out this way had it not been for his enduring love when we were young and I needed rescuing.

Recipes

Mem's White Bread

Note: When I was growing up, *Mem* was known as the best bread baker in our church district. I learned how to bake *Mem's* white bread, but it wasn't until I was baking professionally that I wrote down the recipe. Here is the closest I have come to duplicating *Mem's* bread, including her way of teaching me what the temperature of the water or milk should be when adding the yeast.

Mix together in a large mixing bowl:

½ cup sugar

1 tablespoon salt

2 tablespoons butter

1½ cups hot milk

While the hot milk is dissolving the sugar and melting the butter, mix together in a small bowl:

1 cup lukewarm water (the same temperature as you would use to give a newborn baby a bath)

1 tablespoon sugar

2 tablespoons yeast

Proof the yeast until it becomes nice and foamy. Meanwhile, cool the milk mixture with ice cubes until it becomes lukewarm. (If it's too hot, it will kill the yeast.) When it becomes lukewarm (same temperature as for proofing the yeast), add the yeast mixture and stir.

Sift into the milk mixture, 1 cup at a time:

10 cups white flour

At first this mixture will be lumpy until you add more flour; then it should become nice and smooth. Beat well, and keep sifting in flour, about a cup at a time. The more you stir it at this point, the easier it will be to knead the dough later. When the dough forms a ball, it is ready to be kneaded.

Turn the dough out onto a clean counter with sifted flour on it to knead it. You want the dough to be soft and yielding but not too sticky. I knead my dough for 10 minutes after I've stirred in all the flour that I can. Turn dough into a greased bowl and cover with a clean, lint-free towel. Let rise about an hour, then punch down and let rise again for 1 hour.

The dough is now ready to form into loaves or rolls. Or you can make it into sticky buns (see recipe below). For bread, grease 2 pans and form dough into loaves. Let rise about 1 hour. Preheat oven to 450 degrees. When the dough has risen, place loaves in hot oven and bake for 5 minutes at 450 degrees. Then turn oven temperature to 350 degrees and bake another 40 minutes.

Sticky Buns

Sticky Bun Stuff

Mix together in a saucepan and bring to a boil:

- ¼ **cup butter**
- ⅔ **cup brown sugar**
- **1 tablespoon corn syrup**
- **2 tablespoons water**
- **1 tablespoon vanilla**
- **Pecans or walnuts (optional)**

Pour the Sticky Bun Stuff into 3 9-inch pie pans. Add pecans or walnuts if desired.

Sticky Buns

Mix together and set aside:

- **1½ cups white sugar**
- **2 tablespoons cinnamon**

Grease a clean counter with butter. Without punching it down, place on the greased counter and roll out to about ¼ inch thick:

- **1 batch of** *Mem*'s **White Bread dough: (p. 330)**

Smooth all over the dough:

- **softened butter (about ½ cup)**

Pour the white sugar and cinnamon over the butter and spread it all over the dough. Roll it up like a jelly roll. On a cutting board, cut the roll into slices just under 2 inches thick. Place in the pie pans on top of the Sticky Bun Stuff. Cover and let rise for 45 minutes to an hour.

Preheat oven to 425 degrees. Place sticky buns low into the oven, second to the bottom rack. Bake for 5 minutes, and then lower the temperature to 350 degrees and bake until golden brown (about 35–40 minutes).

Remove from oven and let sit 5 minutes. Turn a large plate upside-down over the top of the pan of sticky buns and turn over. The sticky buns should separate from the pan. Scrape any excess syrup and spread over the top of the buns. Serve while warm.

Pie Crust Made Simple

Note: If *Mem* was the best *bread* baker, Olin Clara was the best *pie* baker. I was fortunate to learn her pie crust method when she took me under her wing when I was a young girl. One summer picnic, Olin Clara brought the pie of all pies. I was in "peach pie heaven" that day. When I baked professionally in Shelburne, Vermont, for nine years, the summer pies I made were modeled after Clara's peach pie. I have also made variations with blueberries or raspberries or both. Each time I eat one of these ambrosia delights, I think of Clara. I have found a way to use a food processor to make the pie crust. I am including that here.

Sift into a food processor:

3¼ cups flour, sifted

½ teaspoon salt

Add and process until no chunks of fat are left in the crumbs:

4 ounces frozen lard, cut into slices or small chunks

Add and repeat this process:

4 ounces frozen butter, sliced (one stick)

For 2 crusts, measure 2½ cups crumbs into a mixing bowl. Add and mix only until dough forms:

¼ cup cold water

Use more water if needed, 1 tablespoon at a time. If dough is too moist, dunk it into the dry crumbs and work them into the dough until the right consistency.

Form two balls of dough and roll out. For a peach pie, make many holes in the crust before forming the crust in the pie pan and fluting the edges. Chill the crust in the freezer. It actually works best to go from the freezer directly to the oven. Preheat the oven to 450 degrees while the crust is chilling. Bake for 10–12 minutes or until golden brown.

Freeze remaining crumbs for later use. Simply add water and roll out when you want to make pie crust later. I keep lard and butter frozen in 4-ounce portions so that when I want to make pie crusts they are ready to use.

~✿~

Olin Clara's Peach Pie

Filling

Peel and dice:

1 heaping quart fresh peaches, peeled and diced

Mix in a saucepan and heat to boiling:

1 cup sugar

1 cup water

Mix to make a paste:

⅓ cup cornstarch or Clear Gel

½ cup water

Stir paste into boiling water and sugar. When it boils and thickens, remove from heat. Mixture should be clear and thick.

Add and stir:

½ small box apricot or raspberry gelatin

Pour mixture over peaches and turn into:

1 baked pie crust (see p. 332)

Chill for several hours. Top with Whipped Cream Topping (p. 334) and keep chilled until served. Decorate top of pie with peach slices.

Whipped Cream Topping

Whip with a mixer until thick:

1 cup whipping or heavy cream

Add:

¼ cup sugar

½ teaspoon vanilla

Variations

Peach-Blueberry Pie: Use 2 cups peaches and 2 cups blueberries.

Peach-Raspberry Pie: Use 2 cups peaches and 2 cups raspberries.

Peach-Raspberry-Blueberry Pie: Use 2 cups peaches, 1 cup raspberries, and 1 cup blueberries.

For a real treat, use peaches, blueberries, and both black raspberries and red raspberries.

Decorate tops with whichever fruit is in the pie.

My Favorite Apple Pie

Note: Most of the Amish women I know would cook the apple filling for their pies before baking the pie, so that is how I learned how to make them. Years later, I read how baking an apple pie just the right way is hard to do because the apples like to bake slowly, while the crust likes a hot oven. A flaky crust is created when the fat bakes before the flour, which is what happens in a hot oven (450 degrees). This is also enhanced when the crust is chilled before baking. The solution is to cook the filling beforehand, so you can bake the pie in a hot oven and the apples will not be crunchy.

I think it's great that the Amish women had this all figured out. Because so much of their lives have to do with following tradition, they don't need to know why they do it this way—it's just the way it's done. Being who I am, I like knowing why. So now I'm happy. This is the recipe I've developed over the years. It is pretty fail-safe if I use crisp Cortland apples in the fall. When they start getting mushy later in the season, I switch to Gala apples.

Filling

Peel, core, and dice:

4 cups apples

Mix in a saucepan and heat to boiling:

1 cup water

1 cup sugar

Add apples and bring to a boil again.

Mix together in a small bowl to make a paste and then stir into boiling apple mixture:

⅓ cup cornstarch or Clear Gel

1 teaspoon cinnamon

⅔ cup cold water

When it boils and thickens, remove from heat. Mixture should be nice and clear and thick. Cool partially while making the crust.

Crust

Follow directions for Pie Crust Made Simple (p. 332) for rolling out two crusts. Form one into a pie pan, and make a top for the pie with template or create a pattern on top with a butter knife. This is not just for looks: the crust needs air holes, so the filling doesn't bubble out the sides of the pie. Place these in the refrigerator or freezer to chill.

Wet the edges of the chilled bottom crust with water. Spread 1 table-spoon whole milk or half-and-half over the top crust. Spoon filling into the pie. Place top crust on pie and let mold to the filling. When edges are soft, seal the top crust with the bottom crust by pinching them together all around the edge with your thumbs. Trim edges with butter knife and flute. Place into preheated 450-degree oven (near the bottom) and bake for 20–25 minutes or until golden brown.

For more recipes, go to www.salomafurlong.com/Salomas_Recipes.html. For more on Amish customs, including naming practices and head covering practices, go to www.salomafurlong.com/Amish_Customs.

The Author

Saloma Miller Furlong is the author of the memoir *Why I Left the Amish,* a finalist for the 2011 *ForeWord Reviews* Book of the Year Award. She is also the author of the popular blog *About Amish* (www.aboutamish.blogspot.com). Saloma is featured on the PBS *American Experience* documentaries *The Amish* and *The Amish: Shunned.*

Saloma was born and raised in an Amish community in Ohio. While she and her husband raised their two sons, Saloma baked bread and quilted professionally. When her sons were both enrolled in college, she decided to pursue her lifelong dream of attending college. She was accepted into the Ada Comstock Scholars Program at Smith College in 2004. Her education included research on the Amish with Donald Kraybill and a semester abroad in Germany, where she studied at the University of Hamburg. She graduated from Smith in May 2007 with a major in German studies and a minor in philosophy.

Saloma and her husband, David, live in the Pioneer Valley in Massachusetts.